SERIES EDITOR: JOHN MOORE

ORDER OF BATTLE SERIES: 4

THE ARDENNES OFFENSIVE

VI PANZER ARMEE

NORTHERN SECTOR

BRUCE QUARRIE

First published in Great Britain in 1999 by Osprey Publishing,
Elms Court, Chapel Way, Botley, Oxford OX2 9LP
Email: osprey@osprey-publishing.co.uk

ISBN 1 85532 853 4

Osprey Series Editor: Lee Johnson
Ravelin Series Editor: John Moore
Research Co-ordinator: Diane Moore
Design: Ravelin Limited, Braceborough, Lincolnshire, United Kingdom
Cartography: Chapman Bounford and Associates, London, United Kingdom

Printed through Worldprint Ltd, Hong Kong

99 00 01 02 03   10 9 8 7 6 5 4 3 2 1

FOR A CATALOGUE OF ALL BOOKS PUBLISHED BY OSPREY MILITARY, AUTOMOTIVE
AND AVIATION PLEASE WRITE TO:

The Marketing Manager, Osprey Direct UK., P.O. Box 140, Wellingborough,
Northants, NN8 4ZA, United Kingdom

The Marketing Manager, Osprey Direct USA, P.O. Box 130, Sterling Hts,
MI 48311-0130, USA

VISIT OUR WEBSITE AT:
http://www.osprey-publishing.co.uk

Key to Military Series symbols

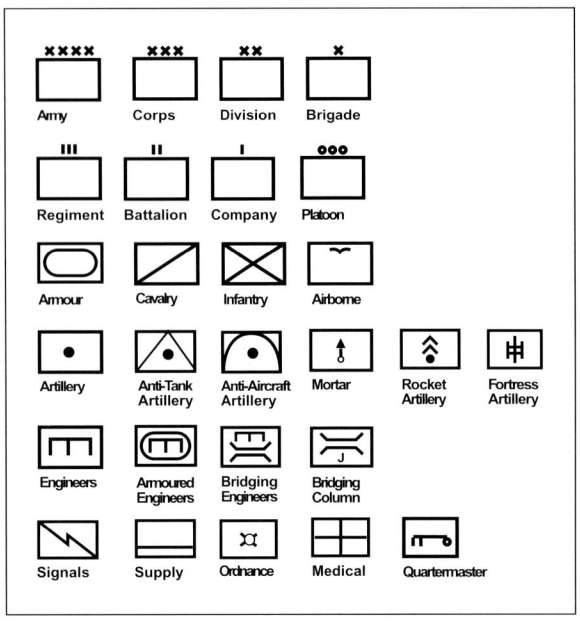

Series style

The style of presentation adopted in the Order of Battle series is designed to
provide quickly the maximum information for the reader.

Order of Battle Unit Diagrams – All 'active' units in the ORBAT, that is those
present and engaged on the battlefield are shown in black. Unengaged and
detached units, as well as those covered in subsequent volumes are
'shadowed'.

Unit Data Panels – These provide a ready reference for all regiments,
battalions, companies and troops forming part of each division or battlegroup
and present during the battle, together with dates of attachment where relevant.

Battlefield Maps – In this volume, German units engaged are shown in red and
Allied units in blue.

Order of Battle Timelines

Battle Page Timelines – Each volume concerns the Order of Battle for the
armies involved. Rarely are the forces available to a commander committed
into action as per his ORBAT. To help the reader follow the sequence of events,
a Timeline is provided at the bottom of each 'battle' page. This Timeline gives
the following information:

The top line bar defines the actual time of the actions being described in that
battle section.

The middle line shows the time period covered by the whole action.

The bottom line indicates the page numbers of the other, often interlinked,
actions covered in this book.

0800 hrs	0900	1000	1100	1200
	pp45-47	48-49 & 52-55	50-51	

Editor's note

All individual battle maps are based on Government Survey 1:50,000 G.S. 4040
series dated 1938 and 1939, revised from aerial reconnaissance 1943, by
permission of the British Library.

CONTENTS

STRATEGY IN THE WEST 4

OPERATION 'HERBSTNEBEL' – Planning 7

SIXTH PANZER ARMEE 20

SIXTH PANZER ARMEE – I SS-PANZER KORPS 26

1 SS-Panzer Division Leibstandarte 'Adolf Hitler' 28

12 SS-Panzer Division ' Hitler Jugend' 32

3 Fallschirmjäger Division 36

12 Volksgrenadier Division 39

277 Volksgrenadier Division 40

I SS-PANZER KORPS' BATTLES – Krinkelt-Rocherath 42

– Büllingen-Dom Bütgenbach 46

– Losheim to La Gleize 50

– Recht-Poteau 58

– Malmédy 60

SIXTH PANZER ARMEE – II SS-PANZER KORPS 62

2 SS-Panzer Division 'Das Reich' 64

9 SS-Panzer Division 'Hohenstaufen' 68

II SS-PANZER KORPS' BATTLES – Salmchâteau 70

– Baraque Fraiture 72

– Manhay-Grandmenil-Erezée 74

– Poteau 77

SIXTH PANZER ARMEE – LXVII KORPS 78

272 Volksgrenadier Division 80

326 Volksgrenadier Division 81

3 Panzergrenadier Division 83

246 Volksgrenadier Division 85

LXVII KORPS' BATTLES – Höfen-Monschau 87

– Elsenborn Ridge 89

THE LUFTWAFFE 92

WARGAMING THE ARDENNES 96

SELECT BIBLIOGRAPHY 96

STRATEGY IN THE WEST

Abwehrschlacht im Westen

On 1 July 1944, Feldmarschall Gerd von Rundstedt, senior commanding officer on the Western Front, telephoned Berlin. He had just received reports from Feldmarschall Erwin Rommel, in effect at this time his executive officer, and General Freiherr Leo Geyr von Schweppenburg, head of Panzergruppe West. The two men had just returned to their commands from an interview with Hitler, having sought a total review of the operational requirements in Normandy. Hitler had refused to listen to either of them and launched into a monologue in which he kept insisting that his new 'miracle weapons' would turn the tide.

Both men were in a foul mood as a result and this communicated itself to von Rundstedt. He was red-faced and choleric himself when he telephoned Hitler's sycophantic lackey, Keitel, in Berlin. Von Rundstedt said he was too old to continue the fight and asked to be replaced by someone younger. His wish was promptly granted after he responded to Keitel's plaintive 'What shall we do?' with 'End the war, you fools!'. Two months later, on 4 September, Gerd von Rundstedt was reinstated. Hitler needed the support of the Army for his latest scheme, and von Rundstedt had been in the Army for 52 years. He was their elder statesman, really the last surviving spokesman with any authority from the pre-Nazi era.

An old-fashioned Prussian aristocrat, he had been a staff officer in the First World War and helped Hitler mould the new army after he repudiated the Treaty of Versailles, even though the two men detested each other. (Von Rundstedt called Hitler 'the Austrian Corporal'.) Later he commanded Heeresgruppen in Poland, France and Russia and then Oberbefehlshaber West, nominally in charge of creating the Atlantic Wall although Rommel did all the work, until he was dismissed in July 1944.

On Hitler's right, his chief of operations, Alfred Jodl, sympathised with the alternative 'kleine lösung' proposed by the generals but was unable to alter the Führer's scheme. On Hitler's left, his chief of staff, Wilhelm Keitel, was a man who never argued and was known as 'The Lackey'. Both men played key roles in assembling the forces for 'Herbstnebel'. (MARS)

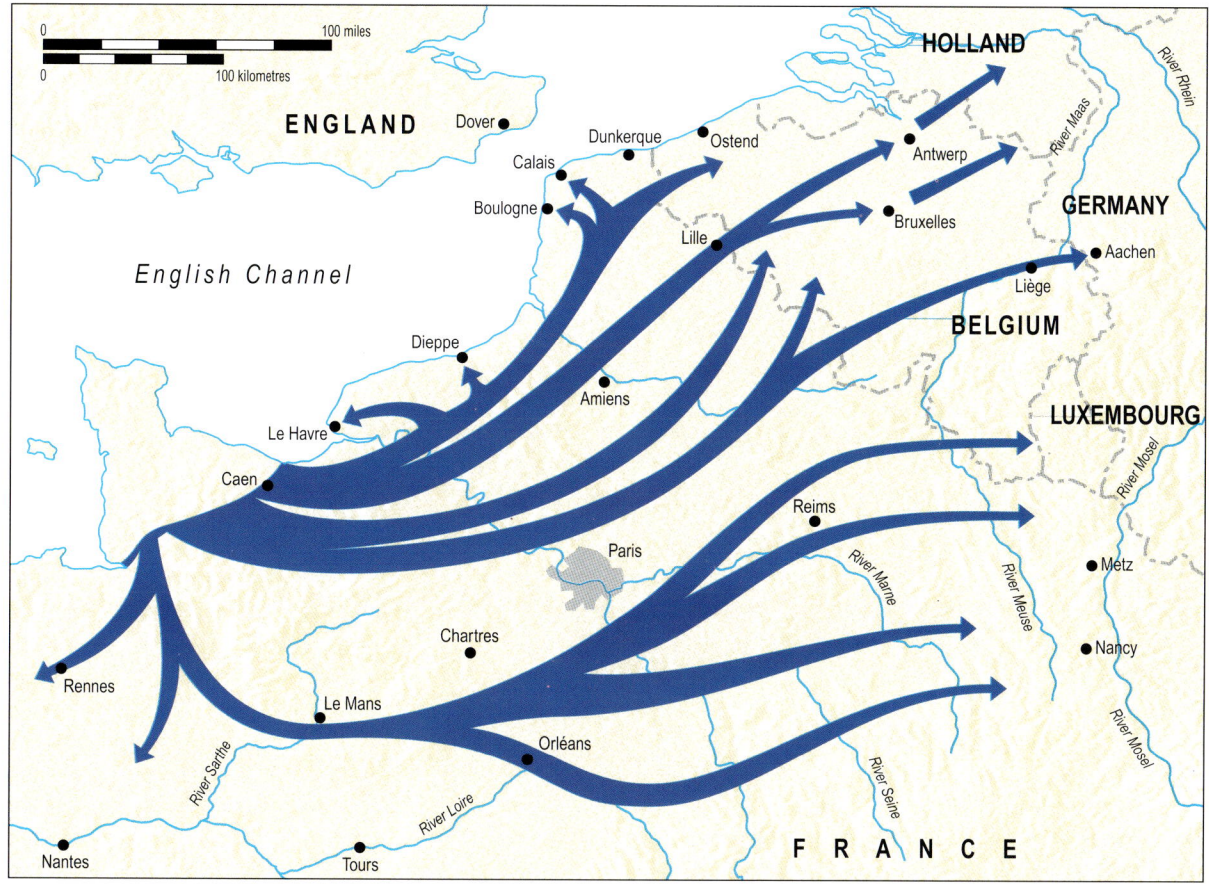

The Allied breakout from Normandy was made on a 'broad front', but as their supply lines lengthened the advance slowed, giving the Germans time to regroup for 'Hertbstnebel'.

Von Rundstedt's chief of staff, Generalleutnant Siegfried Westphal, and his operations officer, Generalleutnant Bodo Zimmerman, takes up the story of Germany's strategy in the west in the autumn of 1944, which is summed up in the operational name, 'Abwehrschlacht im Westen' – 'Defensive battle in the west'.

'Hitler's entire attitude towards German strategy in the west had, since 1942, been based on one conviction,' Zimmerman says. 'Namely, that the battle in the east would not be brought to a quick conclusion and that its developments would be increasingly felt in the west [where] the distances between the Channel and the Ruhr were so short that a successful mass invasion of the former must quickly bring the leading enemy troops to Germany's most vital industrial area.'

By 20 July, the day of the ill-fated bomb plot, Hitler's apprehensions had not yet been realised, but by the end of the month the U.S. First and Third Armies had broken through at St Lô and Avranches; shortly afterwards the British and Canadians had at last removed the plug at Caen and the bulk of the most experienced and best-equipped German forces in the west were decimated trying to escape from the Falaise pocket as the two Allied pincers closed around them. Similarly, the Russians were exploiting their greatest ever summer offensive and Heeresgruppe Mitte was in tatters.

Feldmarschall Günther von Kluge, von Rundstedt's successor, committed suicide as the search for the July bomb plot conspirators widened, and was briefly replaced by Feldmarschall Walter Model until he himself was entrusted with Heeresgruppe B for the Ardennes offensive and Rundstedt was brought back into play.

Model was cast in an entirely different mould from von Rundstedt. Coming from a poor family, he served as a junior infantry officer in the First World War. Progress in the interwar Reichsheer was slow until the Nazis' rise to power, when Model became one of Hitler's most devoted followers. He served as a staff officer in Poland and France, then as CO of 3 Panzer Division and later XLI Korps in Russia. Command of

In November 1944, British troops completed clearing the island of Walcheren, the key to the Scheldt estuary. Antwerp was the ultimate goal of 'Herbstnebel'.
(Imperial War Museum, London)

Ninth Armee followed and in 1943 Model was the driving force behind operation 'Zitadelle', the Kursk offensive. Later, nicknamed 'the fireman of the front', he saved first Heeresgruppe Nord then Heeresgruppe Süd from disaster before taking over OB West after von Kluge's death. In 1945 he committed suicide rather than surrender in the Ruhr pocket.

The strategic situation was further complicated in August 1944 when the Allies also landed on the Mediterranean coast of France, while after the fall of Rome the German situation in Italy was not a happy one either.

'Our decimated divisions,' von Zimmerman continues, 'believed that in the West Wall [the 'Siegfried Line'] they would find a sturdy support. If so, they were greatly mistaken. During the past few years [it] had been systematically and thoroughly plundered for the sake of the Atlantic Wall and in August of 1944 its condition was pitiable.' But the West Wall was not put to immediate test. Eisenhower's strategy was more or less a straight line thrust (despite the need to re-open the Channel ports, especially Antwerp) from Normandy, via Aachen, to the Ruhr. Temporarily distracted by Montgomery's scheme to secure an early crossing of the Rhine by an airborne operation in Holland, the Allied C-in-C could not prevent his principal ground forces from outrunning their over-stretched supply lines.

'In order to appreciate the psychological condition which existed at this time,' says Westphal, 'it is important to realise that the majority of the Germans both at home and at the front had not yet recognised Hitler as the criminal that he was. Despite deep sympathy for the victims of 20 July, the overwhelming mass of the German people still regarded it as their plain duty to accept their fate in silence and to go on working, suffering and dying for the sake of Germany's war effort. They saw no alternative. Only this can explain the fact that, despite well-nigh non-stop Allied air raids, the railways continued to function... while German arms production reached its peak during the autumn of 1944.' (In August, 869 tanks and 744 assault guns.)

It is interesting that Westphal blames three people for Germany's desperate strategic situation. Heinrich Himmler, Reichsführer-SS and head of the so-called 'Replacement Army' since 21 July when General-oberst Friedrich Fromm was executed for his complicity in the bomb plot, came first on Westphal's list, for the 'reign of terror' in Germany. Reichsmarschall Hermann Göring, head of the Luftwaffe, came second for 'recklessly sacrificing... the élite of the air force', for not drawing 'the correct technical conclusions... from the defeat in the Battle of Britain' which resulted in 'experimentation continuing for years on end' when 'what was clearly needed was the immediate production of a high-class fighter 'plane which would provide the answer to the coming Allied air offensive.' Westphal's third target, though, was Hitler himself, for his 'constant interference' in everything.

Nevertheless, he continues, in the early autumn of 1944 'The German armies were granted a brief respite when at last they had reached the German frontiers, for the Allies did not press on at once. Thus, what had seemed most unlikely turned out to be possible after all, and a new defensive front was created.' The West Wall was 'feverishly re-armed with such weapons as were available'. But then, 'the months of September, October and November saw further reverses. Aachen was the first large German town to fall into enemy hands... Lorraine and most of Alsace, together with the fortresses of Metz and Strasbourg, were also lost. 'Yet,' he says with obvious pride, 'despite all the attempts of the Americans to break through, particularly in the Aachen area, the front held.'

'Meanwhile,' Westphal concludes, 'in circumstances of greatest secrecy, an operation was being prepared which was to astonish not only the enemy but also the population of Germany... '

OPERATION 'HERBSTNEBEL'

Planning

Quite when Hitler conceived the operation finally codenamed 'Herbstnebel' ('Autumn Mist') is unclear, but that it was in the wake of the 20 July 1944 bomb attack on his life is not in doubt. 'Panzer Leader' Heinz Guderian, in *Erinnerungen eines Soldaten*, says of him at this time that, 'His mind remained active but there was something unhinged about this activity because it was dominated by constant wanderings [and] with the tenacity of a fanatic he grabbed at the last straw which, he imagined, would save him... from disaster'.

Adolf Hitler. An unstable mind became totally deranged after the attempt on his life and he believed 'Herbstnebel' might retrieve the war Germany had already lost. (U.S. Signal Corps)

The first written record of Hitler's grandiose concept occurs in a Luftwaffe officer's diary entry for 16 September following a routine conference at the *Wolfsschanze*; by coincidence, the same day that Allied paratroops were assembling to descend on Eindhoven, Nijmegen and Arnhem. Hitler would be given further cause that Christmas to have the U.S. 82nd and 101st Airborne Divisions in mind...

The plan had obviously begun to gel more fully in Der Führer's imagination a week later, after the Allies' precipitate attempt to force a crossing of the Rhine was already engraved in legend as the 'bridge too far'. On 25 September Hitler reviewed the overall strategic situation with Feldmarschall Wilhelm Keitel and Generaloberst Alfred Jodl – chief of staff and operations officer of the Oberkommando der Wehrmacht

(OKW) respectively – and told them that 'we have to get out of being endlessly... on the retreat, and grasp the initiative ourselves'.

The Soviet summer offensive, Hitler continued, had run its course and the front was now stable, as it was in Italy, but counter-offensives in either of these theatres would not be possible in the immediate future. The opportunity lay in the west, he considered, because the Allies had already reached the end of their supply lines' tether from the Channel ports and the momentum of their advance had slowed to a crawl

Gerd von Rundstedt. He already knew the cause was futile but obeyed orders – then passed them on to others to carry out, even when he realised their efforts would be in vain. (U.S. Signal Corps)

because of the lack – in particular – of fuel for their tanks. Perhaps this thought also came back to him that Christmas... Given this situation, Hitler explained to Keitel and Jodl, an offensive by between 20 and 30 Panzer and Volksgrenadier divisions would inflict heavy losses on the Allies and stabilise the western front so that stronger forces could subsequently be sent to the east. Many people, including high-ranking officers in the Wehrmacht such as Manteuffel, have theorised from this that Hitler intended to inflict such damage in the west that the United States and Britain would sue for a separate peace, leaving the Wehrmacht to deal with the real problem in Russia. If Hitler genuinely believed this – which is possible, given his state of mind – he was, of course, living in a 'pipe dream' because all the Allies

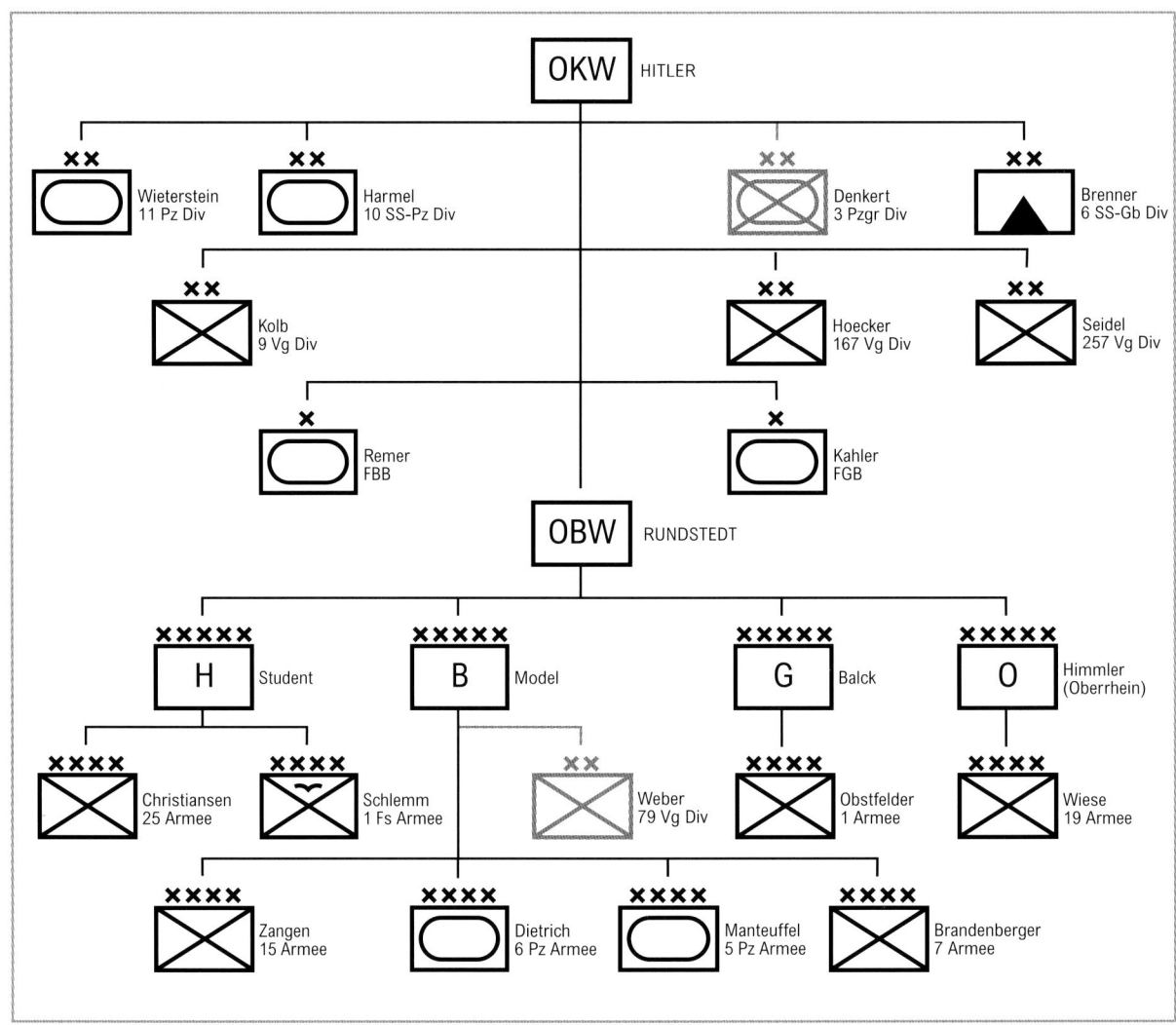

concurred that no solution short of complete surrender was acceptable.

Regardless of this hypothesis, Hitler retained sound judgement in some areas. He admitted that there were dangers in the plan, in that allocating personnel and tank production to such an offensive would leave the eastern front dangerously weak; and he recognised that it would have to be timed for a period when weather conditions would hamper the Allied air operations which had caused so many casualties in the wake of D-Day. He also asserted that the most stringent security precautions would have to be taken to prevent the Allies getting wind of the plan. Hitler estimated, over-optimistically, that it would take six to eight weeks to assemble the strike force and that the offensive should be planned to begin towards the end of November when there would be a new moon.

Hitler told Jodl to set the ball rolling by drafting a plan and ordering the withdrawal of I and II SS-Panzer Korps from the front, while Keitel was to calculate fuel and ammunition requirements. Jodl came up with five ideas on 9 October, none of which met with Hitler's approval, but elements of two could, it was thought, be combined. The revised plan submitted two days later, which called for a thrust through the U.S. First Army in the Ardennes to Antwerp, cutting off the Allied forces in Holland and northern Belgium, was sufficiently 'daring', in Jodl's words, to appeal to Hitler's lurid imagination. The reason for withdrawing forces from other sectors of the front was to be concealed under a code-name suggesting a passive motive: 'Wacht am Rhein' ('Watch on the Rhine').

Three armies were to be used in the offensive under the overall command of Feldmarschall Walter Model's Heeresgruppe B: in the north, SS-Oberstgruppenführer Josef 'Sepp' Dietrich's Sixth Panzer, including the two SS-Panzer Korps in which Hitler placed such faith; in the centre, General der

Panzertruppen Hasso von Manteuffel's Fifth Panzer; and in the south, General der Panzertruppen Erich Brandenberger's Seventh. In each sector the Volksgrenadiers, plus the two Fallschirm divisions which could be pulled out of reserve, were to make the initial breakthrough, then establish hard shoulders against intervention from the U.S. Ninth Army in the north and Third Army in the south. The Panzers would themselves then head straight for the Meuse, cross it and, following the line of the Albert Canal on their right flank, carry on to Brussels and Antwerp.

This plan was presented to Generalleutnant Siegfried Westphal, chief of staff to Feldmarschall Gerd von Rundstedt (who had been called out of retirement to head Oberbefehlshaber (OB) West), and

Model was a man of strong beliefs. After Paulus surrendered Sixth Armee to the Russians at Stalingrad, Model said capitulation was unthinkable for a German Field Marshal, and took his own life rather than surrender in the Ruhr pocket. (U.S. Signal Corps)

Hitler's 'grosse lösung' and the 'kleine lösung' of his generals. In retrospect, the Führer should have accepted the latter, less ambitious, plan.

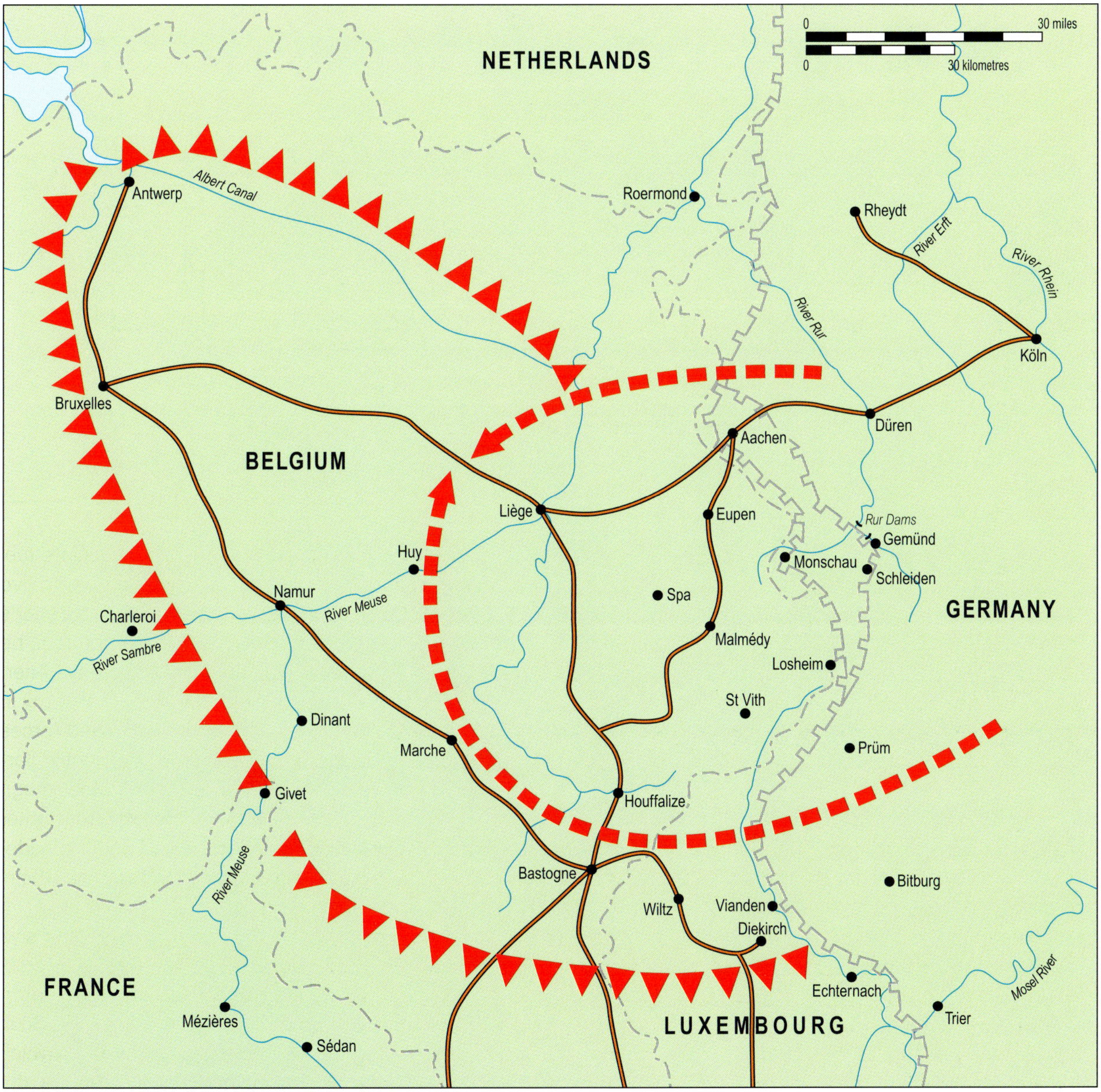

9

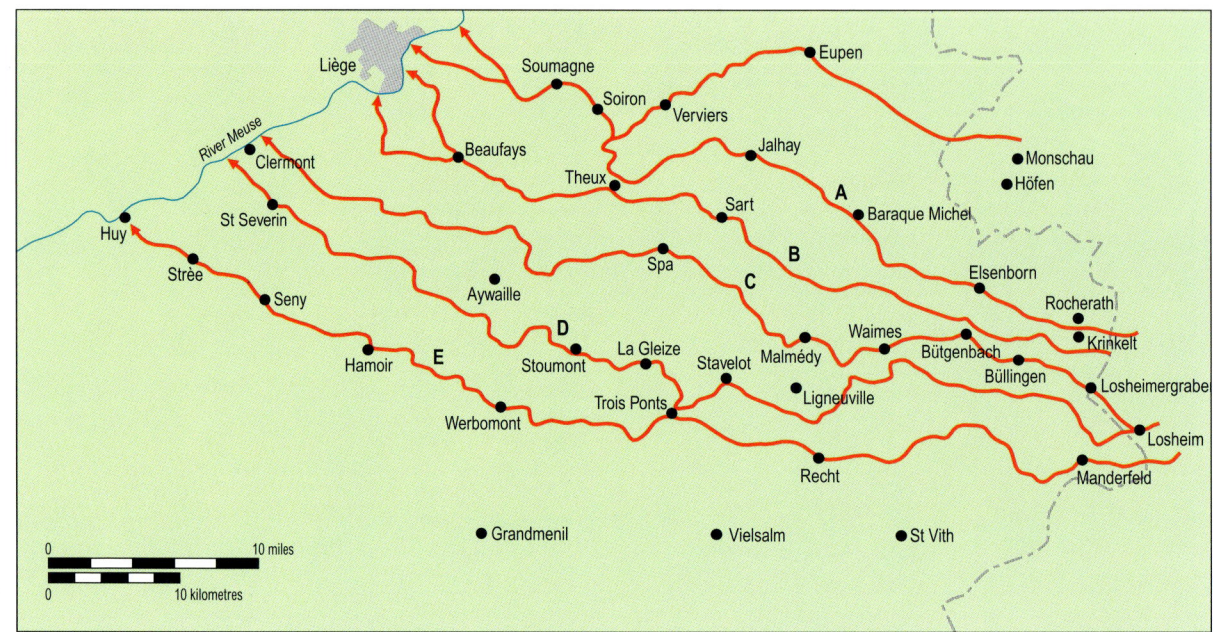

to General Hans Krebs, Model's chief of staff, on 22 October, the day after the fall of Aachen. Both men had to swear, on pain of death, not to divulge the plan or discuss it with anyone except 'predetermined personnel'. Model's reaction when briefed by Krebs was characteristically blunt: 'This plan,' he said, 'hasn't got a damned leg to stand on.' Von Rundstedt

Sixth Panzer Armee's intended routes to the River Meuse. The most northern Rollbahn was reserved for LXVII Korps. Rollbahns A, B & C were assigned to 12 SS-Panzer Division while Rollbahns D & E were intended for 1 SS-Panzer Division. In fact, because 'Hitler Jugend' got embroiled on the northern shoulder, Kampfgruppe 'Peiper' used parts of C, D and E.

VOLKSGRENADIER DIVISION
(c. 10,000 – 12,000 men)
Stabs Kompanie (Staff Company) including Landkarte (Map copying) and Feldgendarmerie (Military Police) Züge (platoons)
(c.200 men)

VOLKSGRENADIER (People's Rifle) REGIMENT
(c.2,000 men)
Stabs Kompanie (c.200 men) including Nachrichten (Signals), Pionier (Engineer), Fahrrad (Bicycle) and Maschinengewehr (Machine-Gun) Züge (10 x LMG [MG34 or '42])

I (1st) Volksgrenadier Abteilung (Battalion) (Fahrrad)
(c.700 men)
Stabs Kompanie (2 x LMG)
1, 2 & 3 Grenadier (Rifle) Kompanien (each 9 x LMG)
4 Hilfs (Support) Kompanie (1 x HMG, 8 x LMG, 6 x 8cm GrW 34 & 4 x 7.5cm leIG 18, 37 or 42)

II (2nd) Volksgrenadier Abteilung (Fuß) (Foot) (c.700 men)
Stabs Kompanie (2 x LMG)
5-8 Kompanien as above
(NB. No 9-12 Kompanien)

'13' Artillerie Kompanie (4 x 12cm sGrW 42, 4 x 7.5cm leFK 18 or 38 & 5 x LMG) (c.180 men)

'14' Panzerjäger Kompanie (54 x Panzerfaust/Panzerschreck & 4 x LMG) (c.180 men)

VOLKS-ARTILLERIE (People's Artillery) REGIMENT
(Pferde) (Horse-drawn) (c.2,400 men)
Stabs Kompanie (c.100 men) (1 x LMG)

I Bataillon (c.500 men)
Stabs Kompanie (2 x LMG)
1-3 Batterien (each 6 x 7.5cm leFK 18 or 38 or 7M85 [rare])

II & III Bataillonen (each c.500 men)
Stabs Kompanien
4-7 Batterien (each 6 x 10.5cm leFH 18, 18M, 18/40 or variants)

IV Bataillon (c.650 men)
Stabs Kompanie
8 & 9 Batterien (each 6 x 15cm sFH 18 or 36)

VOLKSGRENADIER DIVISION (continued)

PANZERJÄGER (Anti-tank) ABTEILUNG (mot) (c.450 men)
Stabs Kompanie (4 x LMG)
1 & 2 Kompanien (each 14 x StuG III/IV or Jagdpanzer
  with 7.5cm L/43, L/48 or L/70)
3 Kompanie (12 x towed 7.5cm PaK 40 or
  7.62cm PaK 36/39 [r])
Versorgungs Kolonne (Supply Column) (3 x LMG)

FLAK (Anti-aircraft) ABTEILUNG (mot) (c.750 men)
Stabs Kompanie (4 x LMG)
1 & 2 Batterien (each 4 x 8.8cm Flak 18, 36 or 37)
3 Batterie (6+ x 2cm Flakvierling)

FÜSILIER BATAILLON
(Ersatz and Aufklärungs or Reserve/Replacement and
Reconnaissance Battalion) (Number of men variable)
1, 2 or 3 Kompanien (Fahrrad) (each 2 x HMG, 8 x LMG,
  2 x 8cm GrW 34 & 2 x 7.5cm leIG 18 or variants)

NACHRICHTEN (Signals) ABTEILUNG (mot) (c.350 men)
Stabs Kompanie
Fernsprech (Telephone) Kompanie (5 x LMG)
Funk (Radio) Zug (4 x LMG)
Versorgungs Kolonne (2 x LMG)

PIONIER (Engineer) ABTEILUNG (Fahrrad) (c.600 men)
Stabs Kompanie
1 & 2 Kompanien (each 2 x HMG, 9 x LMG, 2 x 8cm GrW 34
  & 6 x Flammenwerfer [Flamethrower])

VERSORGUNGS 'REGIMENT'
  (c.1,400 men)
Stabs Kompanie
Verwaltungs (Food and Pay) Kompanie
Fleischerei (Butcher's) Kompanie
Bäkerei (Baker's) Kompanie
Feldpost (Field Post) Kompanie (mot)
Werkstatt (Workshop) Kompanie (mot)
Veterinär (Veterinary) Kompanie
Versorgungs Kolonne (Pferde)
Transport Kompanie (Pferde)
Transport Kompanie (mot)
2 x Sanitäts Kompanien (1 mot and 1 Pferde)
2 x Feld-Krankenwagen Kolonnen (field ambulance columns,
  horse-drawn)

himself said later that 'all, absolutely all conditions for the possible success of such an offensive were lacking'.

Nevertheless, the energetic Model's next step was to summon Dietrich, Manteuffel and Brandenberger to his headquarters (in a former drying-out clinic for alcoholics!) at Fichtenhain, just outside Krefeld, on 27 October. Feldmarschall von Rundstedt was also

Even as late as 1944 the majority of German infantry divisions had to rely on horse-drawn transport. This caused endless delays in getting supplies to the front. (Bildarchiv)

present and, like Westphal and Krebs before them, each of the army commanders had to sign an unprecedented document swearing total secrecy before Model divulged the plan.

Model and von Rundstedt had, in the intervening few days between their own briefings and this conference, independently thought up alternative plans which might have achieved more tangible results. These they also now brought out for discussion and Manteuffel, who was particularly concerned that Brandenberger's relatively weak forces in the south would be unable to withstand a concerted counter-attack by Patton's Third Army, agreed that a less ambitious scheme was the answer. Not surprisingly, Brandenberger himself concurred, and even Dietrich was later to comment bitterly that 'All [Hitler] wanted me to do was cross a river, capture Brussels, then go on and take Antwerp! And all this in the worst time of the year through the Ardennes where the snow is waist deep and there isn't room to deploy four tanks abreast let alone Panzer divisions. Where it doesn't get light until eight and it's dark again at four!'

The five men and their staffs spent several hours hammering out what came to be known as the 'kleine lösung' – the 'small solution'. This envisaged a pincer movement by one Panzer Armee out of the West Wall north of Aachen and by the second through the

PANZERGRENADIER DIVISION
(c. 12,000 men)
Stabs Kompanie including Landkarte and Feldgendarmerie Züge (3 x LMG)

PANZER ABTEILUNG (c.420 men)
Stabs Kompanie (3 x 7.5cm StuG III/IV)
1-3 Kompanien (each 11 x 7.5cm StuG III/IV &
  3 x 10.5cm StuH)

GRENADIER REGIMENT (mot)
  (c.3,000 men)
Stabs Kompanie (c.180 men) including Nachrichten, Kraftrad
  (Motorcycle) and Artillerie Züge (3 x 7.5cm leIG 18 or similar
  & 5 x LMG)

I Grenadier Abteilung (c.800 men)
Stabs Kompanie
1, 2 & 3 Kompanien (each 4 x HMG, 18 x LMG &
  2 x 8cm GrW 34)
4 Kompanie (4 x 12cm sGrW 42, 3 x 7.5cm leIG 18 or
  similar & 2 x LMG)

II & III Grenadier Abteilungen
  As above, but companies numbered 5-8 and 9-12

13 Artillerie Kompanie (6 x 15cm sFH 18 auf Gw III/IV
  'Hummel')
14 Panzerjäger Kompanie (18 x Panzerfaust/Panzerschreck &
  12 x LMG)
15 Flak Kompanie (12 x 2cm towed Flak 38)

ARTILLERIE REGIMENT (mot)
  (c.1,500 men)
Stabs Kompanie (c.80 men) (at least one tank & 2 x LMG)

I Bataillon (c.500 men)
Stabs Kompanie (at least one tank or StuG, 3 x 2cm Flak &
  2 x LMG)
1 & 2 Batterien (each 6 x 10.5cm leFH 18 auf Gw II 'Wespe')
3 Batterie (6 x 15cm sFH 18 auf Gw III/IV 'Hummel')

II Bataillon
Stabs Kompanie (as above)
4 & 5 Batterien (each 6 x towed 10.5cm leFH 18)

III Bataillon
Stabs Kompanie (as above)
6 & 7 Batterien (each 4 x towed 15cm sFH 18)
8 Batterie (4 x towed 10cm sK 18)

PANZER-AUFKLÄRUNGS ABTEILUNG (c.500 men)
Stabs Kompanie including Nachrichten Zug
1 Spähwagen (Armoured car) Kompanie (6 x SdKfz 233 or
  234/3 [7.5cm StuK L/24] & 18 x SdKfz 222 [2cm KwK])
2, 3 & 4 Kraftrad Kompanien (each 18 x m/c with LMG,
  2 x 8cm GrW 34 & 3 x Panzerfaust/Panzerschreck)
5 Hilfs Kompanie (3 x 7. 5cm PaK 40, 2 x 7.5cm leIG 18 &
  6 x LMG)

PANZERJÄGER ABTEILUNG (c.600 men)
Stabs Kompanie including 3 x towed 7.5cm PaK 40 and
  Nachrichten Zug
1 & 2 Kompanien (each 14 x 7.5cm Jagdpanzer IV/70)
3 Kompanie (12 x towed 7.5cm PaK 40)

FLAK ABTEILUNG (mot) (c.600 men)
Stabs Kompanie (2 x LMG)
1 & 2 Kompanien (each 4 or 6 x 8.8cm Flak 18 or 36)
3 Kompanie (12 x 2cm Flakvierling on halftracks)

PIONIER ABTEILUNG (mot) (c.750 men)
Stabs Kompanie including Nachrichten and Werkstatt Züge
1, 2 & 3 Kompanien (each 18 x LMG & 6 x Flammenwerfer)
Brückenkolonne (B) (Bridging Column with Brückengerät B) +
Versorgungs Kolonne

NACHRICHTEN ABTEILUNG (mot) (c.500 men)
Stabs Kompanie
Fernsprech Kompanie (8 x LMG)
Funk Kompanie (8 x LMG)
Versorgungs Kolonne

VERSORGUNGS 'REGIMENT' (mot)
Verwaltungs Truppe
Fleischerei Kompanie
Bäckerei Kompanie
Feldpost Kompanie
2 x Werkstatt Kompanien
Nachschub Truppe
5 x Transport Kompanien
2 x Sanitäts Kompanien
2 x Krankenwagen Kompanien

Ardennes, pinching off most of the U.S. First and Ninth Armies in the Maastricht-Liège salient. If this succeeded, Model argued when he submitted the revised plan to OKW, then Antwerp was still a possible goal.

Despite the validity of the Generals' arguments, it was perhaps predictable that Hitler would remain adamant, and Jodl followed up a written command that the original plan was unalterable with a visit to Model's headquarters on 3 November. Model and Manteuffel argued cogently, sensing that Jodl was, at heart, on

their side, but he insisted that the 'grosse lösung' must stand. (In his memoirs, incidentally, Manteuffel confuses this meeting with the earlier one in October.)

Only minor changes to Hitler's plan were agreed, the most important being that the projected date for the start of the offensive, 25 November, was too early and that the necessary forces could not be assembled – given the need to move them up secretly, and mostly by night – until the middle of December. Some troop movements could not be concealed, however,

FALLSCHIRM-DIVISION
(c. 10,000 – 12,000 men)
Stabs Kompanie including Landkarte Zug

FALLSCHIRMJÄGER REGIMENT
(2,400 men)
Stabs Kompanie including Nachrichten Zug (c.100 men)

I Abteilung (c.700 men)
Stabs Kompanie
1, 2 & 3 Kompanien (each 12 x LMG, 3 x 5cm leGrW 36 &
   3 x 8cm GrW 34)
4 Kompanie (12 x LMG)
5 Kompanie (2 x 7.5cm LG 40 plus Nachrichten & Pionier Züge
   [4 x LMG])

II & III Abteilungen (each c.700 men)
Stabs Kompanien & 6-15 Kompanien as above
6 Kompanie (3 x 7.5cm PaK 40 & 9 x 5cm PaK 38 or up to
   36 Panzerfaust/Panzerschreck) (c.100 men)
7 Kompanie (2 x 10.5cm IG 40 or 42 plus 2 x leichte
   Versorgungs Kolonnen) (c.100 men)

FALLSCHIRM-ARTILLERIE REGIMENT
(c.1,000 men)
Stabs Kompanie including Nachrichten Zug (c.100 men)

I Bataillon (c.400 men)
Stabs Kompanie & Nachrichten Zug
1 & 2 Batterien (each 4 x 10.5cm IG 40 or 42)

II Bataillon (c.400 men)
Stabs Kompanie & Nachrichten Zug
3 & 4 Batterien as above

FALLSCHIRM-AUFKLÄRUNGS ABTEILUNG (c.300 men)
Stabs Kompanie
1 & 2 Kompanien (each 9 x LMG & 2 x 8cm GrW 34)

FALLSCHIRM-PANZERJÄGER ABTEILUNG (c.350 men)
Stabs Kompanie
1 Kompanie (missing from 3 Fallschirm-Division) (12 x
   7.5cm StuG III/IV)
2 Kompanie (12 x towed 5cm PaK 38 or 7.5cm PaK 40)

FALLSCHIRM-FLAK ABTEILUNG (c.500 men)
Stabs Kompanie
1 Kompanie (4-6 x 8.8cm Flak 18 or 36)
2 Kompanie (4-12 x 2cm Flakvierling)

FALLSCHIRM-PIONIER ABTEILUNG (c.400 men)
Stabs Kompanie
1 & 2 Kompanien (2-9 x LMG, 2 x 8cm GrW 34 &
   6 x Flammenwerfer)

FALLSCHIRM-NACHRICHTEN ABTEILUNG (c.200 men)
Stabs Kompanie
Fernsprech Kompanie
Funk Kompanie

FALLSCHIRM-SCHWERE MÖRSER BATTERIE (c.100 men)
(6 x 12cm sGrW 42)

FALLSCHIRM-VERSORGUNGS ABTEILUNG
Stabs Kompanie
Verwaltungs Kompanie
Fleischerei Kompanie
Bäckerei Kompanie
Feldpost Kompanie
Werkstatt Kompanie
2-3 x Transport Kolonnen
2 x Sanitäts Kompanien
2 x Krankenwagen Kolonnen

and these were deliberately scheduled to take place in daylight when, it was actually hoped, they would be spotted by Allied aerial reconnaissance.

After the fall of Aachen, it was obvious that the next American offensive would be – as it in fact was – through the Hürtgen Forest north of Monschau and across the Rur into the Saar-Palatinate, heading for Köln, Bonn and the confluence of the Rhein and Mosel at Koblenz. Thus, it would be apparent to the Allies that German troops would be moved into this sector, as part of 'Wacht am Rhein', to repel them. For this reason, Sixth Panzer Armee's railheads were much further to the north-east of their launch-off points than was really desirable.

One major problem encountered during 'Herbstnebel' was ammunition shortages which restricted the ability of the field artillery to support attacks. (Bildarchiv)

13

FALLSCHIRM-SCHÜTZE KOMPANIE

(144 men)

Stabs Zug (Hauptmann or Oberleutnant & Feldwebel & 7 men
including radio operator)

---

1 Zug (Leutnant & Unterfeldwebel)
1/1 Trupp (Obergefreiter or Gefreiter & 9 men)
2/1 Trupp (Obergefreiter or Gefreiter & 9 men)
3/1 Trupp (Obergefreiter or Gefreiter & 9 men)
4/1 Trupp (Unteroffizier & 12 men)
  1 x MG 42 (3 men)
  1 x 5cm leGrW 36 (3 men)
  1 x 8cm GrW 34 (5 men)
  1 x Panzerfaust/Panzerschreck (1 or 2 men)

2 Zug (Leutnant & Unterfeldwebel)
1/2 Trupp (Obergefreiter or Gefreiter & 9 men)
2/2 Trupp (Obergefreiter or Gefreiter & 9 men)
3/2 Trupp (Obergefreiter or Gefreiter & 9 men)
4/2 Trupp (Unteroffizier & 12 men)
  1 x MG 42 (3 men)
  1 x 5cm leGrW 36 (3 men)
  1 x 8cm GrW 34 (5 men)
  1 x Panzerfaust/Panzerschreck (1 or 2 men)

3 Zug (Leutnant & Unterfeldwebel)
1/3 Trupp (Obergefreiter or Gefreiter & 9 men)
2/3 Trupp (Obergefreiter or Gefrelter & 9 men)
3/3 Trupp (Obergefreiter or Gefreiter & 9 men)
4/3 Trupp (Unteroffizier & 12 men)
  1 x MG 42 (3 men)
  1 x 5cm leGrW 36 (3 men)
  1 x 8cm GrW 34 (5 men)
  1 x Panzerfaust/Panzerschreck (1 or 2 men)

Officers carried pistols as symbols of authority; NCOs, MP40 SMGs; riflemen, assault rifles, either FG 42 or StG 44, plus hand grenades and magnetic anti-tank mines.
Because the FG 42 was always in short supply, these would mainly be carried by the more experienced men. In addition, many men preferred captured weapons which were regarded as status symbols.
The 1, 2 and 3 Truppe each also had 1 x MG 42.

The deception worked, but the results to the offensive were nothing short of catastrophic. As soon as the Allies realised what the German intentions were, and the skies cleared, the railways became principal targets and trains had to spend the daytime

The railheads for troops and supplies for Sixth Panzer Armee. Keitel estimated that no fewer than 50 trains would be needed for ammunition alone. Many had to spend the daylight hours hiding in tunnels from Allied air attacks.

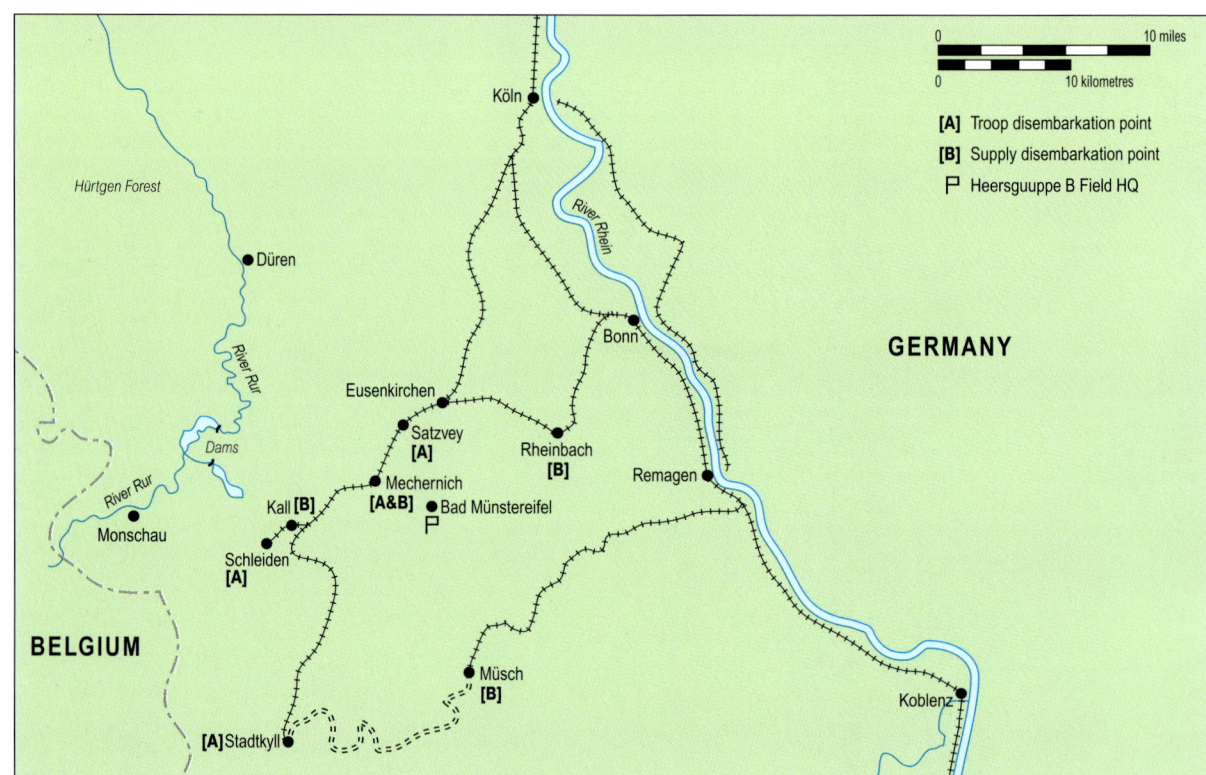

hours sheltering in the numerous tunnels. The Allied air forces put their main effort into interdiction raids against the German railheads and bridges over the Rhein and Mosel and this, coupled with poor traffic control on the ground, meant that supply columns could take five days to travel from the Rhein to the divisional reloading points behind the front line. Time after time the Panzer divisions were delayed waiting for the fuel tankers to struggle through to them along narrow, congested roads whose surfaces had been churned up by the tanks' own tracks.

Other parts of the deception plan were also successful, such as moving headquarters (on paper and with a skeleton staff) to one place but the troops and tanks to another. This way, the Allies were led to believe that Sixth Panzer Armee was assembling northwest of Köln rather than south of Monschau.

Radio traffic was also choreographed, and total radio silence was imposed on all new divisions moving into the Eifel region. Thus, even though the Germans did not know that British cryptanalysts had cracked the 'Enigma' code, they did not give the 'Ultra' team at Bletchley Park a single clue to work on. All communications were sent in sealed packets by despatch rider, and had to be signed for by the addressee in person. Knowledge of the real purpose of the various troop movements was restricted to as few people as possible for as long as possible; Korps' commanders were

not briefed until 11-12 December, divisional commanders on the 13th and the commanders of the Panzer kampfgruppen which would spearhead the assault, and other regimental commanders, on the 14th.

All tank and artillery movements towards the real front line were made by night with teams of engineers following to erase their track and tyre marks, and once in their assembly areas, the vehicles and guns themselves were carefully camouflaged against aerial observation. Senior officers operating anywhere near the front line, studying the lie of the land, for example, had to remove or conceal any identifying insignia. Panzer officers had to swap their black tunics for infantry field grey. Unit insignia on vehicles was similarly obscured and command pennants were removed from staff cars. Charcoal was issued so that there would be no revealing smoke from bivouac fires.

Despite all the careful planning, though, when the assault actually began with a massive bombardment by all the 1,600 artillery pieces in the three armies at 0530 on Saturday 16 December, the state of readiness of Model's forces was far from complete. In Sixth Panzer Armee, only the four SS-Panzer divisions had

Generalleutnant Wolfgang Pickert's III Flakkorps put 21 batteries of 8.8cm anti-aircraft guns at the disposal of Sixth Panzer Armee during 'Herbstnebel'.
(Bildarchiv)

SS-PANZER DIVISION
(c. 13,000 – 15,000 men)
Stabs Kompanie (2 x PzKpfw V), Kapelle (Band), Landkarte Zug, Feldgendarmerie Zug
(4 x 2cm Flakvierling auf Gw IV 'Wirbelwind', 6 x Kraftrad [6 x LMG], 4 x HMG & 6 x LMG) (c.450 men)

SS-PANZER REGIMENT
(c.1,600 men)
Stabs Kompanie including Nachrichten Zug, 2 x PzKpfw IV or
V and 8 x 3.7cm Flak auf Gw IV 'Ostwind' (c.120 men)
Werkstatt Kompanie (c.200 men)

I Abteilung (c.500-600 men)
Stabs Kompanie including 2-8 x PzKpfw V, 3 x 2cm Flakvierling
auf Gw IV 'Wirbelwind' & 12 x LMG
1, 2, 3 & 4 Kompanien (each 14-17 x PzKpfw V and/or
PzKpfw IV)
Versorgungs Truppe (5 x LMG)

II Abteilung (c.500 men)
Stabs Kompanie as above but PzKpfw IV
5 & 6 Kompanien (each 14 x PzKpfw IV)
7 & 8 Kompanien (each 10-14 x 7.5cm Jagdpanzer IV/70)
Versorgungs Truppe (5 x LMG)

I SS-PANZERGRENADIER REGIMENT
(c.2,000 men)
Stabs Kompanie (SdKfz 250 & 251 half-tracks) including
Nachrichten Zug and Kraftrad Zug (6 x LMG) (c.160 men)

I Abteilung (all SdKfz 251 half-tracks) (c.850 men)
Stabs Kompanie including Versorgungs Zug (4 x LMG)
1, 2 & 3 Kompanien (each 2 x 7.5cm PaK 40, 7 x 2cm Flak 38,
2 x 8cm GrW 34, 4 x HMG & 29 x LMG)
4 Kompanie (6 x 7.5cm PaK 40, 4 x 12cm sGrW 42,
2 x HMG & 4 x LMG)

II Abteilung (all truck-mounted) (c.850 men)
Stabs Kompanie as above
5, 6 & 7 Kompanien (each 2 x 8cm GrW 34, 4 x HMG &
18 x LMG)
8 Kompanie (6 x 2cm Flak 38, 4 x sGrW 42 & 2 x HMG)
(NB: No 9-14 Kompanien)
15 Kompanie (6 x 15cm auf Gw III/IV 'Hummel' or sIG 33 or
10.5cm auf Gw II 'Wespe')
Pionier Kompanie (24 x Flammenwerfer, 1 x 2cm Flak 38,
2 x 8cm GrW 34, 2 x HMG & 27 x LMG)

II SS-PANZERGRENADIER REGIMENT
As above except both abteilungen as II/I and Pionier Kompanie
only (16 x Flammenwerfer and 12 x LMG)

SS-PANZER ARTILLERIE REGIMENT
(c.1,600 men)
Stabs Kompanie (2 x LMG) (c.90 men)

I Bataillon (c.550 men)
Stabs Kompanie (1 x Wespe, 3 x 2cm Flak 38 & 2 x LMG)
1 & 2 Batterien (each 6 x Wespe)
3 Batterie (6 x Hummel)

II Bataillon (c.450 men)
Stabs Kompanie as above
4 & 5 Batterien (each 6 x towed 10.5cm leFH 18)

III Bataillon (c.500 men)
Stabs Kompanie as above
6 & 7 Batterien (each 4 x towed 15cm sFH 18)
8 Batterie (4 x 17cm K18)

SS-PANZER AUFKLÄRUNGS ABTEILUNG (c.500 men)
Stabs Kompanie including Nachrichten Zug
1 Spähwagen Kompanie (26 x SdKfz 221 & 16 x SdKfz 231)
2 (leichte) Kompanie (SdKfz 251s) (2 x 7. 5cm PaK 40,
2 x 8cm GrW 34 & 44 x LMG)
3 Kompanie (2 x 7.5cm PaK 40, 7 x 2cm Flak 38,
2 x 8cm GrW 34, 4 x HMG & 29 x LMG)
4 Kompanie (6 x 7.5cm PaK 40, 6 x 8cm GrW 34,
5 x LMG & Pionier Zug [13 x LMG])
Versorgungs Kompanie (5 x LMG)

SS-PANZERJÄGER ABTEILUNG (c.500 men)
Stabs Kompanie (3 x 7.5cm Jagdpanzer IV/70)
1 & 2 Kompanien (each 10 x 7.5cm Jagdpanzer IV/70)
3 Kompanie (12 x towed 7.5cm PaK 40)
Versorgungs Kompanie (3 x LMG)

SS-PANZER FLAK ABTEILUNG (c.750 men)
Stabs Kompanie (2 x LMG)
1 & 2 Kompanien (each 6 x towed 8.8cm Flak 18 or 36 &
3 x 2cm Flak 38)
3 Kompanie (9 x 3.7cm Flak 36 or 37)
4 Kompanie (4-12 x 2cm Flakvierling on half-tracks)

SS-PANZER PIONIER ABTEILUNG (c.850 men)
Stabs Kompanie (4 x LMG & 4 x Flammenwerfer)
1 Kompanie (mot) (4 x HMG, 36 x LMG & 4 x 8cm GrW 34)
2 Kompanie (SdKfz 251s) (2 x HMG, 43 x LMG, 2 x 8cm GrW
34 & 6-8 x Flammenwerfer)
Brückenkolonne (K)

SS-PANZER NACHRICHTEN ABTEILUNG (c.500 men)
Stabs Kompanie
Fernsprech Kompanie
Funk Kompanie
Versorgungs Kompanie (2 x LMG)

SS-PANZER NEBELWERFER ABTEILUNG (c.500 men)
Stabs Kompanie (1 x LMG)
1, 2 & 3 Batterien (each 6 x 15cm WGr 41)
Versorgungs Kompanie (1 x LMG)

SS-VERSORGUNGS ABTEILUNG (mot)
Stabs Kompanie
1, 2, 3, 4 & 5 Transport Kolonnen
Werkstatt Kompanie

<table>
<tr><td>

SS-PANZER DIVISION (continued)

SS-NACHSCHUB & WERKSTATT ABTEILUNG
Stabs Zug
Versorgungs Kompanie (mot)
Fleischerei Kompanie (mot)
Bäckerei Kompanie (mot)
Feldpost Kompanie (mot)
1, 2 & 3 Werkstatt Kompanien (mot)
Ersatz Kompanie (mot)

SS-SANITÄTS ABTEILUNG (mot)
1 & 2 Sanitäts Kompanien
1, 2 & 3 Krankenwagen Kolonnen

</td><td>

PANZER REGIMENT ORDER OF MARCH

I Abteilung
1/I (1 Kompanie/I Abteilung) (PzKpfw V):
   Tanks numbered 100, 101 [1 Kompanie Zug]
   111-115 [1 Zug], 121-125 [2 Zug] & 131-135 [3 Zug]
2/I (2 Kompanie/I Abteilung) (PzKpfw V):
   Tanks numbered 200, 201, 211-215, 221-225 & 231-235
3/I (3 Kompanie/I Abteilung) (PzKpfw V):
   Tanks numbered 300, 301, 311-315, 321-325 & 331-335
4/I (4 Kompanie/I Abteilung) (PzKpfw V):
   Tanks numbered 400, 401, 411-415, 421-425 & 431-435

Stab Zug (PzKpfw V): I00-I01 (-I08)

Regiment Stab: Tanks numbered R01-R08

Werkstatt Kompanie

II Abteilung
Stab Zug (PzKpfw IV): II00-II01 (-II08)
5/II (5 Kompanie/II Abteilung) (PzKpfw IV):
   Tanks numbered 500, 501, 511-515, 521-525 & 531-535
6/II (6 Kompanie/II Abteilung) (PzKpfw IV):
   Tanks numbered 600, 601, 611-615, 621-625 & 631-635
7/II (7 Kompanie/II Abteilung) (Jagdpanzer IV/70):
   Tanks numbered 700, 701, 711-715, 721-725 & 731-735
8/II (8 Kompanie/II Abteilung) (Jagdpanzer IV/70):
   Tanks numbered 800, 801, 811-815, 821-825 & 831-835

Versorgungs Truppe (I & II)

</td></tr>
</table>

been properly rested and refitted, and even they were understrength in tanks. Many vehicles had already seen long and arduous service, and regular mechanical breakdowns had to be expected which would serve to block the already congested Rollbahns. (This was particularly true of the halftrack artillery tractors.)

In the infantry divisions, large numbers of personnel had been drafted in, to make up numbers, from the Luftwaffe and Kriegsmarine – unwilling and untrained

The end of a dream. Even though many were poorly-trained and ill-prepared for the conditions they would meet in the Ardennes, the Volksgrenadiers often fought with a surprising passion this late in the war. (Bildarchiv)

foot sloggers even if they did have the advantage of a much higher proportion of automatic weapons, such as the StG44 assault rifle, than the Americans. Moreover, the veteran cadres were tired, many of them having only recently been withdrawn from the ferocious fighting around Aachen and in the Hürtgen Forest. Despite this, morale was, by all accounts, surprisingly high. The men knew their backs were against the wall, knew that the Allies required their unconditional surrender, and were determined to make that requirement as difficult as possible to achieve. Besides, the Führer had pulled rabbits out of hats before, hadn't he, and even now the V-2 rockets were falling on London and Antwerp. Thus, the stage was set and the players in place for Adolf Hitler's great gamble.

Following pages – **When finalising 'Herbstnebel', the Germans knew that the U.S. First Army was thin on the ground, with divisions holding 20-30 mile fronts. They did not know precisely what lay in front of Sixth Panzer Armee, but estimated between five and seven divisions, including two armoured. What lay west of the Meuse was a mystery.**

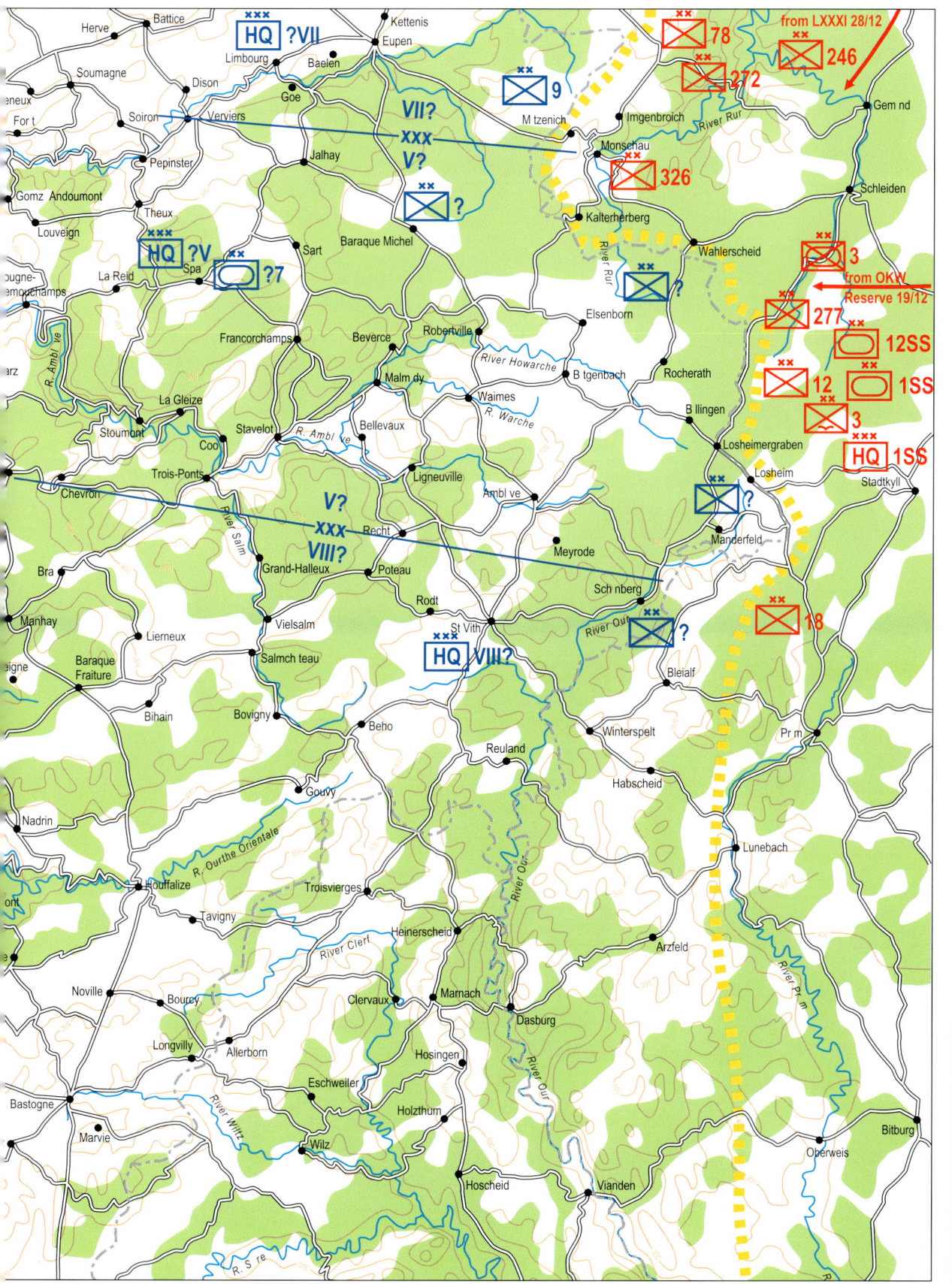

SIXTH PANZER ARMEE

Since it was assumed – erroneously, as events proved – that SS-Oberstgruppenführer 'Sepp' Dietrich's Sixth Panzer Armee would spearhead the drive across the River Meuse, it had a greater number of tanks, tank destroyers and artillery pieces than General Hasso von Manteuffel's Fifth Panzer Armee, and only slightly fewer assault guns. During the first 24 hours of the offensive Dietrich could field between 357 and 377 Tiger Is and IIs, Panthers and PzKpfw IVs; approximately 215 Jagdpanthers, Jagdpanzer IV/70s and 38(t) Hetzers; 112 Sturmgeschütze, 685 artillery pieces and 340 Nebelwerfers. Additionally, Sixth Panzer Armee also later received

SS-Oberstgruppenführer Josef 'Sepp' Dietrich, commander of Sixth Panzer Armee, held the highest SS rank beneath that of Reichsführer Heinrich Himmler.
(U.S. Signal Corps)

SIXTH PANZER ARMEE

SS-Oberstgruppenführer Josef Dietrich

Stabschef: *SS-Brigadeführer Fritz Krämer*

I SS-Panzer Korps (Priess)
II SS-Panzer Korps (Bittrich)
LXVII Korps (Hitzfeld)
150 Panzer Brigade (Skorzeny)
394 & 667 Sturmgeschütze Brigaden
217 Sturmpanzer Abteilung
683 Panzerjäger Abteilung (mot.Z) (Gillenberger)
301 schwere Panzer Abteilung (Fkl) (Krämer)
506 schwere Panzer Abteilung (Lange)
519 schwere Panzerjäger Abteilung
388, 402 & 405 Volks-Artillerie Korps
4, 9 & 17 Volks-Werfer Brigaden
428, 1098, 1110 & 1120 schwere Mörser Batterien
1123 Festungs-Artillerie Batterie
62, 73 & 253 Pionier Bataillonen
59 & 798 Baupionier Bataillonen
655 Pionier-Brücken Bataillon
I/403 & II/406 Brückenkolonnen (B)
602, 967 & 968 Brückenkolonnen (B)
175, 844, 851 & 895 Brückenkolonnen (J)
4 Brigade, Organisation Todt

Fifteenth Armee's 902 Sturmgeschütz Brigade with 20 vehicles and 1000 and 1001 Sturmörser Kompanien with, respectively, three and four 38cm Sturmtigers.

Despite this apparent strength, and Dietrich's encouraging words to his troops on the eve of battle, when he told them, 'the Führer has placed us in a decisive position', he was actually very unhappy and rounded forcefully on Generaloberst Alfred Jodl, Hitler's operations officer, after he received his orders for 'Herbstnebel'. 'I'm a general,' he shouted, 'not a bloody undertaker.'

Dietrich's Sixth Panzer Armee began forming at Paderborn in September 1944 with its staff largely constituted from survivors of XII Korps which had been destroyed in Russia. Dietrich's second in command was the very capable SS-Brigadeführer Fritz Krämer, former chief of staff of I SS-Panzer Korps in Normandy and commander of 12 SS-Panzer Division from September to November 1944.

One of Dietrich's more unorthodox subordinates was SS-Obersturmbannführer Otto Skorzeny, the vainglorious commander of '150 Panzer Brigade'. Skorzeny had been appointed to this post by Hitler and, under the codename Operation 'Greif', entrusted with forming and deploying a force of American speaking troops in captured uniforms and vehicles to sow confusion and panic behind Allied lines through spreading rumours and conducting acts of sabotage. They were also supposed to

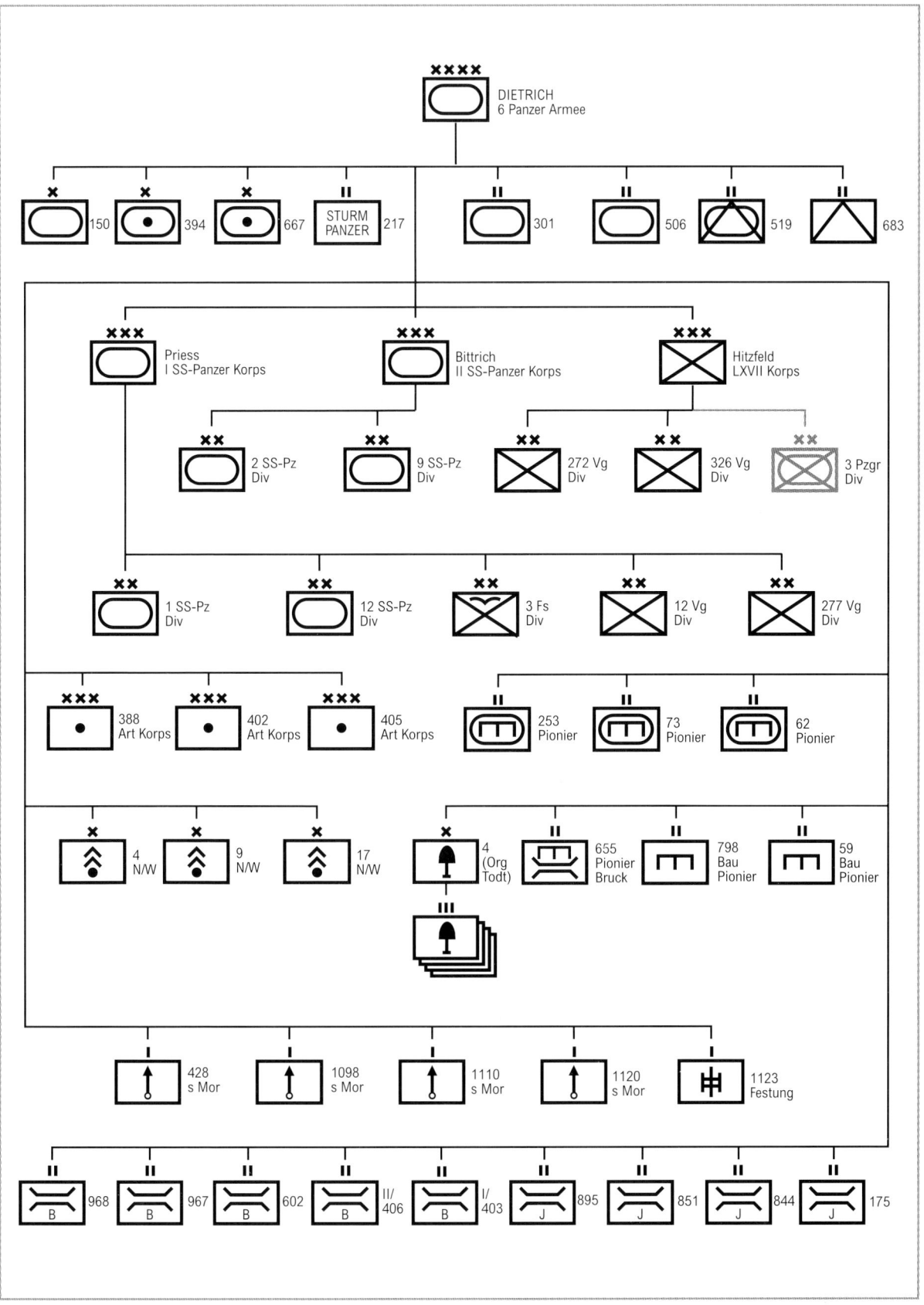

capture intact bridges across the Meuse. There proved a dearth of suitable volunteers and few of Skorzeny's men could speak colloquial English, while captured vehicles were also elusive because those units which had them preferred to hang on to them. The 'Brigade' was a mere shadow of what it was supposed to have been and ended up fighting as a 'line' formation trying to extricate Kampfgruppe 'Peiper' from its predicament, while many of the 'Einheits Kommando' saboteurs acting in its van were caught and executed.

SS-Obersturmbann-führer Otto Skorzeny claimed in his postwar memoirs that the idea behind operation 'Greif' was his. It was not. It was Hitler's.
(U.S. Signal Corps)

---

150 PANZER BRIGADE
SS-Obersturmbannführer Otto Skorzeny

Kampfgruppe X (Hardieck)
Kampfgruppe Y (Scheff)
Kampfgruppe Z (Wolf)

Model's operational orders for Sixth Panzer Armee made everybody's role quite clear. 'The Sixth Panzer Armee will break through the enemy front to the north

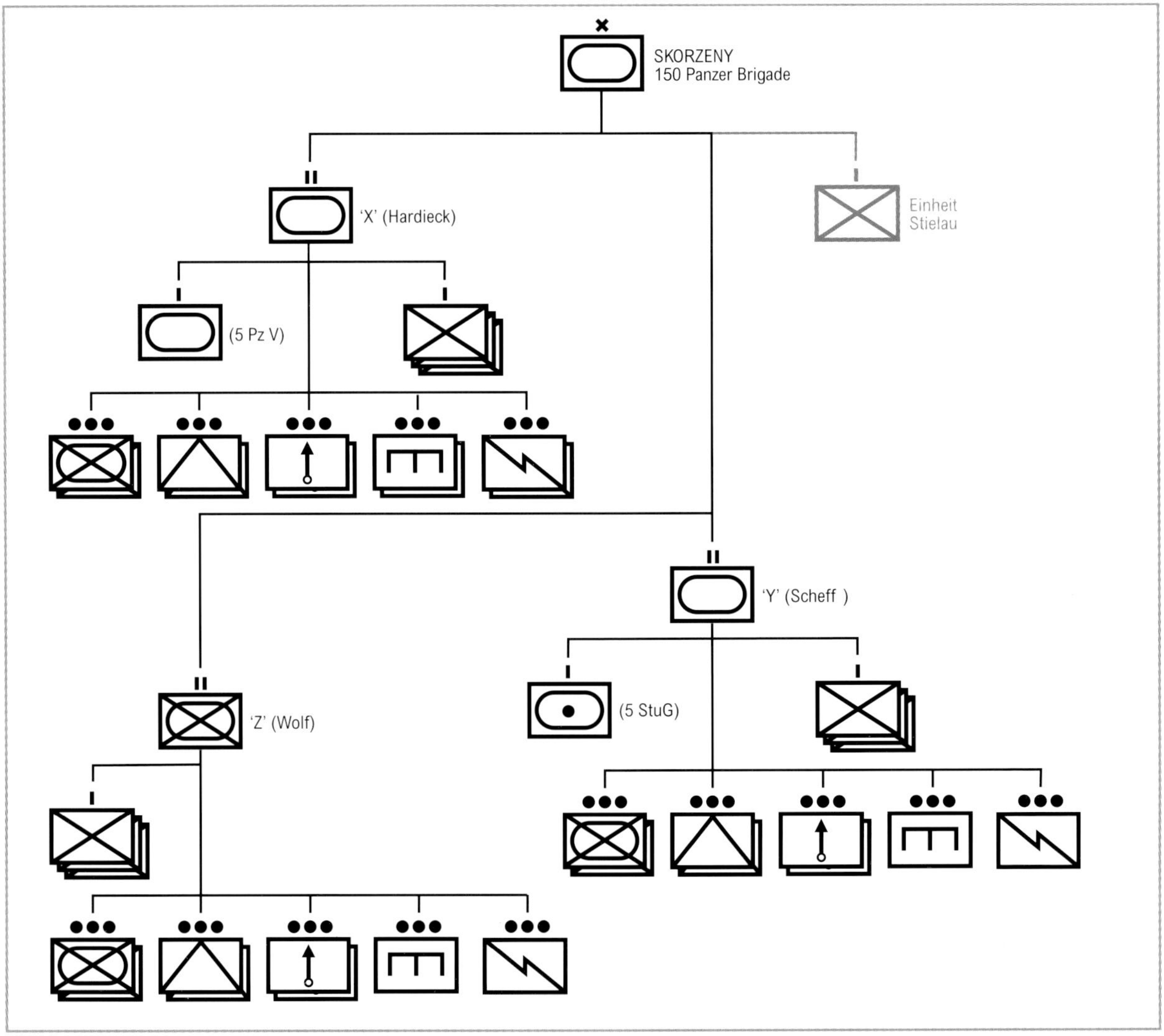

SKORZENY
150 Panzer Brigade

'X' (Hardieck)

Einheit Stielau

(5 Pz V)

'Y' (Scheff)

'Z' (Wolf)

(5 StuG)

VI PANZER ARMEE RESERVE

---

schwere Panzer Abteilung (Fkl) 301
Stabs Kompanie including 3 x 2cm Flakvierling auf Gw IV
 'Wirbelwind'
1, 2 & 3 Kompanien (total 22 x PzKpfw VI Tiger II)
Werkstatt Kompanie (only two Züge) (3 x Bergepanther)
Versorgungs Kompanie (mot)

schwere Panzer Abteilung 506
Stabs Kompanie as above
1, 2 & 3 Kompanien (total 22 x PzKpfw VI Tiger I)
Werkstatt Kompanie (5 x Bergepanther)
Versorgungs Kompanie (mot)

Sturmgeschütze 'Brigaden' 394 & 667
 (each one Kompanie, 4 x StuG)

Sturmpanzer Abteilung 217
 (attached to 12 Volksgrenadier Division)
 1 & 2 Kompanien (each 4 x Brummbär)

Panzerjäger Abteilung (mot) 683
Stabs Kompanie
1, 2 & 3 Kompanien (each 12 x 8.8cm PaK 43)

Festungs Artillerie Batterie 1123
 (6 x 17cm K18)

schwere Mörser Batterien 428, 1098, 1110 and 1120
 (each 6 x 21cm Mörser 18 or 38)

Pionier Bataillonen 62, 73 and 253
Stabs Kompanien (each 5 x LMG)
1, 2 & 3 Kompanien (each 2 x HMG, 18 x LMG,
 2 x 8cm GrW 34 & 6 x Flammenwerfer)

Pionier-Brücken Bataillon 655
Stabs Kompanie (5 x LMG)
1, 2 & 3 Kompanien (each 6 x LMG)

Bau-Pionier Bataillonen 59 and 798
Stabs Zug (1 x LMG)
1, 2 & 3 Kompanien (each 6 x LMG)
4 Kompanie (2 x LMG)
Transport Kolonne (2 x LMG)

Brückenkolonnen (B) 602, 967, 968, 403
 (I Abteilung only) and 406 (II Abteilung only)
 (Each abteilung 4 x Kompanien, 4 x pontoon bridges)

Brückenkolonnen (J) 175, 844, 851 and 895
 (Each abteilung 4 x Kompanien, 4 x girder bridges)

---

of the Schnee Eifel and will resolutely thrust forward on its right flank with its fast-moving units for the Meuse crossing points between Liège and Huy in order to capture these intact in conjunction with Operation 'Greif'. Following this, the army will drive forward to the Albert Canal between Maastricht and Antwerp. The penetration of the Volksgrenadiers through the Hohes Venn will be supported by the paratroop operation 'Stösser'.'

The latter was another ill-planned ingredient in the 'Herbstnebel' concept: a battalion-sized Kampfgruppe commanded by the former CO of 6 Fallschirmjäger Regiment, Oberst Friedrich Freiherr von der Heydte, was to capture the important crossroads at Baraque Michel on Rollbahn A ahead of 12 SS-Panzer Division. Once the mobile forces had achieved their penetration, Model's orders continued, the Volksgrenadiers were to establish a secure right flank to safeguard the Panzer divisions' lines of communication, at which point the infantry would come under Fifteenth Armee control.

Given such a complex situation to contend with, Dietrich was fortunate to have a capable staff because, although he was idolised by his men, he was uneducated and under normal circumstances could not have realistically expected to rise much above the rank of sergeant. Born in Bavaria in 1892, Dietrich enlisted in the Imperial German Army in 1911. By 1917 he had mastered the skills of a motor mechanic, and with the rank of Oberfeldwebel entered one of the first German tank battalions, a fact he remained proud of all his life.

Like many of his contemporaries, Dietrich was disillusioned at the end of World War 1 and sought a scapegoat for Germany's defeat. This made him an ideal recruit for the fledgling Nazi Party. His physique and mentality also suited him perfectly during Hitler's rise to power and in 1928 Dietrich became commander of the Führer's Schutzstaffel (SS) bodyguard. This was given the name Leibstandarte 'Adolf Hitler' in 1933 and from that moment on, Dietrich's career was inextricably linked with his command, his rank increasing each time the Leibstandarte was enlarged until he reached the pinnacle of Oberstgruppenführer, the SS equivalent of Field Marshal.

At heart, though, Dietrich remained an NCO throughout. Ignorant, coarse and a heavy drinker, he was detested by the Army hierarchy but gradually won their reluctant admiration, and the championship of men of the calibre of Guderian and Manstein, for his gutsy determination in battle. It was this leadership

Göring (left) promised Jodl and Keitel that the Luftwaffe would be able to provide adequate support for Sixth Panzer Armee, but most of the fighters had to be used to defend the railheads. (Bildarchiv)

VOLKS ARTILLERIE KORPS
(3,326 men, 414 light and 111 heavy trucks)
Stabs Kompanie
Beobachtungs (Observation) Kompanie

I Bataillon
  Stabs Kompanie (each 2 x LMG)
  1-3 Batterien (each 6 x 7.5cm PaK 40)
II Bataillon
  Stabs Kompanie
  4-6 Batterien (each 6 x 8.8cm PaK 43)
III Bataillon
  Stabs Kompanie
  7-9 Batterien (each 6 x 10.5cm leFH 18)
IV Bataillon
  Stabs Kompanie
  10 & 11 Batterien (each 6 x 15cm sFH)
V Bataillon
  Stabs Kompanie
  12 & 13 Batterien (each 6 x 12.2cm sFH(r))
VI Bataillon
  Stabs Kompanie
  14 & 15 Batterien (each 3 x 21cm Mrs 18)
  16 Batterie (3 x 17cm K18)

---

quality which caused him to be adored by his men even when he gave them almost suicidal tasks.

Dietrich appreciated that the task entrusted to Sixth Panzer Armee was far from easy. Apart from the weather – which would, at least, save his tanks from the attentions of the dreaded 'Jabos' – his forces had 72 miles to cover before they reached the Meuse and a further 53 miles to go before they entered Antwerp. It had taken the Panzer divisions nearly three days to reach the Meuse in the summer of 1940; how much longer would it take in the depths of winter? Fuel was also in desperately short supply and the speedy capture of one or more Allied POL depots was essential if the momentum of the advance was to be maintained. Indeed, a not uncommon sight in the Ardennes was a tank towing trucks whose fuel tanks had been drained.

On top of this, the grain of the land was against a speedy advance, restricting the Panzer divisions to their assigned Rollbahns. These were narrow, in many places single-track roads, which meant that each Kampfgruppe would straggle over several miles rather than being concentrated in force. The so-called main roads also featured many hairpin bends, and were often built into steep hillsides which would cause enormous problems for the slower-moving towed artillery and bridging trains.

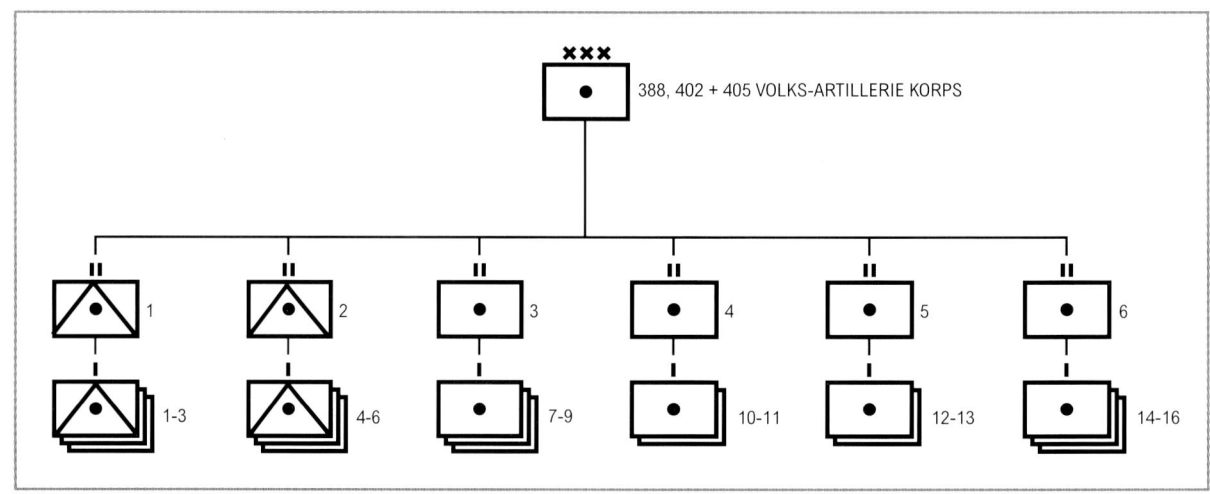

Oberst Friederich Freiherr von der Heyte led the ill-fated operation 'Stösser'. A lawyer by profession, he later became a Fellow of the Cargenie Endowment for International Peace.
(U.S. Signal Corps)

VOLKS-WERFER BRIGADE
(2,933 men, 276 light and 109 heavy trucks)
Stabs Kompanie (3 x LMG)
Nachrichten Kompanie (2 x LMG)
Park Kompanie

---

1 Regiment
  Stabs Kompanie (2 x LMG)
  I & II Bataillonen
  Stabs Kompanien (each 1 x LMG)
  Versorgungs Kompanien (each 1 x LMG)
  1-6 Batterien (each 6 x 15cm WGr 41)
  III Bataillon
  Stabs & Versorgungs Kompanien
  7-9 Batterien (each 6 x 21cm WGr 42)
2 Regiment
  Stabs Kompanie
  I & II Bataillonen
  Stabs & Versorgungs Kompanien
  1-6 Batterien (each 6 x 15cm WGr 41)
  III Bataillon
  Stabs & Versorgungs Kompanien
  7-9 Batterien (each 6 x 30cm WkrS 42)

Given these circumstances, even 'Sepp' Dietrich appreciated that a spirited resistance by a token American force at one of the many choke points on Sixth Panzer Armee's route to the Meuse could seriously delay his timetable. He was right, but Model's orders to his two Panzer Armee commanders were nonetheless unequivocal: the infantry were to be used to achieve the initial breakthrough, after which the tanks were to stop for nothing in their westward drive until they reached the Meuse, ignoring their flanks and bypassing enemy strongpoints to be mopped up later. The Panzer commanders did, however, have flexibility to use side roads or logging tracks if a Rollbahn was blocked or congested with other traffic.

The failure of Sixth Panzer Armee to come even close to its first objective, crossing the Meuse, can be attributed in part to all the above factors: weather, terrain, fuel, disjointed planning and American resistance, often where least expected. In any case, once the Allies had regained the initiative and the outcome was certain, Sixth Panzer Armee ceased to exist. Between 20 and 24 January 1945 its residual SS-Panzer elements were withdrawn eastwards to form the nucleus of a new Sixth SS-Panzer Armee to fight in Hungary. What else remained which had not already been absorbed by Fifteenth Armee was re-allocated to Fifth Panzer Armee.

'Sepp' Dietrich himself was tried after the war for his complicity, as overall commander, in the Malmédy massacre. He was released from gaol in 1955, and lived out the rest of his life in Ludwigsburg, dying in April 1966.

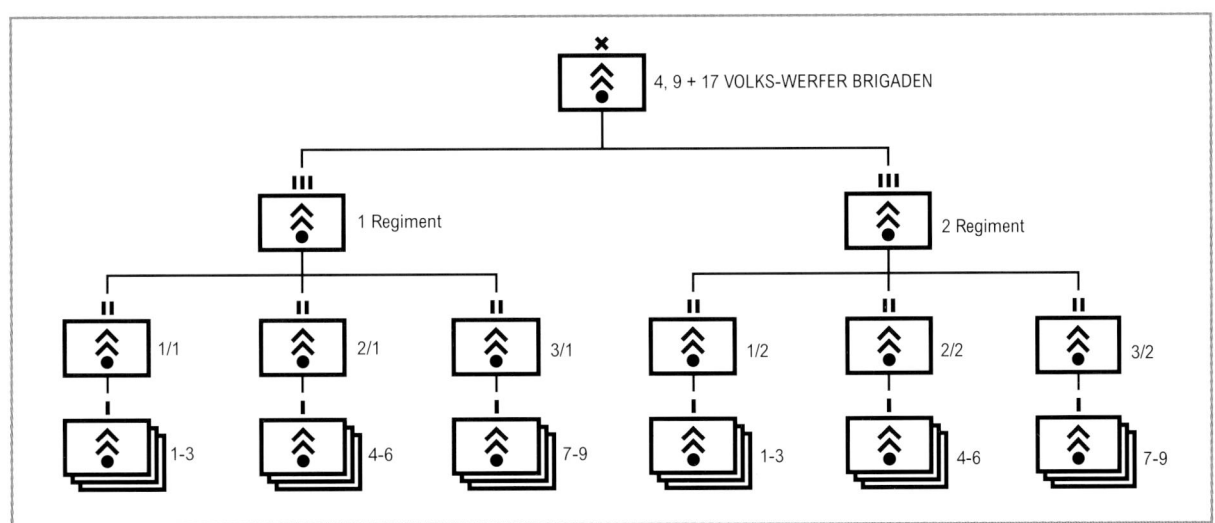

SIXTH PANZER ARMEE

I SS-PANZER KORPS

SS-Gruppenführer Hermann Priess' Korps, reinforced for the initial assault phase of 'Herbstnebel' by one paratroop and two infantry divisions, was expected by Hitler to achieve the decisive breakthrough in the Ardennes. Priess was well used to such expectations, having commanded 3 SS-Panzer Division 'Totenkopf' in Russia until July 1944 and then the Leibstandarte for a short while after Theodor Wisch was wounded. Nevertheless, he must

SS-Gruppenführer Hermann Priess was a highly experienced and respected leader, having earlier commanded both 1 and 3 SS-Panzer Divisions in the field.
(U.S. Signal Corps)

I SS-PANZER KORPS
SS-Gruppenführer Hermann Priess
Stabschef: *SS-Obersturmbannführer Rudolf Lehmann*

---

1 SS-Panzer Division Leibstandarte 'Adolf Hitler' (Mohnke)
12 SS-Panzer Division 'Hitler Jugend' (Kraas)
3 Fallschirmjäger Division (Wadehn)
12 Volksgrenadier Division (Engel)
277 Volksgrenadier Division (Viebig)
(Attached from Armee Reserve)
4 Volks-Werfer Brigade (51 and 53 Regimenten)
9 Volks-Werfer Brigade (14 and 54 Regimenten)
388 and 402 Volks-Artillerie Korps

---

have read Dietrich's operational orders for his Korps with misgivings.

'On Day Zero at 0600 I SS-Panzer Korps will break through the enemy positions in the sector Hollerath-Krewinkel with its infantry divisions. It will then thrust to beyond the Meuse in the sector Liège-Huy with 12 SS-Panzer Division on the right and 1 SS-Panzer Division on the left.

The Korps will so deploy itself as to be able, according to the situation, either to continue the penetration in the direction of Antwerp, or to be prepared for the defence of the right flank.' Then, Dietrich's orders continued: 'Bridges on the Meuse will be taken in undamaged condition by ruthless and rapid penetrations. This will be accomplished by specially organised forward detachments, under the command of suitable officers.'

Five Rollbahns had been allocated to Priess' Panzer divisions compared with only two for both of Fifth Panzer Armee's Panzer Korps: A, B and C in the north for 12 SS-Panzer Division and D and E to their south for 1 SS-Panzer Division. The Schwerpunkt, or centre of gravity, lay on Rollbahns C and D with the bulk of the two divisions' tanks concentrated in Kampfgruppe 'Kühlmann' and Kampfgruppe 'Peiper' – the 'specially organised forward detachments'.

On Rollbahn A, which wound from Rocherath and Elsenborn through the Hohes Venn, the critical crossroads at Baraque Michel would, it was intended, be seized by von der Heydte's paratroop battalion. In fact the paratroop operation was a disaster, 12 SS-Panzer Division became embroiled in costly close-quarter fighting around Rocherath and Büllingen, Kampf-gruppe 'Peiper' only managed to get as far west as Stoumont before becoming stalled, out of fuel, and Kampfgruppe 'Hansen' to their south only got as far as Wanne.

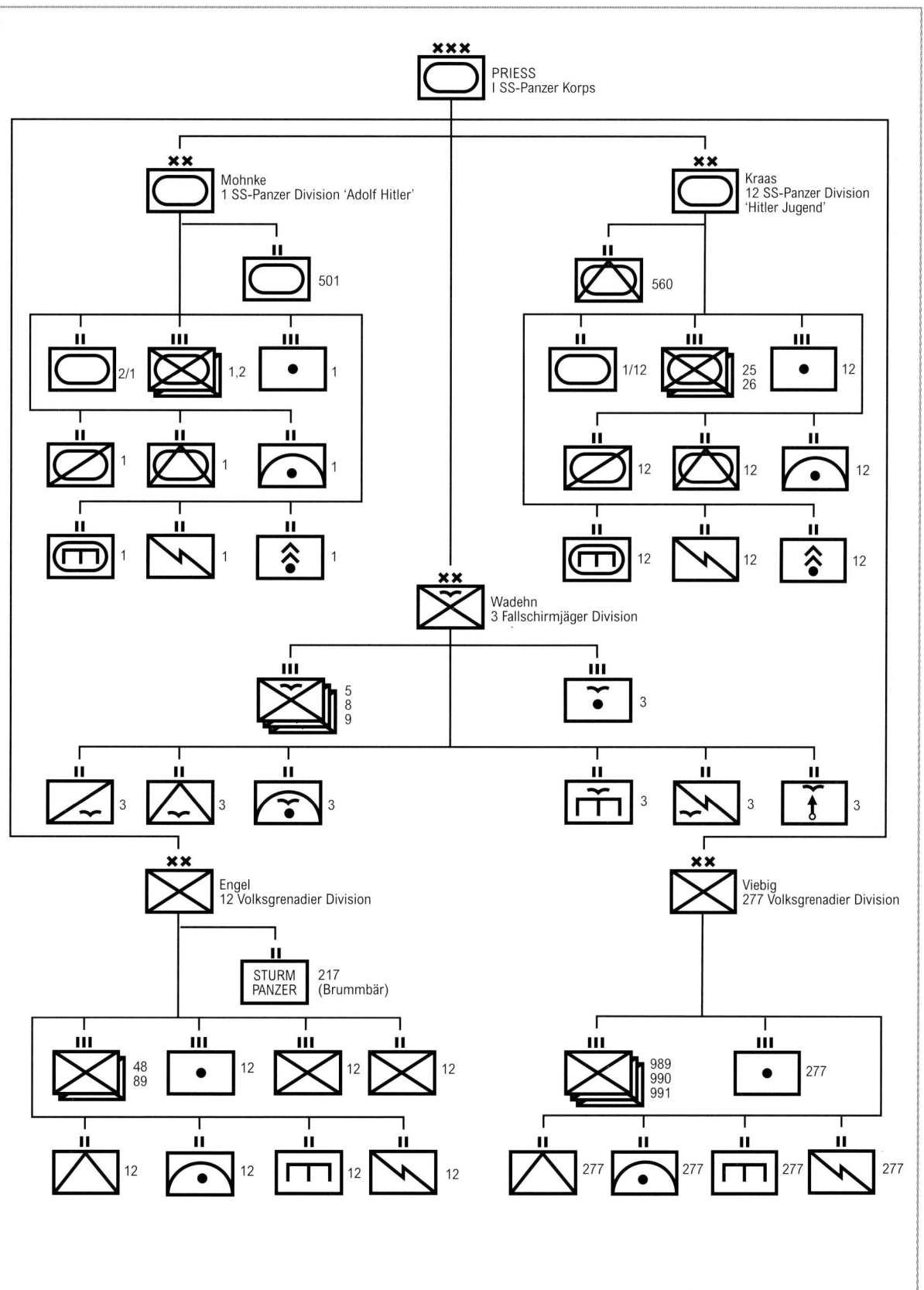

PRIESS
I SS-Panzer Korps

Mohnke
1 SS-Panzer Division 'Adolf Hitler'

Kraas
12 SS-Panzer Division 'Hitler Jugend'

501

560

2/1

1,2

1

1/12

25
26

12

1

1

1

12

12

12

1

1

1

12

12

12

Wadehn
3 Fallschirmjäger Division

5
8
9

3

3

3

3

3

3

3

Engel
12 Volksgrenadier Division

Viebig
277 Volksgrenadier Division

STURM
PANZER

217
(Brummbär)

48
89

12

12

12

989
990
991

277

12

12

12

12

277

277

277

277

1 SS-Panzer Division Leibstandarte 'Adolf Hitler'

Hitler entrusted the task of spearheading the drive across the Meuse to his beloved Waffen-SS bodyguard division, a situation which was far from novel to the veterans in its ranks.

The Leibstandarte was almost up to full strength when it assembled in the vicinity of Stadtkyll during the nights of 13 and 14 December, because Hitler had specifically ordered priority for the refitting of the SS-Panzer divisions which had been so badly mauled in Normandy. Joachim 'Jochen' Peiper, CO of its 1 SS-Panzer Regiment, considered the standard of the new personnel to be 'pretty good', but his own regiment was missing its I Abteilung. SS-Sturmbannführer Werner Pötschke's II Abteilung could muster 17 PzKpfw V Panthers in each of its first two companies (instead of a full establishment of 22) and 17 PzKpfw IVs in its third and fourth. They were to form the vanguard of Kampfgruppe 'Peiper', beefed up by approximately 30 Tiger IIs in SS-Obersturmbannführer Heinz von Westernhagen's 501 schwere SS-Panzer

---

1 SS-Panzer Division Leibstandarte 'Adolf Hitler'

SS-Oberführer Wilhelm Mohnke

Stabs Kompanie

II/1 SS-Panzer Regiment (Pötschke)
1 SS-Panzergrenadier Regiment (Hansen)
2 SS-Panzergrenadier Regiment (Sandig)
1 SS-Panzer Artillerie Regiment (Steineck)
1 SS-Panzer Aufklärungs Abteilung (Knittel)
1 SS-Panzerjäger Abteilung (Rettlinger)
1 SS-Panzer Flak Abteilung
1 SS-Panzer Pionier Abteilung
1 SS-Panzer Nachrichten Abteilung
1 SS-Panzer Nebelwerfer Abteilung
1 SS-Panzer Nachschub Truppe
1 SS-Panzer Werkstatt Truppe
1 SS-Panzer Verwaltungs Truppe
1 SS-Panzer Sanitäts Truppe
501 schwere SS-Panzer Abteilung (attached)
84 Flak Abteilung (Luftwaffe) (attached)

SS-Oberführer Wilhelm Mohnke. Like all the divisional commanders at this stage of the war, he had extensive combat experience as a regimental officer.
(U.S. Signal Corps)

Abteilung. Additionally, SS-Hauptsturmführer Rettlinger's 1 SS-Panzerjäger Abteilung, part of Kampfgruppe 'Hansen', could field 10 Jagdpanzer IV/70s. The bulk of the remainder of the battlegroup comprised SS-Sturmbannführer Josef Diefenthal's III/2 SS-Panzergrenadier Regiment plus a battalion of towed artillery and Major von Sacken's attached Luftwaffe flak battalion. Their route lay via Stavelot and Stoumont to the Meuse between Clermont and Ombret-Rawsa.

Because of the nature of the terrain and the narrowness of the roads, the division could not be deployed in the sort of attack formation it was used to in the wide open spaces of Russia. Its front, and that of 12 SS-Panzer Division, was further restricted by the need to route the advance south of the Elsenborn heights, whose capture was intended to be an infantry task. As a result, the division was split into four Kampfgruppen. The leading two, 'Peiper' on Rollbahn D and 'Hansen' on Rollbahn E (via Vielsalm to Huy) contained most of the armour and motorised infantry, while the artillery was concentrated in the following Kampfgruppe 'Sandig' (behind Peiper on Rollbahn D). The reconnaissance battalion under SS-Sturmbannführer Gustav Knittel was to operate independently, probing ahead for weak points on minor roads and scouting for undamaged bridges. It was anticipated that some, at least, of these could be secured by Skorzeny's disguised commandos, but this proved a forlorn hope.

A further urgent need was to locate Allied POL depots. Because the Germans' own main depots were east of the Rhine, bringing up supplies was taking two or three days and on the morning of 16 December the Leibstandarte only had a quarter of the fuel it needed. This was barely sufficient for the leading Kampfgruppen to advance 40 miles before they would be stranded.

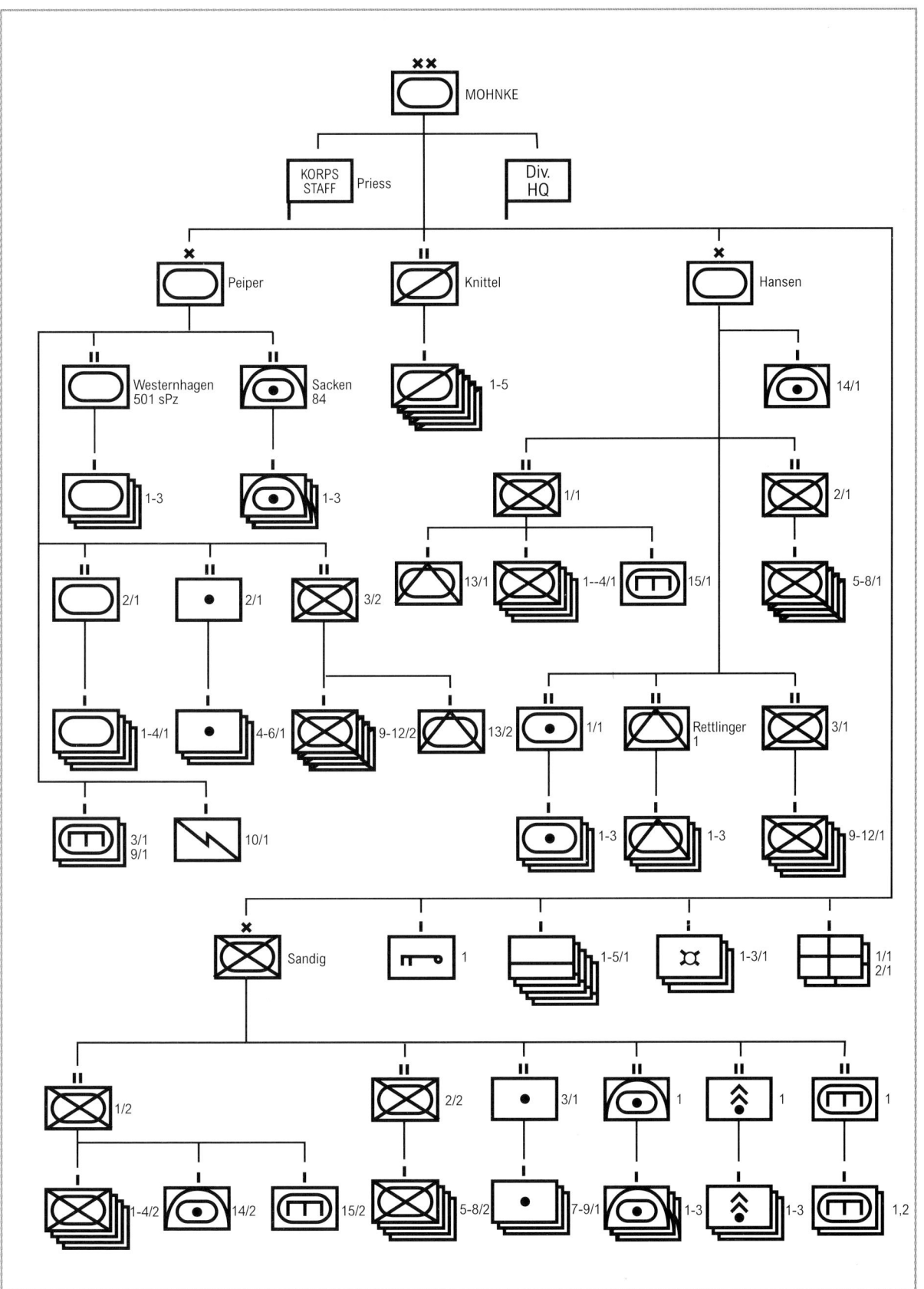

Kampfgruppe 'Peiper'
SS-Obersturmbannführer Joachim Peiper

Stabs Kompanie, 1 SS-Panzer Regiment
II/1 SS-Panzer Regiment (Pötschke)
501 schwere SS-Panzer Abteilung (von Westernhagen)
84 Flak Abteilung (Luftwaffe) (von Sacken)
III/2 SS-Panzergrenadier Regiment (Diefenthal)
II/1 SS-Panzer Artillerie Regiment (Schlett)
13/2 SS-Panzergrenadier Regiment (Sturmgeschütz Kompanie)
3/1 SS-Panzer Pionier Abteilung
9/1 SS-Panzer Regiment (Pionier Kompanie)
10/1 SS-Panzer Regiment (Nachrichten Kompanie)

SS-Obersturmbannführer Joachim Peiper commanded 1 SS-Panzer Regiment.
He preferred to be called 'Jochen' because Joachim sounded Jewish. (U.S. Signal Corps)

in 1923, and enlarged and retitled ten years later after Hitler's accession to power. It was prominent in the Röhm Purge and the Austrian Anschluss and took part in the Polish campaign of 1939. It was next prominent in the invasion of the west in May/June 1940, during which it was responsible for the massacre of British PoWs at Wormhoudt.

Kampfgruppe 'Hansen'
SS-Standartenführer Max Hansen

Stabs Kompanie, 1 SS-Panzergrenadier Regiment
I/1 SS-Panzergrenadier Regiment
13/1 SS-Panzergrenadier Regiment (Sturmgeschütz Kompanie)
14/1 SS-Panzergrenadier Regiment (Flak Kompanie)
15/1 SS-Panzergrenadier Regiment (Pionier Kompanie)
II/1 SS-Panzergrenadier Regiment
III/1 SS-Panzergrenadier Regiment
I/1 SS-Panzer Artillerie Regiment
1 SS-Panzerjäger Abteilung (Rettlinger)

SS-Standartenführer Max Hansen, commander of 1 SS-Panzergrenadier Regiment.
(U.S. Signal Corps)

The Leibstandarte's commander, SS-Oberführer Wilhelm Mohnke, was the division's fourth CO, stepping into the shoes of Dietrich, Wisch and, most recently, Priess, whom he succeeded when the latter became his Korps commander. Mohnke himself had previously commanded 26 SS-Panzergrenadier Regiment, 12 SS-Panzer Division, in Normandy.

The Leibstandarte's origins dated back to the 'Stosstruppe Hitler', a 200-strong bodyguard created

Enlarged to the size of a motorised division for the invasion of Russia, the Leibstandarte first fought in the short Yugoslav/Greek campaign in April 1941. Then,

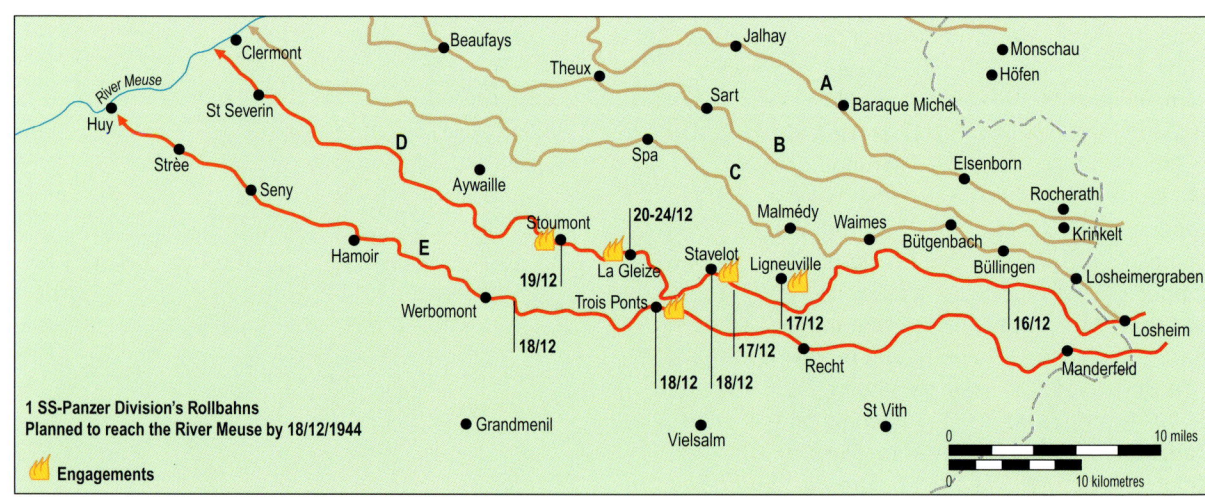

1 SS-Panzer Division's Rollbahns
Planned to reach the River Meuse by 18/12/1944

🔥 Engagements

SS-Standartenführer
Rudolf Sandig
commanded 2
SS-Panzergrenadier
Regiment.
(U.S. Signal Corps)

Kampfgruppe 'Knittel'
SS-Sturmbannführer Gustav Knittel

---

1 SS-Panzer Aufklärungs Abteilung

Kampfgruppe 'Sandig'
SS-Standartenführer Rudolf Sandig

Stabs Kompanie, 2 SS-Panzergrenadier Regiment
I/2 SS-Panzergrenadier Regiment
14/2 SS-Panzergrenadier Regiment (Flak Kompanie)
15/2 SS-Panzergrenadler Regiment (Pionier Kompanie)
II/2 SS-Panzergrenadier Regiment
III/1 SS-Panzer Artillerie Regiment
1 SS-Panzer Flak Abteilung (Ullerich)
1 SS-Panzer Nebelwerfer Abteilung
1 SS-Panzer Pionier Abteilung (Scheler)

---

command of 1 SS-Panzer Regiment in 1944. By this stage of the war he had seen it all but even his experience was insufficient to win Hitler his victory in the Ardennes – although he did miss a golden opportunity to alter the course of the battle, if not its outcome.

At the time Kampfgruppe 'Peiper' reached Büllingen, encroaching on 12 SS-Panzer Division's Rollbahn C, it could have swung north and wrapped up the American 99th and 2nd Infantry Divisions on Elsenborn ridge from the flank and rear. But Peiper was at least rewarded with the capture of a fuel dump which yielded 50,000 gallons and allowed him to continue driving west. Not far enough though, and even the award of the Swords to go with the Oakleaves to his Knights Cross cannot have given much satisfaction.

advancing into Russia in July along the Black Sea coast, it battled its way to Rostov where it was decimated during the Soviet winter counter-offensive. Withdrawn to France for rehabilitation as a Panzergrenadier division, it participated in the occupation of Vichy in 1942 before returning to Russia in spring 1943 as part of the newly-created I SS-Panzer Korps. Victory at Kharkov was followed by defeat at Kursk, after which the Leibstandarte was briefly posted to Italy before returning to the Russian front, upgraded to a full Panzer division, at the end of 1943.

Decimated once more in the Kamenets-Podolsk pocket, it was recuperating in Belgium and approximately back up to strength when the Allies landed in Normandy in June 1944. The division suffered heavily, particularly at Mortain, and was withdrawn to Siegburg in Germany to begin refitting for 'Herbstnebel'.

Mohnke briefed his Kampfgruppe commanders on 14 December; Otto Skorzeny was also present because SS-Obersturmbannführer Willi Hardieck's Kampfgruppe X, 150 Panzer Brigade, was to lend its support to Peiper's force. It was the first time Peiper and the others realised fully what they were being let in for, even though Peiper had a pretty shrewd idea.

A Berliner, Peiper had won the Iron Cross in France in 1940 and rapidly rose to command of III/2 SS-Panzergrenadier Regiment in Russia, winning the Knights Cross early in 1943 before being promoted to

SS-Sturmbahnführer
Gustav Knittel,
commander of 1 SS-Panzer Aufklärungs
Abteilung.
(U.S. Signal Corps)

Much later, on Bastille Day, 1976, Peiper was murdered by former members of the French Resistance who thought his punishment inadequate. But this was still far in the future when Hitler finally called off the Ardennes offensive in January 1945. The Leibstan-darte was pulled back to Bonn and in February 1945 was in Hungary where its further failure in the Lake Balaton offensive caused Hitler to order the removal of the division's prestigious cuff titles. 'Sepp' Dietrich refused to pass the order on and withdrew the Leibstandarte into Austria where, in May, it surrendered to US troops near Steyr. From a strength of 19,700 men prior to D-Day, it had a mere 1,500 survivors with 16 tanks.

12 SS-Panzer Division 'Hitler Jugend'

Assigned to I SS-Panzer Korps' three northern-most Rollbahns, it was 12 SS-Panzer Division's misfortune to become embroiled in a costly battle of attrition which left it with no chance of achieving any of its primary objectives.

The Schwerpunkt of the division's assault lay along Rollbahn C leading through Büllingen, Malmédy and Spa to the Meuse at Aigremont. Three Kampfgruppen were assigned this route. In the van was Kampfgruppe 'Kühlmann', commanded by SS-Sturmbannführer Herbert Kühlmann, CO of 12 SS-Panzer Regiment. As with Kampfgruppe 'Peiper', this had only one tank battalion, SS-Sturmbannführer Arnold Jürgensen's I SS-Panzer Abteilung with 19 Panthers in each of its first two companies and 19 PzKpfw IVs in its third and fourth. As a result Kampfgruppe 'Kühlmann' was beefed up by the Army's 560 schwere Panzerjäger

---

12 SS-Panzer Division 'Hitler Jugend'

SS-Standartenführer Hugo Kraas

Stabs Kompanie

I/12 SS-Panzer Regiment (Jürgensen)
25 SS-Panzergrenadier Regiment (Müller)
26 SS-Panzergrenadier Regiment (Krause)
12 SS-Panzer Artillerie Regiment
12 SS-Panzer Aufklärungs Abteilung (Bremer)
12 SS-Panzerjäger Abteilung
12 SS-Panzer Flak Abteilung
12 SS-Panzer Pionier Abteilung
12 SS-Panzer Nachrichten Abteilung
12 SS-Panzer Nebelwerfer Abteilung
12 SS-Panzer Nachschub Truppe
12 SS-Panzer Werkstatt Truppe
12 SS-Panzer Verwaltungs Truppe
12 SS-Panzer Sanitäts Truppe
560 schwere Panzerjäger Abteilung (Heer) (attached)

SS-Standartenführer Hugo Kraas had risen to command 'Hitler Jugend' after combat experience as a regimental officer with the Leibstandarte.
(U.S. Signal Corps)

Abteilung. Even this had only three understrength companies, the first with Jagdpanthers and the other two with Jagdpanzer IV/70s, totalling 25 vehicles. The battlegroup also included a company of Sturmgeschütze and III/26 SS-Panzergrenadier Regiment in SdKfz 251 half-tracks.

Kampfgruppe 'Kühlmann' was followed along Rollbahn C by the division's reinforced 12 SS-Panzer Aufklärungs Abteilung commanded by SS-Sturmbann-führer Gerhardt Bremer. At the rear followed Kampf-

gruppe 'Krause', commanded by SS-Obersturmbann-führer Bernard Krause, CO of 26 SS-Panzergrenadier Regiment, with his I and II Abteilungen and most of the divisional artillery and flak guns.

Rollbahn B, following a line between Rocherath and Büllingen via Franchimont to the Meuse just south of Liège, was allocated to Kampfgruppe 'Müller' which principally comprised the whole of SS-Sturmbann-führer Siegfried Müller's 25 SS-Panzergrenadier Regiment plus towed artillery and the division's 12 SS-Panzerjäger Abteilung with 22 Jagdpanzer IV/70s. Müller's I/25 Abteilung was assigned to Rollbahn A, its orders to join up with von der Heydte's paratroop battlegroup at the Baraque Michel crossroads deep in the heavily forested Hohes Venn and defend the westernmost bastion of the 'northern shoulder' against encroachment from Lieutenant-General William Simpson's Ninth Army.

Rollbahn A, if followed to the Meuse, would have taken Müller to Liège, but Hitler had expressly forbid-den an attack on the city, which was expected to be heavily defended, or any attempts at crossing the river to its north, despite the fact that the banks here are lower and more suitable for bridging than those further south. As events transpired, this would have been a forlorn hope anyway, despite the enthusiasm of the

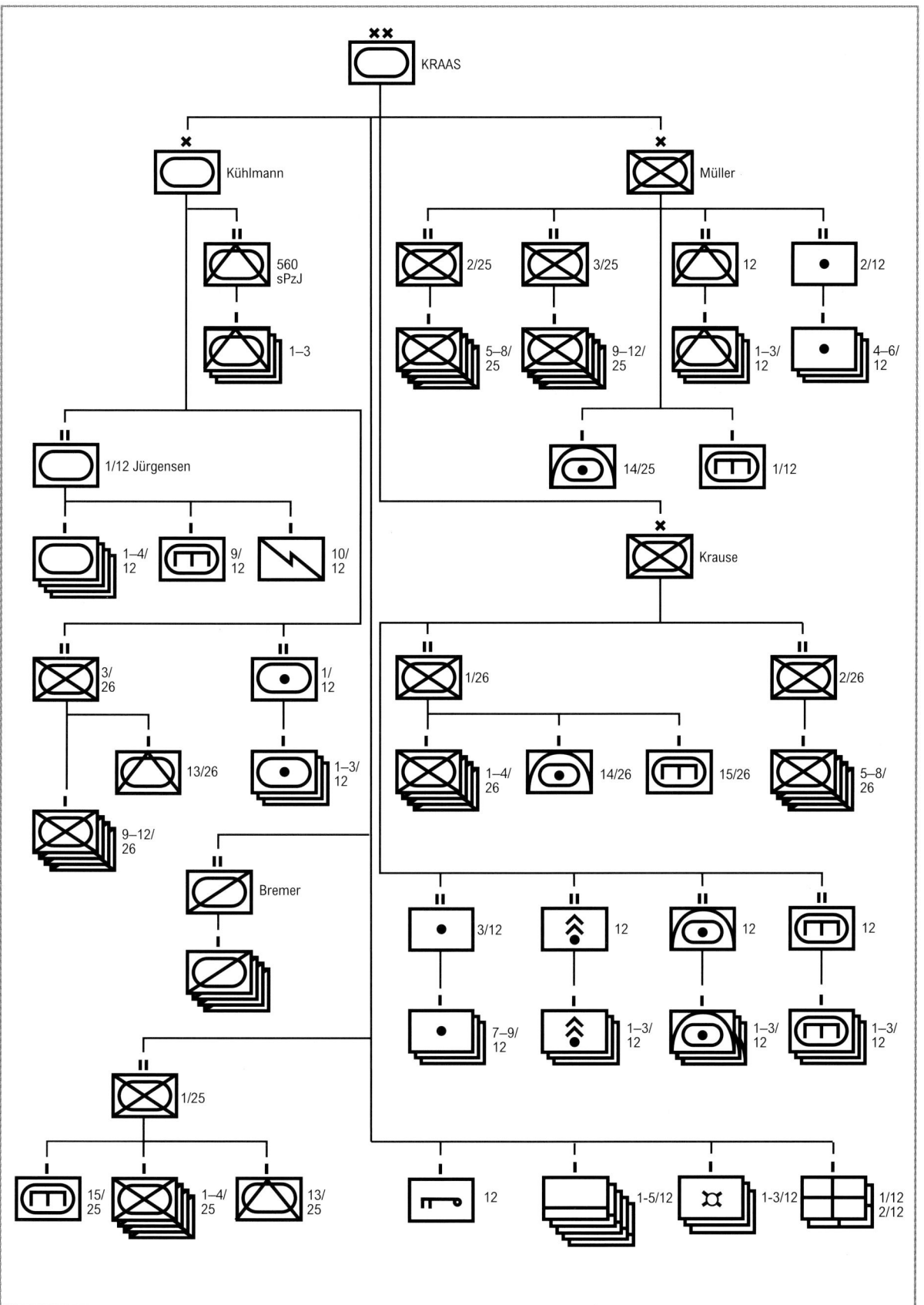

Kampfgruppe 'Kühlmann'
SS-Sturmbannführer Herbert Kühlmann

Stabs Kompanie, 12 SS-Panzer Regiment
I/12 SS-Panzer Regiment (Jürgensen)
9/12 SS-Panzer Regiment (Pionier Kompanie)
10/12 SS-Panzer Regiment (Nachrichten Kompanie)
560 Panzerjäger Abteilung
III/26 SS-Panzergrenadier Regiment
13/26 SS-Panzergrenadier Regiment
 (Sturmgeschütz Kompanie)
I/12 SS-Panzer Artillerie Regiment

Kampfgruppe 'Müller'
SS-Sturmbannführer Siegfried Müller

Rollbahn A
I/25 SS-Panzergrenadier Regiment
13/25 SS-Panzergrenadier Regiment
 (Sturmgeschütz Kompanie)
15/25 SS-Panzergrenadier Regiment (Pionier Kompanie)

Rollbahn B
Stabs Kompanie, 25 SS-Panzergrenadier Regiment
II/25 SS-Panzergrenadier Regiment
III/25 SS-Panzergrenadier Regiment
14/25 SS-Panzergrenadier Regiment (Flak Kompanie)
12 SS-Panzerjäger Abteilung
II/12 SS-Panzer Artillerie Regiment
1/12 SS-Panzer Pionier Abteilung

17 and 18-year-olds of 12 SS-Panzer Division who had been taught by their instructors to be 'fighters, not soldiers'.

They employed teenage gang-warfare tactics, dressed outlandishly (but very practically) in U-boat 'leathers', and painted their girlfriends' names all over their tanks. Nevertheless, they had already showed they could fight with fanatical passion, and a deep rivalry had developed between themselves and the 'old soaks' of the Leibstandarte because they used the former's key symbol crossed with a runic 'S' as their unit identification. (The word 'Dietrich' in German means 'skeleton key'.)

The idea for a hand-picked division plucked from the flower of German youth – the Hitlerjügend organi-sation – originated with Artur Axmann, the Hitler Youth leader, in January 1943. Gottlob Berger, responsible for most recruitment into the Waffen-SS, was so

entranced by the idea that he asked to be appointed divisional commander. Fortunately, saner heads pre-vailed and a regimental commander from the Leibstandarte, SS-Brigadeführer Fritz Witt, was appointed instead.

The division was officially called into being on 24 June 1943 at Beverloo in Belgium and the original 10,000 volunteers, formed around an experienced cadre of officers and NCOs from the Leibstandarte and other divisions, began intensive training before being posted to France in April 1944. 12 SS-Panzer Division was based just outside Paris in June and was one of the first units rushed to Normandy.

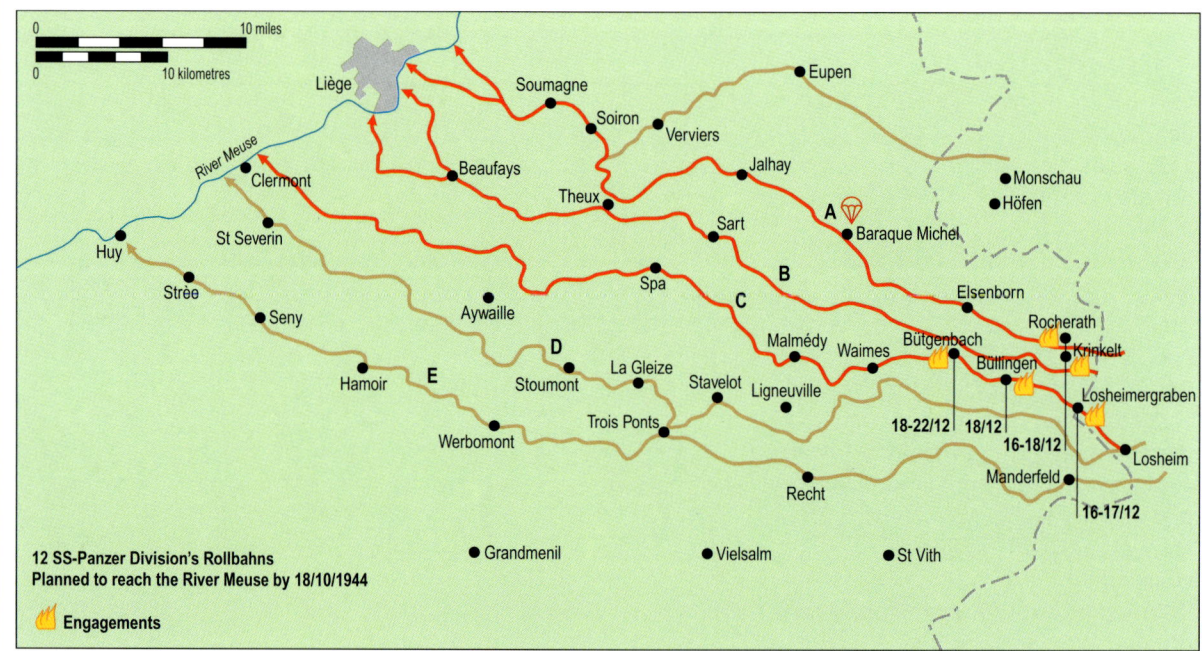

12 SS-Panzer Division's Rollbahns
Planned to reach the River Meuse by 18/10/1944

🔥 Engagements

Kampfgruppe 'Krause'
SS-Obersturmbannführer Bernard Krause

Stabs Kompanie, 26 SS-Panzergrenadier Regiment
Stabs Kompanie, 12 SS-Panzer Artillerie Regiment
I/26 SS-Panzergrenadier Regiment
14/26 SS-Panzergrenadier Regiment (Flak Kompanie)
15/26 SS-Panzergrenadier Regiment (Pionier Kompanie)
II/26 SS-Panzergrenadier Regiment
III/12 SS-Panzer Artillerie Regiment
12 SS-Panzer Nebelwerfer Abteilung
12 SS-Panzer Flak Abteilung
12 SS-Panzer Pionier Abteilung

PzKpfw V Panther Ausf Gs of an unidentified SS Abteilung take temporary refuge beneath snow-laden trees on one of the Rollbahns. (U.S. Signal Corps)

Here, fighting alongside the Army's veteran 21 Panzer Division, the 'Hitler Jugend' fanatics played a vital role in stalling Montgomery's attacks on Caen and preventing an early Allied breakout from the beachhead. In a single engagement on their first day in action they knocked out 28 Allied tanks for the loss of only two of their own and the vigour of their opposition had a demoralising effect on the unfortunate Canadian 3rd Division. Unluckily, Fritz Witt was killed by naval gunfire on 16 June and the CO of the division's Panzer Regiment, SS-Oberführer Kurt 'Panzer' Meyer, took over.

Kampfgruppe 'Bremer'
SS-Sturmbannführer Gerhardt Bremer

12 SS-Panzer Aufklärungs Abteilung

Meyer rapidly restored the division's morale after their popular commander's death and it continued to defy Montgomery until Caen finally fell in July. On the 11th of that month the 'Hitler Jugend' Division was withdrawn from the front line and sent to Falaise. By this time it had suffered over 60% casualties and had only a third of its 150 tanks still operational. Undaunted, the division fought on and, following the American breakout through Avranches, helped hold open the 'neck' of the Falaise pocket to allow many of the survivors from other units to escape.

By 21 August the division had been reduced to a mere 300 men and 10 tanks and was pulled back to Aachen. During the retreat Kurt Meyer was captured and SS-Gruppenführer Fritz Krämer ('Sepp' Dietrich's chief of staff for 'Herbstnebel') took over temporary command.

The division was only partially rebuilt by the time of the Ardennes offensive and fought under SS-Standartenführer Hugo Kraas, a former commander of the Leibstandarte's 2 SS-Panzergrenadier Regiment. (Ironically, it was SS-Oberführer Wilhelm Mohnke, former CO of what was now Bernard Krause's 26 SS-Panzergrenadier Regiment, who now himself commanded the Leibstandarte. So much for filial rivalry!)

Trying to advance along its assigned Rollbahns, the 'Hitler Jugend' Division encountered unexpectedly tough opposition from the 'green' American 99th Infantry Division which took a drastic toll of the Panzers as they tried to help the Volksgrenadiers to broach Elsenborn ridge, and eventually the division was pulled out to help Fifth Panzer Army in the battle west of St Vith. Müller's I/25 SS-Panzergrenadier Abteilung on Rollbahn A never got a chance to get near von der Heydte's paratroops, who had to abandon their mission and individually make their own best way back to German lines.

After the failure of the Ardennes assault and being repulsed at St Vith, 12 SS-Panzer Division was sent to Hungary alongside the 1, 2 and 9 SS-Panzer Divisions where it took part in the abortive Lake Balaton offensive. Still under command of Hugo Kraas, it finally surrendered to American troops near Enns in Austria. From a strength of 21,300 men prior to D-Day there were only 455 survivors.

3 Fallschirmjäger Division

Paratroops, as paratroops, were only used in one comparatively small-scale and ill-advised episode during the Ardennes offensive: Operation 'Stösser'. The remainder of the paras in 3 Fallschirm-Division, and 5 Fallschirm-Division in the southern sector, fought as line infantry to clear a path for the Panzers, protect their flanks and try to subdue opposition left in their wake.

After the invasion of Crete in 1941, which had only succeeded by the narrowest margin and at terrible cost, Hitler had forbidden any further large-scale parachute operations. Thus, even though fresh Fallschirm divisions were still being created as late as 1944, they were paratroops in name only and the bulk of their personnel had never made even a single jump. However, so impressed had Hitler been with the performance of his paras in France, particularly at Carentan and during the siege of Brest, that he gave them important roles in 'Herbstnebel'.

One key element was supposed to have been 'Stösser'. Oberst Friedrich Freiherr von der Heydte, a hero of Crete and Carentan, was entrusted by Hitler with forming a battlegroup to capture the Baraque Michel crossroads in front of 12 SS-Panzer Division's route along Rollbahn A. He was not allowed to choose men from his own 6 Fallschirmjäger Regiment in case security was compromised, and had to settle for a scratch force from various regiments, many of whom had never made a jump, let alone at night. The crews

---

3 Fallschirmjäger Division
Generalmajor Karl Wadehn
Stabs Kompanie

---

5 Fallschirmjäger Regiment
8 Fallschirmjäger Regiment
9 Fallschirmjäger Regiment (Hoffmann)
3 Fallschirm Artillerie Regiment
3 Fallschirm Aufklärungs Abteilung
2/3 Fallschirm Panzerjäger Abteilung (mot)
3 Fallschirm Flak Abteilung
3 Fallschirm Pionier Abteilung
3 Fallschirm Nachrichten Abteilung
3 Fallschirm schwere Mörser Batterie
3 Fallschirm Nachschub Truppe
3 Fallschirm Werkstatt Truppe
3 Fallschirm Verwaltungs Truppe
3 Fallschirm Sanitäts Kompanie

---

of the Ju 52 transport aircraft were similarly inexperienced, and the drop was hopelessly inaccurate.

The battlegroup was organised in four infantry companies, a support company and signals and supply platoons, totalling 870 men. At dawn on 17 December, only about 150 men had managed to rally around their commander, who had jumped with a broken arm. Moreover, not one radio remained intact. All the paras could do was lie low while stragglers gradually swelled their ranks to about 300. But, with no food and no sign

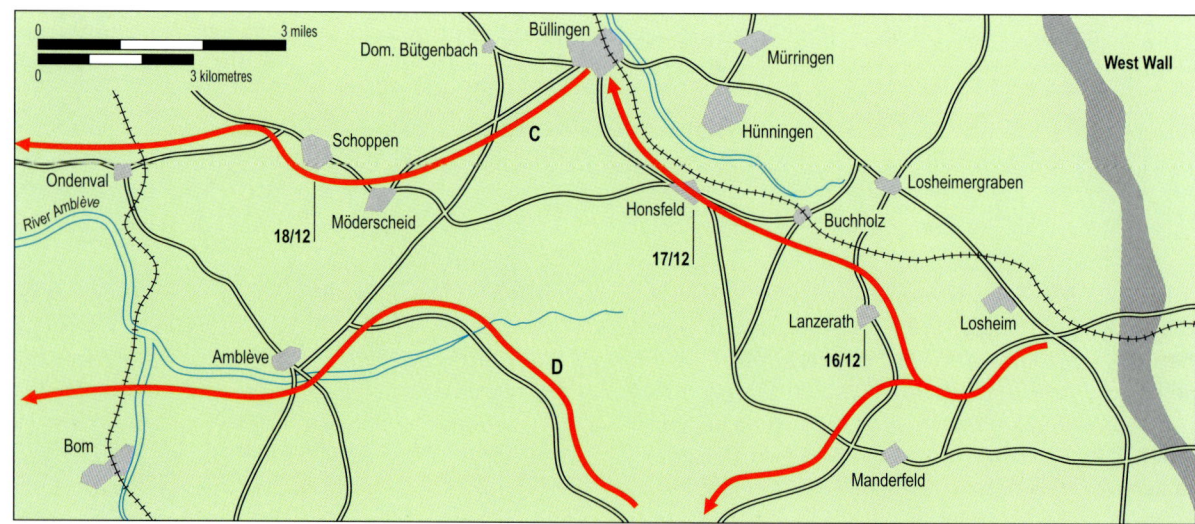

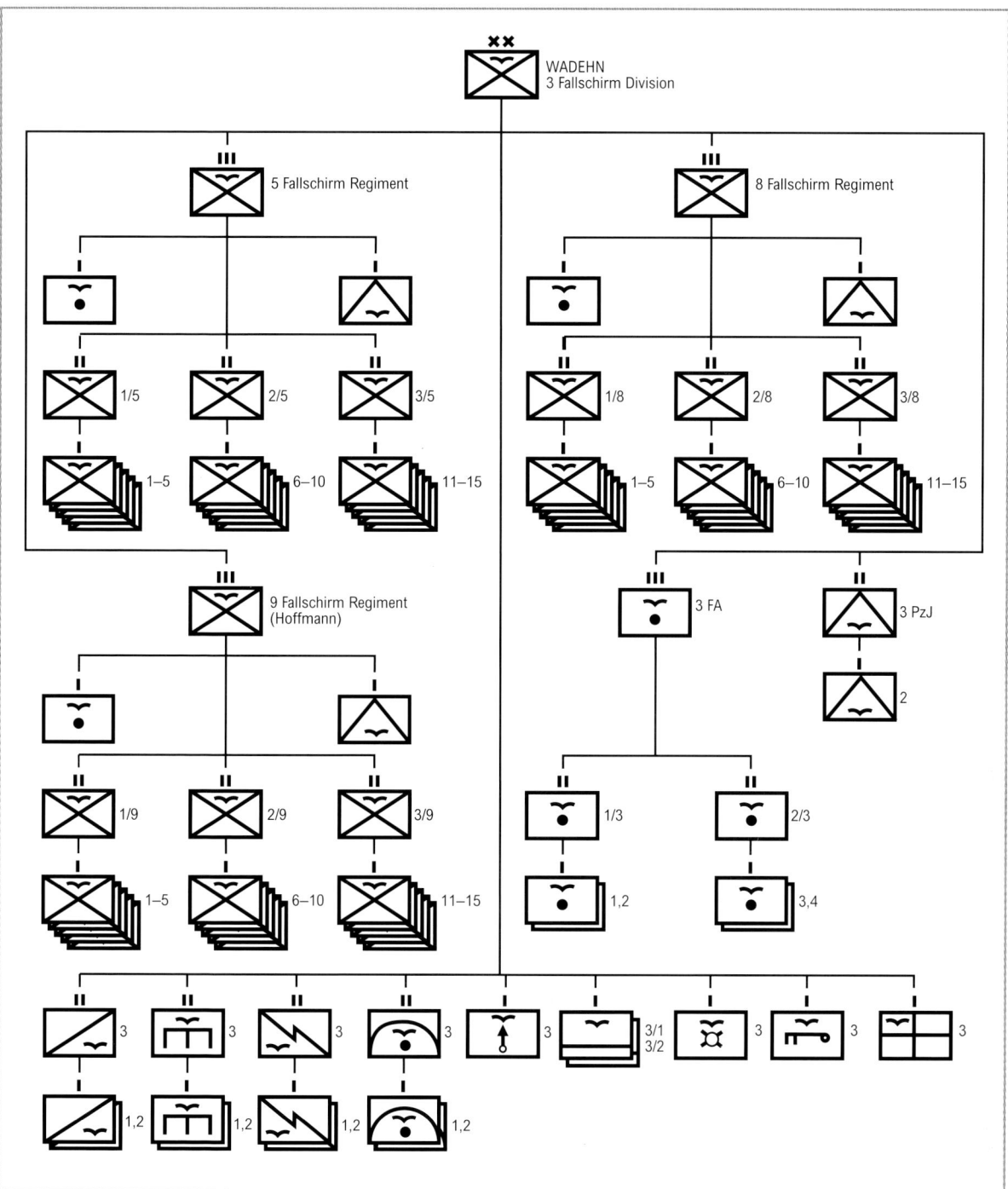

of the SS Panzers, von der Heydte had no option but to abandon his mission on 20 December and order his men to make their own way back to friendly lines. He himself was captured two days later.

3 Fallschirm-Division had a slightly luckier story. It was a late war formation but still had considerable battle experience by December 1944. Formed at Reims in France in October 1943 around a cadre from 1 Fallschirm-Regiment, it was at full strength of 17,000 men in June 1944. Rushed to Normandy, commanded by Generalmajor Richard Schimpf, the division fought hard in front of St Lô and incurred heavy losses in the close-quarter bocage battles during the American breakout.

By mid-July the division had suffered 65% casualties together with the loss of most of its heavy

Fallschirmjäger on a Tiger II tank on the road near Kaiserbaracke between St Vith and Malmédy.

equipment, and the bulk of the survivors was trapped in the Falaise pocket, most being captured. Schimpf was severely wounded but some of his men carried him to safety and temporary command was assumed by Generalleutnant Eugen Meindl. Meindl was himself then wounded in the escape from the pocket but, so desperate was the Wehrmacht's manpower shortage that the depleted division was kept in the line until September, when it was again surrounded, this time in the Mons pocket.

The handful of men who managed to escape were ordered to Oldenzaal in Holland, now commanded by Generalmajor Karl Wadehn until Schimpf recovered. Most of his staff lacked experience and the bulk of the reconstituted division comprised Luftwaffe ground personnel with limited, if any, combat experience. Many of Wadehn's officers were more accustomed to directing aerial battles and his chief of staff had to be replaced because of incompetence.

At the beginning of the Ardennes offensive when the division assembled at Mechernich it was still only at 75% of establishment; most of its artillery was horse-drawn and it had no assault guns, although 519 schwere Panzerjäger Abteilung was later attached from Armee Reserve; on top of which only two of its infantry regiments had reached their start lines east of

Hallschlag by 16 December, the remainder of the division arriving late the next day.

Despite this inauspicious beginning to the campaign, the paratroops did accomplish their principal objective in 'Herbstnebel', which was to clear a path for Kampfgruppe 'Peiper' on Rollbahn D. Advancing into the Losheim Gap, with Oberst von Hoffmann's 9 Fallschirmjäger Regiment in the van, they pushed the U.S. 14th Cavalry Group back, first to the Manderfeld ridge and then steadily further west, capturing first Buchholz and then Honsfeld for Peiper's Panzers. At this point the division was reassigned to LXVII Korps to take up defensive positions on the northern shoulder of the German advance.

After the Ardennes offensive became a desperate defensive, 3 Fallschirm-Division was transferred to Manteuffel's Fifth Panzer Army under General Schimpf, now recovered from his wounds, and helped hold the Schnee Eifel until virtually annihilated. (Karl Wadehn took over the regiment-sized '8 Fallschirm-Division'.) With Schimpf captured by the Americans on the bank of the Rhine, the last remnants of the division surrendered in the Ruhr pocket in April 1945.

12 Volksgrenadier Division

Rated by both 'Sepp' Dietrich and American intelligence as the best infantry division in Sixth Panzer Armee, the 12th was given the key role of clearing Rollbahn C through Büllingen towards Malmédy for 12 SS-Panzer Division's Kampfgruppe 'Kühlmann'. The grenadiers succeeded in getting through Büllingen but then ran into the freshly arrived U.S. 1st Infantry Division at Dom Bütgenbach. Unable, despite being reinforced by an entire Volks-Artillerie Korps, to make any further headway, the division's commander, Generalmajor Gerhard Engel, arranged a ceasefire for Christmas Day, and the division was later reassigned to Fifth Panzer Armee, replacing 9 SS-Panzer Division in the line opposite the 82nd Airborne Division when Hitler began withdrawing the SS Korps to send them to Hungary.

The 12 Volksgrenadier Division had been nearly at full strength in October 1944 (14,800 men) but, after battling at Aachen, was reduced to about 12,000 by

---

12 Volksgrenadier Division
Generalmajor Gerhard Engel
Stabs Kompanie

---

27 Füsilier Regiment
48 Volksgrenadier Regiment
89 Volksgrenadier Regiment
12 Volks-Artillerie Regiment
12 Füsilier Bataillon
12 Volks-Panzerjäger Abteilung (Holz)
12 Volks-Flak Abteilung
12 Volks-Pionier Abteilung
12 Volks-Nachrichten Abteilung
12 Volks-Nachschub Truppe
12 Volks-Werkstatt Truppe
12 Volks-Verwaltungs Truppe
12 Volks-Sanitäts Truppe
217 Sturmpanzer Abteilung (attached)

Generalmajor Gerhard Engel, one of Hitler's previous aides.
(Christopher Ailsby Historical Archives)

December and, according to Engel, had only six StuG III assault guns (some sources say just two) to complement its largely horse-drawn artillery. It was therefore assigned 217 Sturmpanzer Abteilung whose two companies could themselves, however, field only eight Brummbär between them, and arrived late.

The original 12 Infanterie Division was a pre-war unit recruited in Mecklenberg; during the Polish campaign in 1939 its artillery regiment was briefly commanded by Generaloberst Werner von Fritsch, the former Army C-in-C who had been framed for homosexual behaviour by Reinhard Heydrich and forced to resign. Von Fritsch sought and found death in battle as a way of retrieving his honour.

The 12 Infanterie Division fought well in France, defeating a French attempt to sever the Panzer divisions' lines of communication to where the British Expeditionary Force was trapped at Dunkerque. It was a similar story in Russia where the 12th was the main instrument in the relief of 3 SS-Division 'Totenkopf' in the Demyansk pocket in 1942. However, the division was finally surrounded near Minsk in July 1944 and forced to surrender. But a new 12th was promptly raised as a Volksgrenadier division under Gerhard Engel, who had been one of Hitler's adjutants since 1937. They fought at Aachen, the Emperor Charlemagne's old capital, in October before being transferred to Sixth Panzer Armee for the Ardennes offensive. Engel was seriously wounded during the battle and his place taken by Generalmajor Eugen König until the former's recovery in February 1945.

The 12th remained in the west fighting on the Rur river line against the U.S. Ninth Army, burnt-out but still defiant, until the last remnants of the division were destroyed in the Ruhr pocket in mid-April.

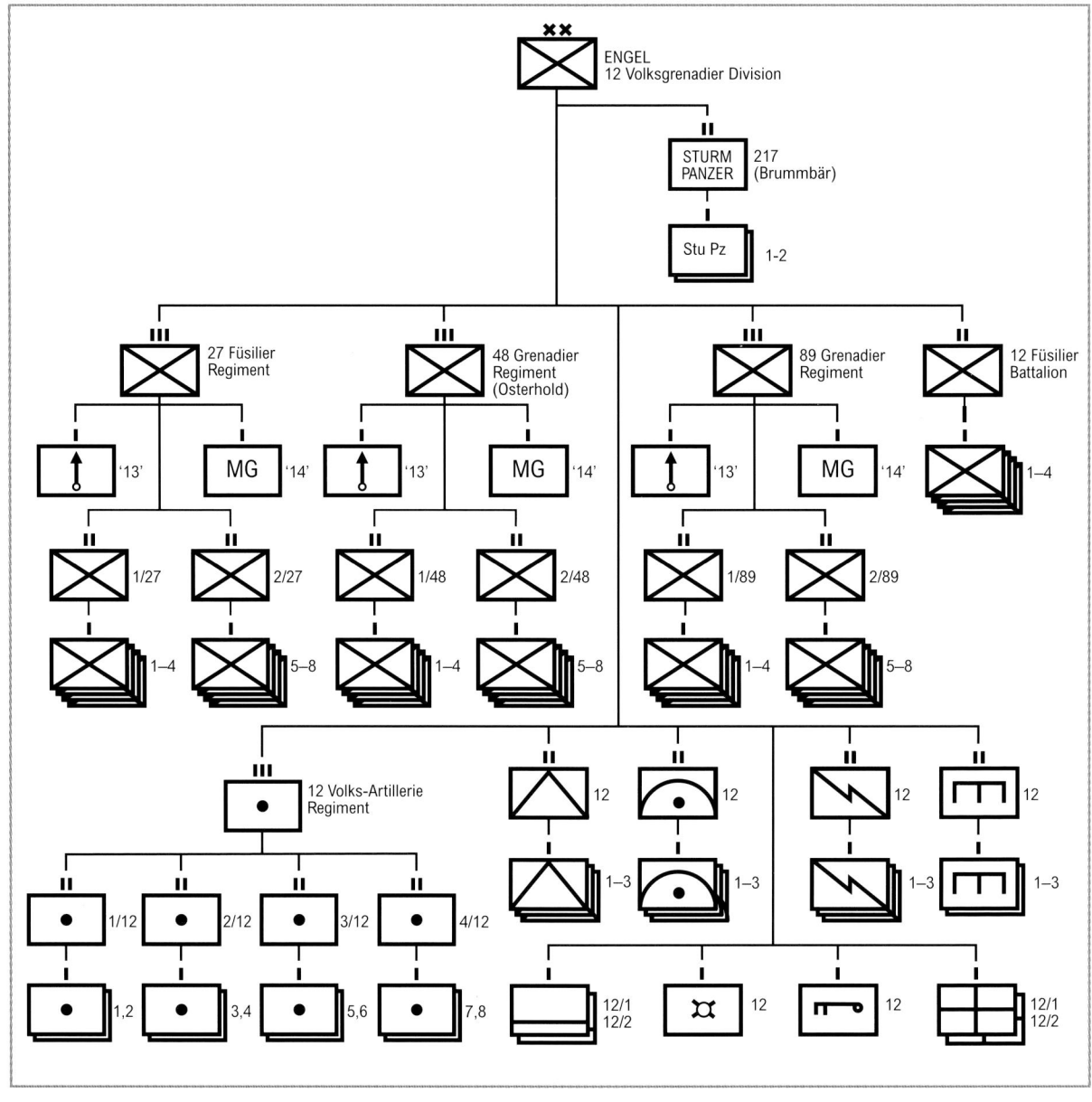

277 Volksgrenadier Division

O berst (later Generalmajor) Wilhelm Viebig's division fought hard on the right flank of I SS-Panzer Korps where it was tasked with capturing the villages of Rocherath and Krinkelt and then clearing the road through Elsenborn towards Baraque Michel to open up Rollbahns A and B for Kampfgruppe 'Müller'. The twin villages were only taken with enormous difficulty after the volksgrenadiers were reinforced by 3 Panzergrenadier Division, but after this

they were unable to make further headway and, transferred to Fifteenth Armee, fell onto the defensive.

An original 277 Infanterie Division was raised in 1940, mostly from elderly reservists, but disbanded without seeing action. A second 277th was raised as a divisional staff only in 1942 but was transformed into a 'proper' division in Westfalia during 1943-44, mainly from Austrian personnel. Its first assignment was on anti-partisan duties in Yugoslavia but in May 1944 it moved to Narbonne in southern France, commanded by Generalleutnant Albert Praum.

Rushed to the Normandy front, 277 Infanterie Division came to the relief of 9 SS-Panzer Division and was heavily engaged as part of II SS-Panzer Korps around Caen in July. The division escaped quite lightly from Falaise, in comparison with many other units, with 2,500 men, even if the majority were rear echelon troops. Praum himself was badly wounded.

The survivors, now commanded by Wilhelm Viebig (a former regimental CO in 112 Infanterie Division), were sent to Hungary for rehabilitation. Here they were absorbed into the largely Croatian 574 Volksgrenadier Division. The unit was renumbered in September and the rebuilt 277 Volksgrenadier Division was at 80% strength when it was ordered west to the vicinity of Losheim. It had a company of 11 Jagdpanzer 38(t) Hetzers, (although some sources indicate only six).

After the Battle of the Bulge the division retreated slowly eastwards, Viebig being captured on 9 March 1945, and surrendered in the Ruhr pocket in April.

277 Volksgrenadier Division
Oberst Wilhelm Viebig
Stabs Kompanie

989 Volksgrenadier Regiment
990 Volksgrenadier Regiment
991 Volksgrenadier Regiment
277 Volks-Artillerie Regiment
277 Füsilier Bataillon
277 Panzerjäger Abteilung
277 Flak Abteilung
277 Pionier Abteilung
277 Nachrichten Abteilung
277 Nachschub Truppe
277 Werkstatt Truppe
277 Verwaltungs Truppe
277 Sanitäts Truppe

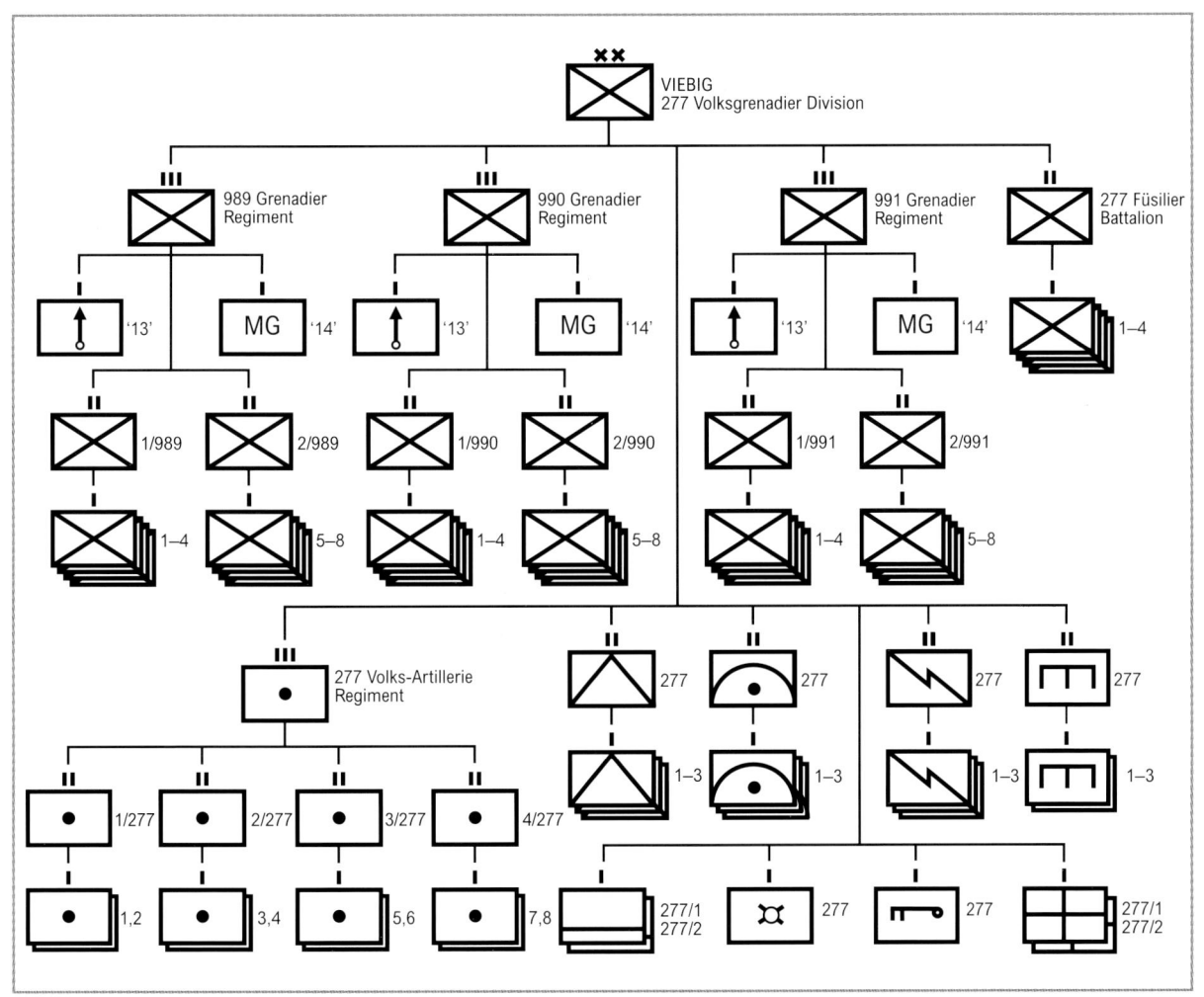

I SS-PANZER KORPS' BATTLES

277 Volksgrenadier Division and Kampfgruppe 'Müller'

Krinkelt-Rocherath – December 16-18

Krinkelt and Rocherath are insignificant dots on most maps of Belgium, and Elsenborn ridge does not appear at all, being simply a name given it by the American defenders in 1944. Yet all three were to play a decisive role in the ultimate defeat of I SS-Panzer Korps.

The 'twin villages', as they are called in most accounts of the battle, were assigned to Oberst Wilhelm Viebig's 277 Volksgrenadier Division. Like all the infantry divisions in front of the Panzer Korps, their role was to clear the path, then follow on in support, mop up bypassed pockets of resistance, and protect the flanks. It was a proven formula practised and used successfully by the Wehrmacht many times in the last five years. That it did not work this time is down to a multiplicity of factors already examined.

Be that as it may, the mixed bag of men constituting Viebig's ranks certainly gave it their best try, hampered by the fact that they were a battalion short at the start of the offensive. And to begin with, things did not seem to be going too badly. Their Korps' commander, Hermann Priess, reported enthusiastically at 0730 hrs on 16 December that 'the enemy outpost positions have been taken and the attack is making excellent progress'. As things turned out, his optimism was unjustified because even though Viebig's 989 Grenadier Regiment on the northern flank, attacking from Hollerath towards Rocherath, quickly penetrated the lines of III/393rd Regiment, 99th Infantry Division, pushing it back three-quarters of a mile, the 989th rapidly began running into problems. The regiment's initial assault, coming hard on the heels of the immense artillery barrage which had severely shaken the 'green' American division, had been helped by searchlights reflected off the clouds, and the attack had momentarily severed the Americans' communications between their 1st and 3rd Battalions.

To the 989th's south, however, 990 Grenadier Regiment fared less well, attacking from Udenbreth and exposed over open fields to fire from I/393rd; its men did not reach the comparative shelter of the woods until after dawn when Viebig released his reserve 991 Regiment to reinforce them. Confused fighting against small but stubborn American platoons continued all day and, even with the extra help, by nightfall on 16 December the grenadiers had still not cleared the woods or threatened Rocherath. Nor had Viebig's reserve 277 Füsilier Bataillon, supported by three StuGs, made much headway against II/394th on the German left. This prompted Priess to unleash SS-Sturmbannführer Siegfried Müller's Kampfgruppe of 12 SS-Panzer Division next morning in an attempt to effect a more rapid breakthrough on to Rollbahn B.

The Americans were also reacting to the threat. Even though Major General Walter E. Lauer's inexperienced troops were putting up a good fight, they could not hold forever against such an unexpected and determined assault, so the uncommitted 26th Regiment of the 1st Infantry Division was transferred from VII to V Corps and ordered to Elsenborn. There, the acting CO, Lieutenant-Colonel Edwin Van Sutherland, was ordered to take his men to Dom Bütgenbach. Meanwhile, Major-General Walter M. Robertson's veteran 2nd Infantry Division, out on a limb having just moved through Lauer's lines for its own assault through the West Wall at Wahlerscheid, towards the Rur and Urft dams, was recalled before Kampfgruppe 'Peiper' reached Büllingen, and Robertson's men began retracing their footsteps to reinforce the beleaguered 99th. It was none too soon for Lauer. III/23rd and a platoon of Shermans from the 741st Tank Battalion had just got into position behind III/393rd on the morning of 17 December, when Viebig's 989 and 990 Regiments together, reinforced by a company of

16/12/1944	18/12	20/12	22/12	24/12	26/12	28/12	30/12	6/1/1945	13/1	20/1	27/1	3/2	7/2
pages 46-59,70-73,77,87-91			60-61,74-76										

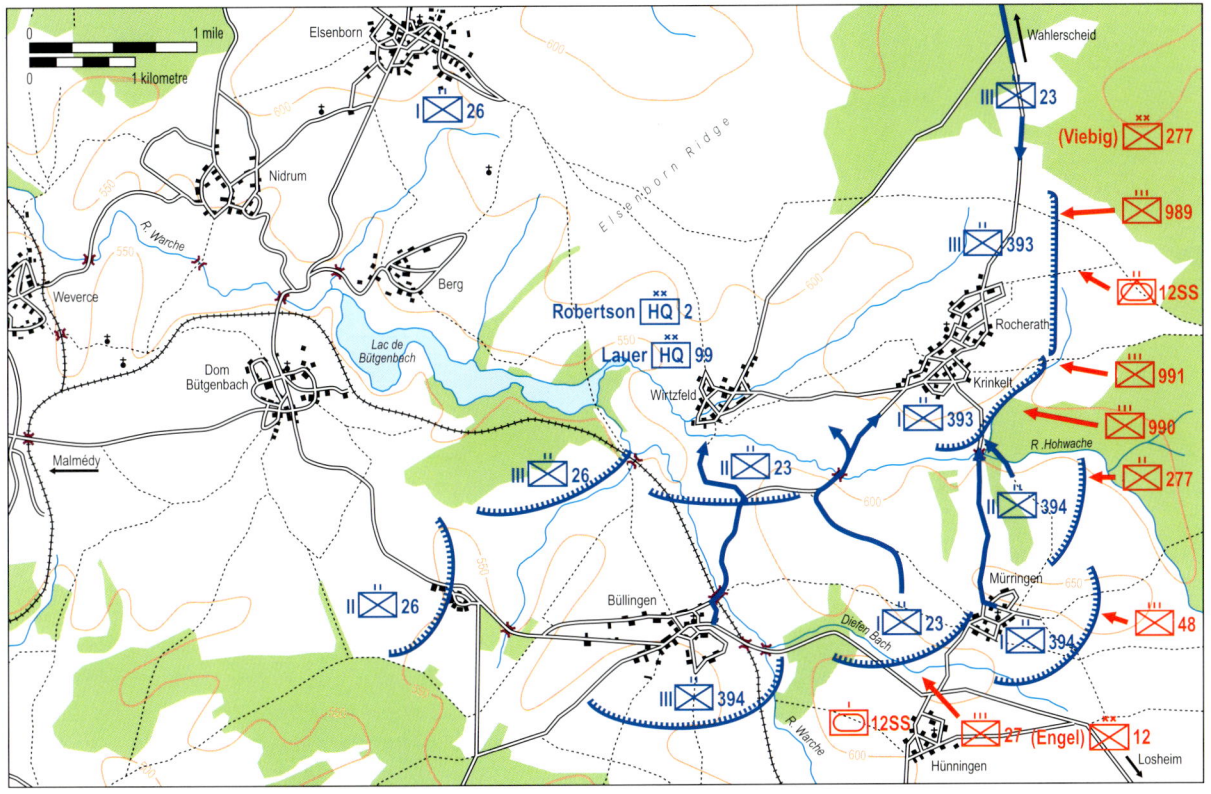

The defence of the 'twin villages' of Krinkelt and Rocherath effectively denied I SS-Panzer Korps access to Rollbahn B and left I/12 SS-Panzer Regiment severely weakened.

Müller's tanks, hit their lines again. One Panther succumbed to a bazooka, but the remainder roamed up and down the thin American line, shelling and machine-gunning. III/393rd, and I/393rd on their right flank, retired with heavy losses through Colonel Paul Tuttle's III/23rd towards Rocherath. Tuttle's men put up a good fight but Müller's tanks were too much, wiping out the platoon of Shermans for the loss of only two Panthers and driving the remaining infantry back towards the village. But Robertson's reinforcements were gradually getting through, and by nightfall on the 17th parts of Colonel Chester Hirschfelder's 9th and Colonel Francis Boos' 38th Infantry Regiments were also in place around Rocherath, Krinkelt and, further south towards Büllingen, at Wirtzfeld.

A bizarre occurrence, almost replicated later at Manhay, took place that night while Lauer's depleted battalions were withdrawing and licking their wounds,

and Robertson's were systematically moving south-west to their aid. (Robertson himself had been as appalled as Sutherland at the confusion when he visited Lauer's headquarters and would shortly be given command of both divisions.) SS-Obersturmführer Helmut Zeiner commanded 1/12 Panzerjäger Abteilung, 12 SS-Panzer Division. Advancing cautiously towards Rocherath through the falling snow at about 1930 hrs, his three leading Panzerjäger IV/70s and about 40 Panzergrenadiers passed unmolested in the dark through the positions of Company B of Lieutenant-Colonel William McKinley's I/9th battalion, 2nd Infantry Division. However, the Americans *had* realised belatedly that Zeiner's vehicles were German, and the following züge were not so lucky. Of the next zug, one succumbed to artillery fire; of the third, two to mines and two to bazookas; of a subsequent company, four out of seven were disabled. But still Zeiner's leading tank destroyers pressed on, evading American dugouts and mines to enter Rocherath and Krinkelt. Here, they quickly despatched three Shermans from the 741st Tank Battalion near the church in Krinkelt.

16/12/1944	18/12	20/12	22/12	24/12	26/12	28/12	30/12	6/1/1945	13/1	20/1	27/1	3/2	7/2
pages 46-59,70-73,77,87-91				60-61,74-76									

A Panther, from 1 Kompanie, I/12 SS-Panzer Regiment, burns alongside the road just south of Krinkelt on 18 December. (U.S. Signal Corps)

By this time shells from both sides were falling all around the villages, endangering friend and foe alike, and the situation was one of total chaos, with no-one sure which way to turn. Battles are confusing enough in daylight; in the dark, with snow falling – as on so many other occasions during the 'battle of the bulge' – it became every man for himself or, as the U.S. Official History records, a 'wild night of fighting'. There was usually no time to take prisoners; they were simply disarmed and told to 'get lost', which most did gladly.

The situation was worsened by the fact that GIs of the 99th Infantry Division were pulling back towards Elsenborn through the defenders from the 2nd, intermingled with the advancing grenadiers. By about midnight, however, the Americans still retained control of the two villages with one exception: Helmut Zeiner, with three surviving Jagdpanzers, about 40 grenadiers and 80 prisoners, was still sitting in the middle of Rocherath. With only ten rounds of ammunition left, he had been lying 'doggo', but as the night wore on he realised he could not wait for daylight to reveal his position. He was unable to make radio contact with his battalion, and did not even know where it was.

At 0600 hrs on 18 December he decided to take a chance. There was still a lot of movement with further reinforcements from the 2nd Infantry Division arriving in a constant stream, so the noise of his vehicles' engines should not alert anyone. He led his tiny force eastwards out of the village just before daybreak and found a place to stop about 300 yards away. Then, just as it was beginning to get light, he saw 'tank after tank' emerging from the forest in a wide formation. Priess had commit-

ted SS-Sturmbannführer Arnold Jürgen-sen's I/12 SS-Panzer Regiment from Kampfgruppe 'Kühlmann' to help Müller take the villages, and the tanks that Zeiner could see were the Panthers of 1 and 3 Kompanien followed by the PzKpfw IVs of 5 and 6 Kompanien, supported by II and III/25th SS-Panzer-grenadier Regiment and the grenadiers of Viebig's 989 Regiment, 277 Volksgrenadier Division. Zeiner's men did not join in the new attack; their vehicles needed rearming and refuelling, and they needed food and sleep.

The unforeseen American resistance in Krinkelt and Rocherath, which they had expected to capture on day one of the offensive, had seriously upset 12 SS-Panzer Division's timetable, and its CO, SS-Standartenführer Hugo Kraas, had told Jürgensen bluntly to get the job done. Their attack first hit the 600-odd men of Lieutenant-Colonel Bill McKinley's I/9th and Company K from III/9th, 2nd Infantry Division, around Rocherather Baracken just to the northeast of Rocherath itself.

The rising sun had drawn a thick mist out of the fields which favoured the defenders, because the tank crews could not see anything to use their main arma-ment on, but the Americans had plenty of bazookas. SS-Untersturmführer Willi Fischer, commanding a Panther in SS-Hauptsturmführer Kurt Brödel's 3 Kompanie, said later that 'it was an absolute deathtrap for panzers'. First Lieutenant John Granville,

16/12/1944	18/12	20/12	22/12	24/12	26/12	28/12	30/12	6/1/1945	13/1	20/1	27/1	3/2	7/2
pages 46-59,70-73,77,87-91				60-61,74-76									

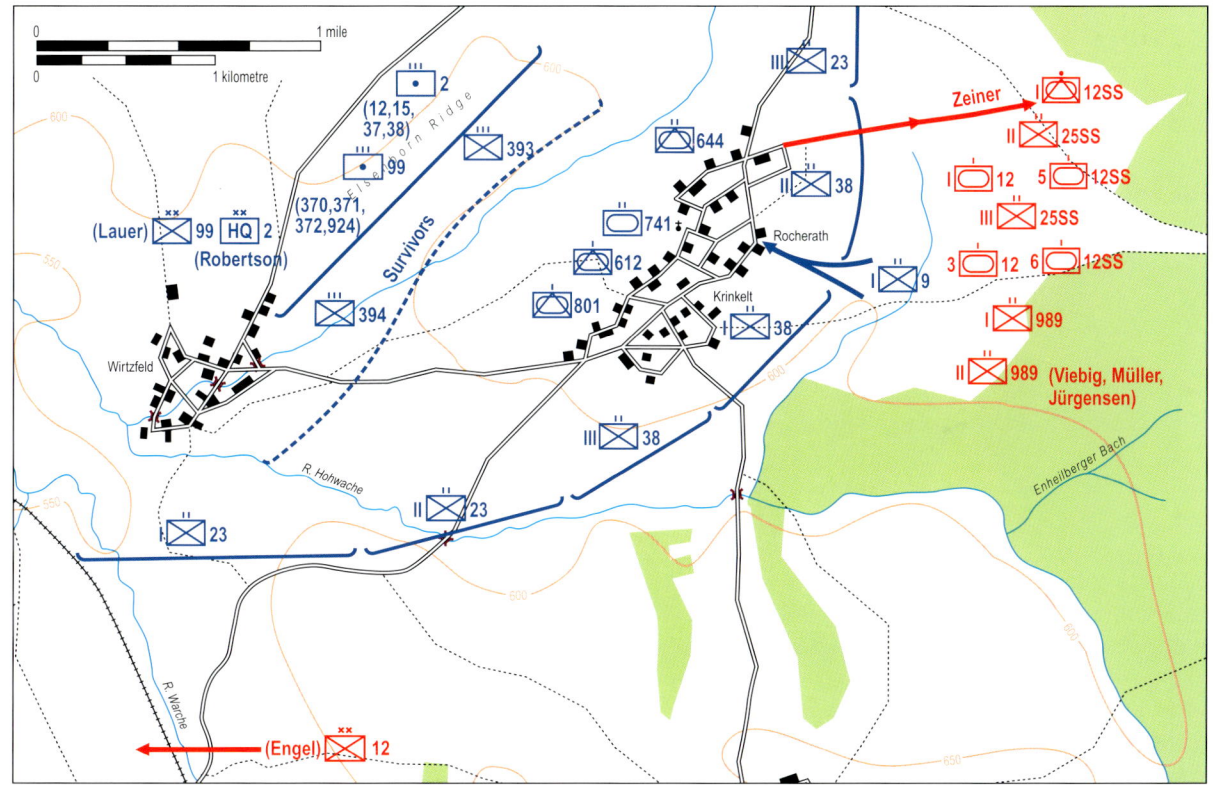

U.S. and German deployments at Krinkelt and Rocherath on 18th December when Jürgensen's tanks so nearly broke through.

McKinley's artillery liaison officer, wasted no time in calling down fire from the 2nd and 99th Infantry Divisions' field guns now deployed on Elsenborn ridge. And when the Panzergrenadiers overran Company A, its commander, First Lieutenant Stephen Truppner, called for fire 'on me'. The German attack here was broken up but Truppner and all except 12 of his men were dead. On the left of the American line, Captain Jack Garvey's Company K in and around a farmhouse was engulfed by Germans and the survivors forced to surrender. By 1100 hrs, when McKinley finally re-ceived the order to withdraw under covering fire from Company A of the 741st Tank Battalion, his I/9th battalion was down to 217 men.

The panzers and panzergrenadiers were now into the two villages, where they found much tougher opposition than during the preceding night. Apart from the 741st Tank Battalion's Shermans, the 38th Infantry Regiment whose lines McKinley retired through was now supported by the 644th Tank Destroyer Battalion's M10s, a company of the 612th Tank Destroyer Battalion's M18s and some towed guns from the 801st. Thus, although at one point Müller's tanks and grenadiers got as far as Colonel Boos' command post in Rocherath, and others as far as I/38th's CP in Krinkelt, that was as far as they got. The Panther in front of Willi Fischer succumbed to a direct hit near the church in Krinkelt but most of its crew got out. Brödel, his company commander, was less lucky and did not escape from his burning tank. Fischer's own Panther had its track blown off and he surrendered to about 20 GIs who surrounded him.

At the end of the day the Americans still held the two villages and Kampfgruppe 'Müller' and Jürgensen's surviving tanks were pulled back to redeploy in support of Kampfgruppe 'Kühlmann' on Rollbahn C at Büllingen and Dom Bütgenbach. The onus of trying to break through over Elsenborn ridge would now be left to Viebig's 277 Volksgrenadier Division supported by a fresh unit, 3 Panzergrenadier Division, released from OKW Reserve.

16/12/1944	18/12	20/12	22/12	24/12	26/12	28/12	30/12	6/1/1945	13/1	20/1	27/1	3/2	7/2
pages 46-59,70-73,77,87-91				60-61,74-76									

I SS-PANZER KORPS' BATTLES
12 Volksgrenadier Division and Kampfgruppe 'Kühlmann'

Büllingen-Dom Bütgenbach – December 16-22

The assault by Generalmajor Gerhard Engel's 12 Volksgrenadier Division began optimistically enough at 0700 hrs on 16 December in the wake of the immense artillery barrage which heralded the start of the offensive, but very quickly bogged down just like that of 277 Volksgrenadier Division to the north. The 'footsloggers' who were supposed to clear the path actually blocked the roads for the tanks and halftracks of the Panzer Kampfgruppen waiting impatiently behind them. Therefore, although Engel's 27 Füsilier Regiment had got into Losheim by 0900 hrs and started following the railway line which winds northwest between Losheim and Losheimergraben towards 12 SS-Panzer Division's Rollbahn C, they encountered an immediate hitch.

When the Wehrmacht had retreated through this sector earlier in the year, they had destroyed the bridge on the Büllingen road over the railway track. Infantry could bypass the obstacle, but not tanks, so Engel's pioniers, helped by some from 3 Fallschirm Division, began trying to effect repairs. They did not work quickly enough for SS-Obersturmbannführer 'Jochen' Peiper, who pushed his own engineers forward to speed the work up.

Meanwhile, Engel's infantry pressed on, led by 27 Füsilier Regiment on the left and 48 Grenadier Regiment on the right (through the woods towards Losheimergraben). The Füsiliers almost immediately ran into trouble at Buchholtz station which was defended by Company L of Major Norman Moore's III/394th battalion, and a solitary M18 of the 801st Tank Destroyer Battalion, both from the 99th Infantry Division. Moore promptly sent Company K to support them. The Füsiliers took cover underneath boxcars on the railway track but the M18 shot these up and, under heavy machine-gun, mortar and smallarms fire, the Füsiliers retired.

Another company of Füsiliers accompanied by two of the division's half-dozen StuGs now tried to outflank the station, but ran into Lieutenant-Colonel Robert Douglas' I/394th. An anti-tank gun took out the leading StuG and heavy mortar fire stopped the infantry in their tracks.

Engel's 48 Grenadier Regiment, meanwhile, had been making slow progress through the woods, which were festooned with barbed wire and mines (again, left over from the earlier German retreat), but finally reached Losheimergraben at about midday. They quickly forced back Companies B and C, I/394th, but Company A held on and by nightfall Douglas' battalion still precariously controlled the crossroads. On a broader scale, the American battalion was out on a limb, because the 14th Cavalry Group had been pushed back in the Losheim gap by 3 Fallschirm Division and contact had been lost with the 106th Infantry Division, in the Schnee Eifel, which was under heavy attack from 18 Volksgrenadier Division (LXVI Korps, Fifth Panzer Army). Douglas could not expect any immediate help from the north either, because the 393rd Infantry Regiment had its own problems around Krinkelt and Rocherath while the 395th on the division's northern flank was covering the withdrawal of Major-General Walter Robertson's 2nd Infantry Division from Wahlerscheid.

The situation became very confused on 17 December when Kampfgruppe 'Peiper' and paras from 3 Fallschirm Division deviated from their planned route to take Buchholtz station, then Honsfeld and then the fuel dump outside Büllingen. These objectives properly belonged to 12 Volksgrenadier and 12 SS-Panzer Division, but they were seriously lagging behind schedule. Much to the surprise of the thin American line blocking the routes to the north, which would have outflanked the 99th Infantry

16/12/1944	18/12	20/12	22/12	24/12	26/12	28/12	30/12	6/1/1945	13/1	20/1	27/1	3/2	7/2
pages 42-45,50-59,70-73,77,87-91				60-61,74-76									

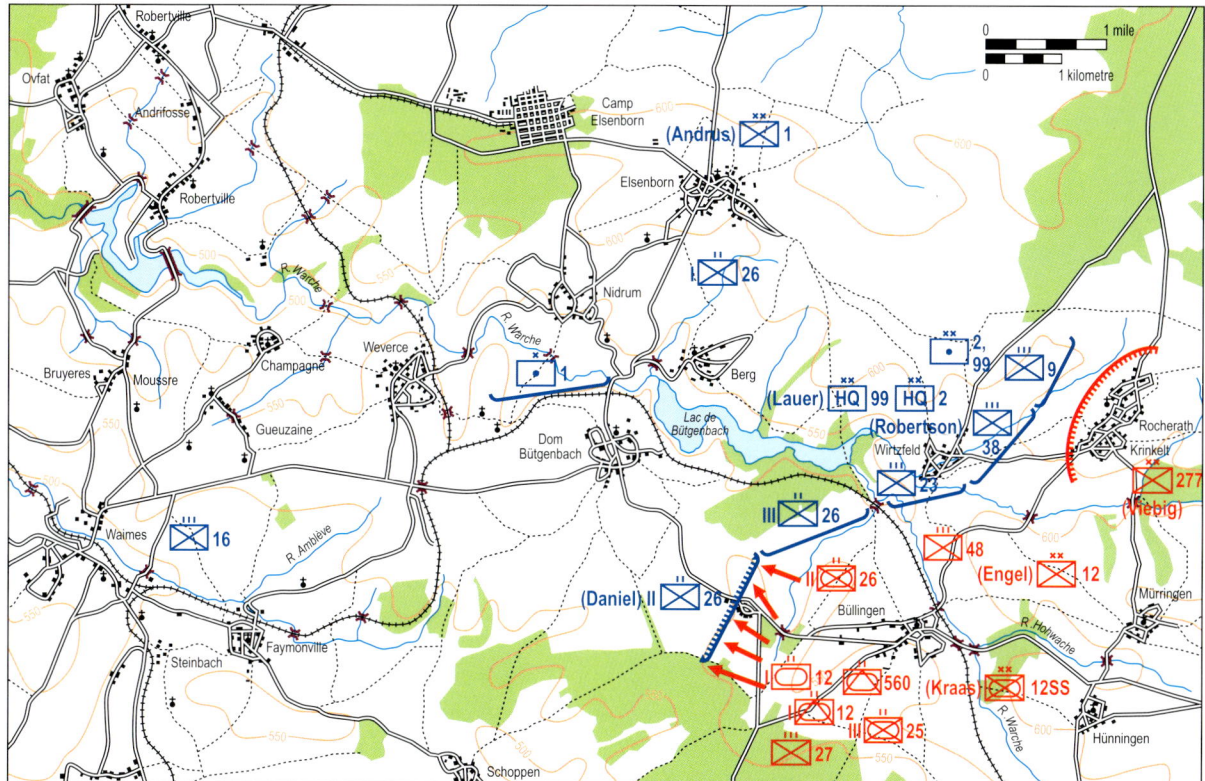

U.S. dispositions on the southern and western shoulder of Elsenborn ridge and the approach routes during successive attacks by 12 Volksgrenadier and 12 SS-Panzer Divisions. All failed to achieve a decisive breakthrough and the assault was abandoned.

Division, Peiper turned south and west towards his original Rollbahn. However, there was no sanguinity in the Allied camp because Losheimergraben had finally fallen.

The costly frontal assault here had been renewed early in the morning by 48 Grenadier Regiment of 12 Volksgrenadier Division, but it was an outflanking manoeuvre from the west by 27 Füsilier Regiment which did the trick, driving a wedge between I and III/394th and forcing the surviving men from Companies B and C into hiding until nightfall; only 20 escaped to rejoin the division. The remainder of the two battalions fell back on Mürringen; II/394th, retiring through the Honsfelder Wald to conform, got lost in the dense forest and dug in to await events.

Engel's Volksgrenadiers, spearheaded again by 27 Füsilier Regiment, now turned their attention on Lieutenant-Colonel John Hightower's freshly-arrived I/23rd from the 2nd Infantry Division, which had established a blocking position at Hünningen a mile south of Mürringen.

By this time, leading elements of 12 SS-Panzer Division had caught up with the infantry over the wall of earth and stone which the pioniers had thrown up across the railway cutting, and about a dozen PzKpfw IVs from an unidentified company moved up through the mist to support the Volksgrenadiers. This was a mistake, because a 76mm anti-tank gun took out four of them with six shots, a remarkable feat under any circumstances.

Engel's Füsiliers launched no fewer than seven determined assaults against Hightower's battalion during the afternoon, but the few men who managed to get into Hünningen were quickly killed or captured. There was intense artillery fire from both sides, the Americans having the advantage of the church tower from which an observer was able to zero in the guns. But, as nightfall approached, the American position was becoming untenable, for they were not only running low on ammunition but were in grave danger

16/12/1944	18/12	20/12	22/12	24/12	26/12	28/12	30/12	6/1/1945	13/1	20/1	27/1	3/2	7/2
pages 42-45,50-59,70-73,77,87-91				60-61,74-76									

47

After his heroic efforts to take Krinkelt and Rocherath, SS-Sturmbannführer Arnold Jürgensen was killed during the later fighting at Dom Bütgenbach.
(U.S. Signal Corps)

of being surrounded. The only solution was to pull back in concert with the 394th through Krinkelt towards Elsenborn, a manoeuvre which was accomplished successfully in the small hours of 18 December.

Finding Hünningen deserted in the morning, Engel wasted no time in speeding the as yet uncommitted 12 Füsilier Bataillon and the remaining five StuGs of Holz's 12 Volks-Panzerjäger Abteilung west to Büllingen, which was only lightly defended and was quickly in German hands. It was not before time, because it had actually been Engel's objective for day one of the offensive. The next target was the village of Dom Bütgenbach and Priess had brought Kampfgruppe 'Krause' forward from Losheimergraben to support the Volksgrenadiers' assault. SS-Obersturmbannführer Bernard Krause's battlegroup had originally been intended to follow that of SS-Sturmbannführer Herbert Kühlmann along Rollbahn C, but Priess put Krause in the van because Kühlmann's Panzer Abteilung was still involved in support of Siegfried Müller's Kampfgruppe at Krinkelt-Rocherath. This unit would shortly disengage and the assault on that sector was handed over to 3 Panzergrenadier Division.

On the American side, 2nd Infantry Division's right flank at Dom Bütgenbach was now protected by Colonel John Seitz's 26th Infantry Regiment, 1st Infantry Division, temporarily commanded by his executive officer, Colonel Edwin Van Sutherland because Seitz was on leave. Sutherland deployed his 2nd Battalion (Lieutenant-Colonel Derrill Daniel) on the high ground in front of Dom Bütgenbach, supported by five M4s from the 745th Tank Battalion and four M10s from the 634th Tank Destroyer Battalion deployed in hulldown positions. Sutherland kept I/26th in reserve at Elsenborn with III/26th on the high ground to Daniel's left; the right flank was screened by the three

battalions of Colonel Frederick Gibb's 16th Infantry Regiment which stretched west to Waimes. The third of Major-General Clift Andrus' 1st Infantry Division regiments, the 18th, was still hunting for von der Heydte's Fallschirmjäger between Malmédy and Eupen.

Krause and Kühlmann spent the rest of 18 December in reconnaissance, having determined that Dom Bütgenbach was occupied when an armoured car probing up the road from Büllingen was shot to pieces. During the night further SS troops arrived and Kühlmann launched III/26 SS-Panzergrenadier Regiment's half-tracks towards the village at 0225 hrs on the 19th, but they got bogged down in the mud and had to be abandoned under heavy artillery fire. A second attempt at 1010 hrs met a similar fate. That ended that day's attack but Hugo Kraas had now made Büllingen the 'Hitler Jugend' Division's headquarters and reinforcements were arriving hourly, including the remnants of Arnold Jürgensen's Panzer Abteilung and the Army's attached 560 schwere Panzerjäger Abteilung with a company of Jagdpanthers.

Kraas and Kühlmann renewed the attack on the 20th, using Engel's by now severely depleted Füsilier battalions on the right flank to probe through the woods towards Wirtzfeld for a weak spot. The main effort was made by Kühlmann's I/26 SS-Panzergrenadier Regiment supported by Hauptmann Heinz Wewers' 1 Kompanie of Jagdpanthers, which attacked across open countryside to the west of the Büllingen road. The infantry again suffered heavily from concentrated shellfire but a few of the Jagdpanthers got into the village – in fact, to within yards of Daniel's command post in the manor house. In the darkness, two drove past a little 57mm anti-tank gun which put well-aimed rounds through their more thinly armoured stern plates, and the rest retired. (Wewers was later to complain about using SP guns without traversing turrets in this type of close-quarters battle.)

Kühlmann launched three further attacks during the morning, hitting Daniel's F, G and E Companies respectively, but his tanks and Jagdpanzers could find little room to manoeuvre and suffered from the attentions of the dug-in tank destroyers, while on each occasion the Panzergrenadiers were badly mauled by accurate artillery and mortar fire.

Next day, 21 December, the assault was even more determined. The division now had the support of an entire Volks-Artillerie Korps to reinforce its own

16/12/1944	18/12	20/12	22/12	24/12	26/12	28/12	30/12	6/1/1945	13/1	20/1	27/1	3/2	7/2
pages 42-45,50-59,70-73,77,87-91				60-61,74-76									

The deployment of the U.S. 26th Infantry Regiment around Dom Bütgenbach and the German attacks on 21-22 December before the withdrawal of 12 SS-Panzer Division. On Christmas Day the CO of 12 Volksgrenadier Division, Gerhard Engel, ordered his men to cease fire for the occasion.

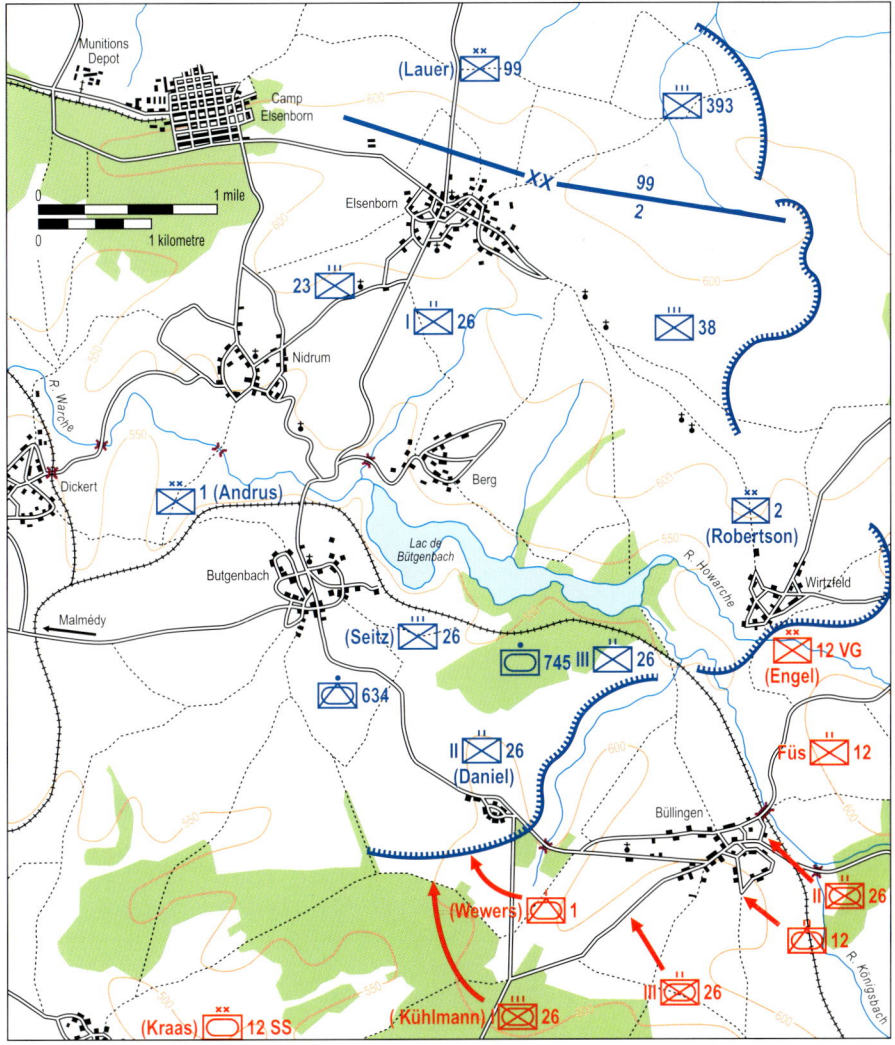

12 SS-Panzer Artillerie Regiment's four battalions in trying to keep the defenders' heads down. Kühlmann mustered all the remaining tanks of Jürgensen's Panzer Abtei-lung, all except one company of 560 Panzerjäger Abteilung, and III/25 SS-Panzergrenadier Regiment on the left, with II/26 SS-Panzergrenadier Regiment on their right supported by Jagdpanzer IV/70s of 12 SS-Panzerjäger Abteilung.

The day opened with a three-hour artillery barrage against the American positions, then the tanks and Jagdpanzers rolled forward, penetrating Daniel's line on his left, knocking out several anti-tank guns and machine-gunning the infantry foxholes. However, they had outstripped their infantry, and American bazooka teams began to take their toll; so did the tank destroy-ers of the 634th hull-down behind the ridge north of the village. The surviving Panzers again fell back.

One last attempt was made on 22 December, using III/26th SS-Panzergrenadier Regiment which had been held in reserve on the 21st, supported by all the surviving tanks and Jagdpanzers and 217 Sturm-panzer Abteilung's Brummbärs which had finally arrived to reinforce 12 Volksgrenadier Division. This time the attack went in from the west just before 1000 hrs, and initially looked as though it was going to succeed because the grenadiers broke through between Daniel's A and K Companies on his right flank. But again the American artillery and tank destroyers prevailed, and that night 12 SS-Panzer Division was pulled out of the line.

16/12/1944	18/12	20/12	22/12	24/12	26/12	28/12	30/12	6/1/1945	13/1	20/1	27/1	3/2	7/2
pages 42-45,50-59,70-73,77,87-91				60-61,74-76									

I SS-PANZER KORPS' BATTLES

Kampfgruppe 'Peiper'

Losheim to La Gleize – December 16-24

These roads 'are only broad enough for a bicycle!' SS-Obersturmbannführer 'Jochen' Peiper was not a happy man. He had just finished a gruelling 50-mile drive, at night, in a 40-ton Panther tank, to find out how long it would take his 1 SS-Panzer Regiment, Leibstandarte 'Adolf Hitler', to cover this distance. 'Too long,' was the kernel of his answer to 'Sepp' Dietrich's chief of staff, SS-Brigadeführer Fritz Krämer, who had asked Peiper the question five days before the beginning of 'Herbstnebel'. The youngest regimental commander in the division used almost the same words when his CO, SS-Oberführer Wilhelm Mohnke, briefed him about his role in the new offensive a couple of days later. The roads, he told Mohnke, were suitable 'not for tanks, but for bicycles'.

Peiper's words were, in a sense, prophetic, because it was the poor state of the roads – about which both Dietrich and Manteuffel were already concerned – that virtually sealed the fate of the German offensive. Limited to narrow, winding tracks running precipitously around steep hillsides or through deep ravines, with dense forest on both sides for much of the route, there was no way to deploy a Panzer force effectively. Peiper estimated that his 5,000-man Kampfgruppe would stretch over ten miles of road, highly vulnerable to any form of counter-attack from the ground and clearly visible to any Allied 'Jabos' (the fighter-bombers which Peiper had experienced so disastrously in the ill-conceived counter-attack at Mortain earlier in the year).

In the event, Kampfgruppe 'Peiper' ended up straggling over about 20 miles of narrow roads, and was totally unable to bring its formidable offensive firepower to bear against any adversary worthy of the name. It was largely isolated groups of American engineers, not tanks and tank-destroyers, which thwarted Peiper's aim of getting 'just one Panzer' over the Meuse end of Rollbahn D.

Could Peiper have rearranged his column to give himself more chance of success? He put his PzKpfw IVs in the van to begin with, followed by the Panthers, with the lumbering Tigers of 501 schwere SS-Panzer Abteilung at the rear. This made sense to a degree; a PzKpfw IV could take on any M4 Sherman (except a British Firefly) at even odds; apart from a fluke, the Panther was more or less impervious to Shermans except from flank or rear, and under the right circumstances could sit back and demolish them with its long-barrelled 7.5cm gun from outside the M4's range. The less-mobile Tigers, with their 8.8cm weapons, also preferred to fight from long range with a clear field of fire.

Peiper's arrangements thus made initial sense, because he did not really envisage any tank-versus-tank encounters until his Kampfgruppe neared the more open terrain when they were closer to the Meuse. He also took the precaution of putting one of his two companies of pioniers (9/1) in the van with his leading tanks, remembering how failure to do so in Normandy had contributed so significantly to the Leibstandarte's crushing defeat. The only snag was, they had no heavy bridging equipment. The bridging columns were all far to the rear, and there was no way that such a unit could hope to overtake an armoured regiment on a road only suitable for bicycles! Instead, it was the 'Verdammt pioniere' of the U.S. Army who thwarted Peiper's ambitions.

Having said that, it was also the 'damned engineers' of his own side which ruined Peiper's timetable on 16 December. With his men shivering in their tanks and half-tracks, Peiper was forced to fume impotently in the field headquarters of 12 Volksgrenadier Division all morning while the infantry

16/12/1944	18/12	20/12	22/12	24/12	26/12	28/12	30/12	6/1/1945	13/1	20/1	27/1	3/2	7/2
pages 42-49,58-59,70-73,77,87-91				60-61,74-76									

A Tiger II from 501 schwere SS-Panzer Abteilung passes prisoners captured at Honsfeld. (US Army)

and engineers of Engel's command, and those of 3 Fallschirm Division, struggled to clear a foothold for the Leibstandarte's tanks past the demolished railway bridge at Losheim. At 1400 hrs, by which time the battle had been raging elsewhere for nearly seven hours, Peiper had waited long enough.

'Es war zum Kotzen' ('It made you puke'), he was later fond of saying, and rough-shouldered his own SS engineers through the Wehrmacht ranks to improvise a couple of crossing points over the deep railway cutting which was holding everything up. This was accomplished by about 1600 hrs and by 2200 hrs even 501 schwere SS-Panzer Abteilung's Tigers had caught up with the rest of the Kampfgruppe around Losheim. Instead of being halfway to the Meuse, they had barely started. But there was some good news.

A radio message told Peiper that a regiment of 3 Fallschirm Division had captured the hill village of Lanzerath. Peiper wasted no time getting his men moving again, off the road and across the fields. Then they ran into a minefield which the paras had failed to clear, losing three tanks and five half-tracks. Peiper

was in an even fouler mood when he tracked down the hapless commander of 9 Fallschirm Regiment, Oberst i.G. von Hoffmann (a middle-aged Luftwaffe general staff officer from Berlin), in the village café at about midnight.

Hoffmann blustered and was later to complain about Peiper's attitude, but he had unforgiveably bedded his men down for the night, waiting for daylight before probing the woods for the 'amis' he was convinced filled them. After his losses in the minefield, Peiper was in no mood for excuses, and radioed I SS-Panzer Korps' CO Hermann Priess for permission to commandeer I/9 Fallschirm Regiment for a dawn attack on 17 December. Unspoken was the understanding that they would be cannon-fodder.

The woods were empty of anything except rabbits!

By this time, only 24 hours into the offensive, Peiper was already running short of fuel, but he remembered what his divisional CO, Mohnke, had told him before the offensive: that there was believed to be a large American POL dump at Büllingen. This lay on 12 SS-Panzer Division's Rollbahn C, but from the sound of heavy gunfire to the northeast, Peiper realised that they, too, must have been held up. Mohnke had also told him that it was permissible to deviate from his own

16/12/1944	18/12	20/12	22/12	24/12	26/12	28/12	30/12	6/1/1945	13/1	20/1	27/1	3/2	7/2
pages 42-49,58-59,70-73,77,87-91				60-61,74-76									

Paratroops of 3 Fallschirm Division hitch a ride on one of II SS-Panzer Abteilung's Panthers. Some paras travelled like this as far as La Gleize. (US Army)

designated Rollbahn if necessary, so Peiper decided to take the chance.

The route lay through Bucholtz, already captured by 9 Fallschirm Regiment, and the village of Honsfeld, but even before they reached Honsfeld the leading Panzers ran into a long column of retreating Americans, who scattered and jammed the roads in their efforts to escape. A brave few attempted to fight back, and Allied fighters appeared, so Peiper left the village for the paras to clear up and urged his Kampfgruppe forward. They reached Büllingen virtually unopposed between 0800 and 0900 hrs on 17 December and captured about 50 GIs who were pressed into service at gunpoint to refill the tanks of the Panzers and half-tracks. Peiper was anxious to leave quickly since he did not want his tanks to get mixed up with those of Kühlmann, spearheading 12 SS-Panzer Division.

This is where Peiper missed an opportunity which could have altered the course of the battle. To the astonishment of the Americans at Wirtzfeld and Dom Bütgenbach, instead of turning north to outflank them, Peiper turned southwest towards Stavelot, now putting the Panthers of II/1 SS-Panzer Regiment under SS-Sturmbannführer Werner Pötschke in the van. With full fuel tanks, they reached Thirimont by noon but then, in order to keep to a reasonable road surface, had to detour through the tiny hamlet of Baugnez en route to Ligneuville and Stavelot.

At this moment, Combat Command R of the U.S. 7th Armored Division was passing through this otherwise insignificant crossroads on its way south to help the beleaguered 106th Infantry Division (VIII Corps) in front of St Vith. The only other Allied troops in the vicinity were companies of Colonel David E. Pergrin's 291st Engineer Combat Battalion in Malmédy, Stavelot and Trois Ponts – the 'Verdammt pioniere'.

At the Baugnez crossroads that afternoon occurred one of the most infamous events of this whole campaign. The precise details have been a source of controversy ever since. What is clear is that Pötschke's tanks came unexpectedly upon a column of vehicles belonging to the unattached US Battery B, 285th Field Artillery Observation Battalion, as they were travelling from Malmédy towards St Vith. The vehicles were

machine-gunned and a number of Americans killed in the initial onslaught. Others surrendered and were later shot after having been disarmed, only 14 badly-wounded men surviving. How many were killed in the massacre, and how many in the preceding firefight is not entirely clear, but about 80 Americans died in all. No matter who gave the orders and who pulled the triggers, what is clear is that unarmed prisoners were ruthlessly and cold-bloodedly butchered.

Kampfgruppe 'Peiper' encountered its first genuine resistance at Ligneuville, which CCR of 7th Armored Division had again just passed through. The opposition came from a scratch force of 9th Armored Division's CCB, also on its way towards St Vith. Peiper had been anxious to reach Ligneuville quickly, for purely personal reasons. A prisoner had revealed that this was the headquarters of General Edward Timberlake, CO of the 49th Anti-Aircraft Brigade. Peiper had captured generals before, but never an American one. Nor was he destined to; Timberlake and his staff vacated the village ten minutes before Kampfgruppe 'Peiper' arrived. As the leading Panther of SS-Untersturmführer Arnt Schmidt neared the bridge over the Amblève on the southern side of Ligneuville, a Sherman opened fire from behind a house, setting the German tank ablaze. Peiper, following behind in a Hanomag half-track, quickly reversed his vehicle into cover and jumped out with a Panzerfaust. (In November 1941 he had saved his company by destroying a Russian T-34 with a single rifle grenade.) But another Panther got a shot in first and the Sherman fell silent. The skirmish lasted a scant few minutes; Schmidt's tank was the only serious casualty and the Americans lost two Shermans and an M10.

While the Kampfgruppe pressed on towards

16/12/1944	18/12	20/12	22/12	24/12	26/12	28/12	30/12	6/1/1945	13/1	20/1	27/1	3/2	7/2
pages 42-49,58-59,70-73,77,87-91				60-61,74-76									

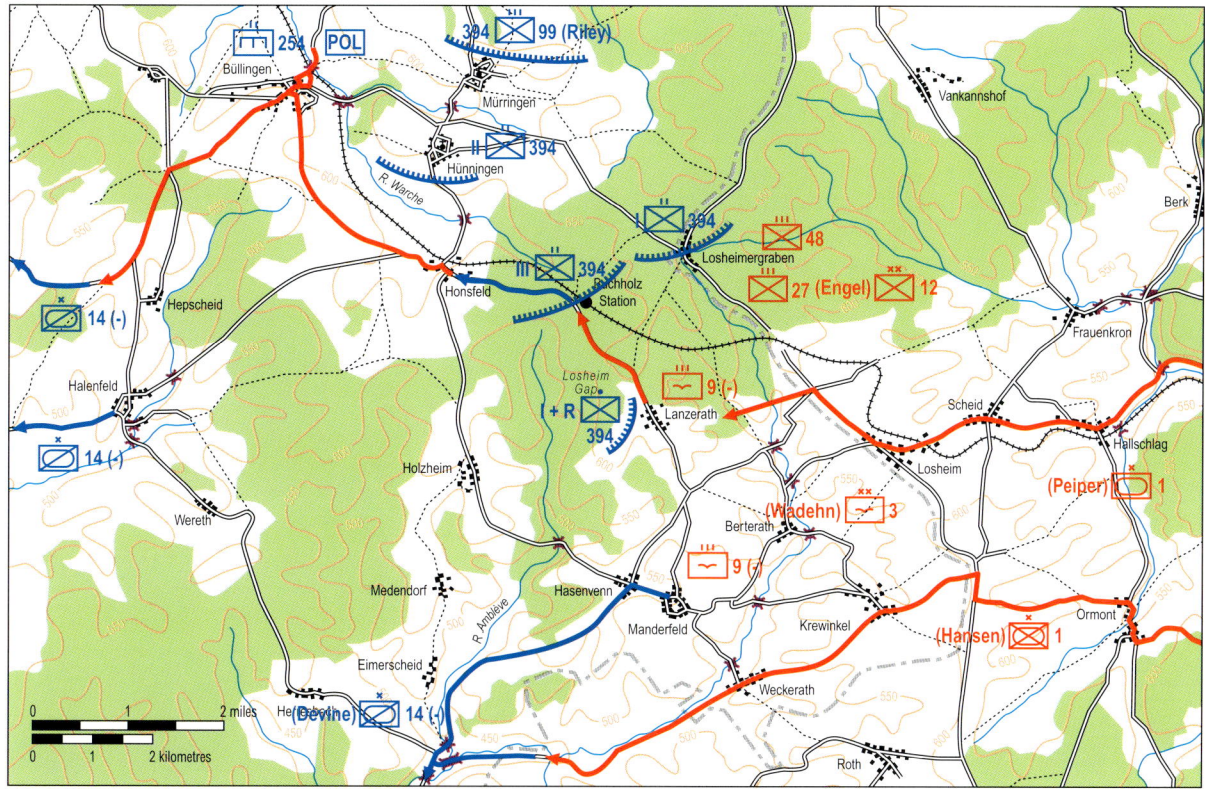

Once he eventually got his Kampfgruppe out of Losheim, Peiper made good progress through Lanzerath and Honsfeld to the U.S. POL depot at Büllingen.

Stavelot, Peiper remained behind in General Timberlake's former headquarters to wait to confer with his divisional CO, Mohnke. As it happened, this was a mistake. The 291st Engineer Combat Battalion had established a roadblock at a bend on the hill sloping down into Stavelot, and as Pötschke's leading Panthers approached at about 1930 hrs, a brave GI let fly a single shot with a bazooka. Not knowing the extent of the opposition he faced in the pitch-black night, Pötschke retired back up the hill to wait for daylight. It was another delay which was to have unforeseen repercussions at a little village called Trois Ponts.

By the time Peiper rejoined his unit at about 0600 hrs on 18 December, the defence of Stavelot had been strengthened by part of the 526th Armored Infantry Battalion and four 76mm anti-tank guns from the 825th Tank Destroyer Battalion – non-divisional troops from

First Army headquarters in Spa. They were commanded by Major Paul Solis.

Peiper began his attack with an artillery barrage on the roadblock, and two of Solis' guns were destroyed as they raced back down the hill towards Stavelot. The road to the stone bridge over the Amblève lay open but Solis had deployed one of his remaining anti-tank guns on the Malmédy road, on the hill to the west of Stavelot, so that it could fire across the river. SS-Hauptsturmführer Krenser's leading Panther was hit immediately but SS-Obersturmführer Hennecke pressed on with the attack. Coming under heavy machine-gun and mortar fire as he led the way across the miraculously intact bridge, Hennecke spotted Solis' other remaining 76mm gun in the market place and veered left up a narrow street leading diagonally towards the Trois Ponts road. Unable to stop the Panzers, the American crew spiked their gun and retreated.

Peiper decided to leave mopping up to the following 3 Fallschirm Division and urged his weary men on. Trois Ponts was a key objective and Peiper was well aware that his timetable was a shambles. He wrote

16/12/1944	18/12	20/12	22/12	24/12	26/12	28/12	30/12	6/1/1945	13/1	20/1	27/1	3/2	7/2
pages 42-49,58-59,70-73,77,87-91				60-61,74-76									

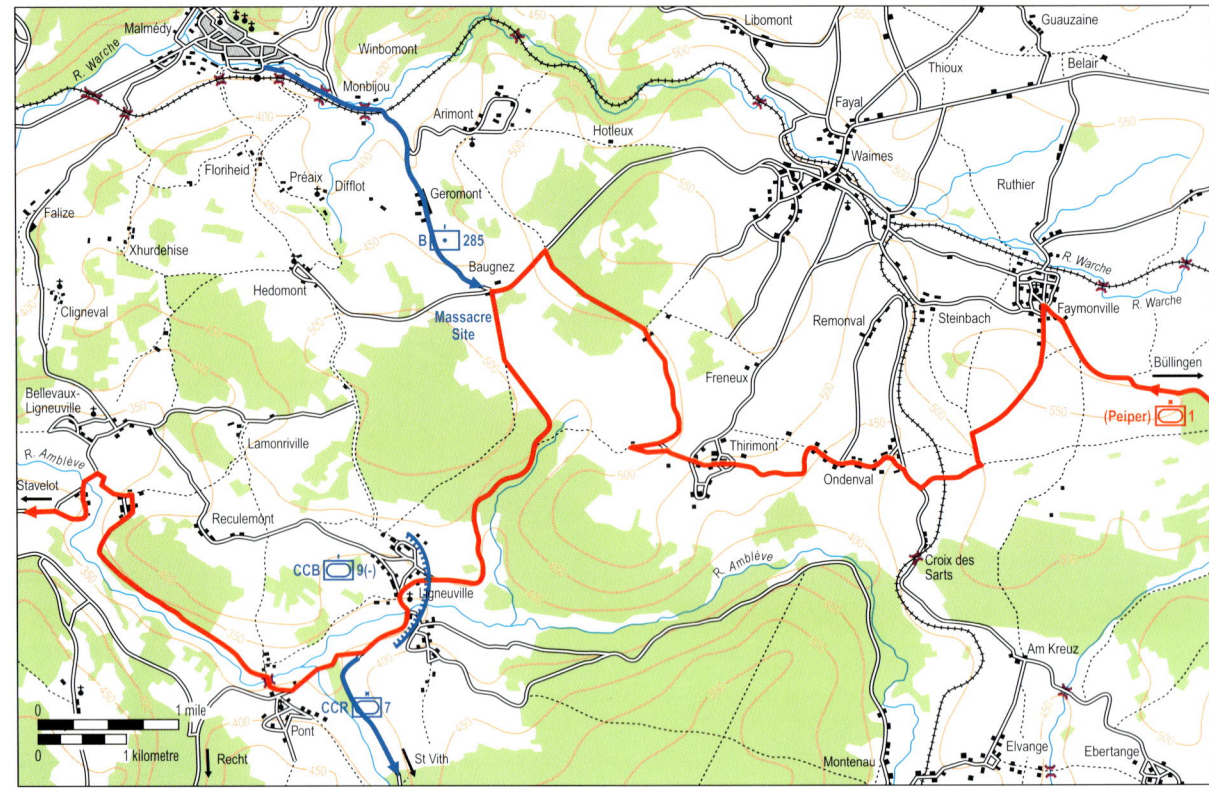

Peiper's circuitous route to Ligneuville, dictated by the terrain, took him through Baugnez where the massacre of American prisoners occurred.

afterwards that, 'My own situation was obscure. Clear was only that things did not develop according to plan. We were low on gas. Food was not worth mentioning. I sensed that my flanks were completely open and had the uneasy feeling that nobody followed either.' What Peiper did not know, or he would certainly not have abandoned Stavelot so casually, was that the Americans had an even larger POL depot on the Francorchamps road to the north of the town. Major Solis ordered the dump destroyed, believing Peiper's tanks were only minutes away. They were actually heading in the opposite direction...

Trois Ponts should actually have been called 'Quatre Ponts' because it is the locus of four bridges; one over the Amblève, two over the Salm and one over the strategically unimportant western tributary, the Bodeux. If the one over the Amblève, and just one of the bridges over the Salm, was intact, Peiper had a clear road towards Werbomont along Rollbahn E.

There was, moreover, another bridge over the Salm about a mile south of Trois Ponts, which could open a 'back door' to the village if the frontal attack failed. He therefore decided on a two-pronged attack and sent a small task force (6 and 7 Kompanien, 1 SS-Panzer Regiment, with PzKpfw IVs, and 3 Kompanie, 1 SS-Panzer Pionier Abteilung) south via Wanne, while the main force approached from the northeast down the narrow, winding road from Stavelot.

This road passed under a sturdy railway viaduct which the officer in charge of the American engineers (of the 291st again), Major Robert B. Yates, decided would take too long to blow. Colonel H. Wallis Anderson, CO of the 1111th Engineer Combat Group and in overall charge of the defence, placed a small 57mm anti-tank gun (abandoned by the 526th Armored Infantry on their way to Stavelot) to cover the approach. Yates concentrated on laying demolition charges on the three main river bridges but wisely detached a platoon to deal with the one further south as well.

As they approached the railway underpass at about 1045 hrs on 18 December, Peiper's men could see GIs

16/12/1944	18/12	20/12	22/12	24/12	26/12	28/12	30/12	6/1/1945	13/1	20/1	27/1	3/2	7/2
pages 42-49,58-59,70-73,77,87-91				60-61,74-76									

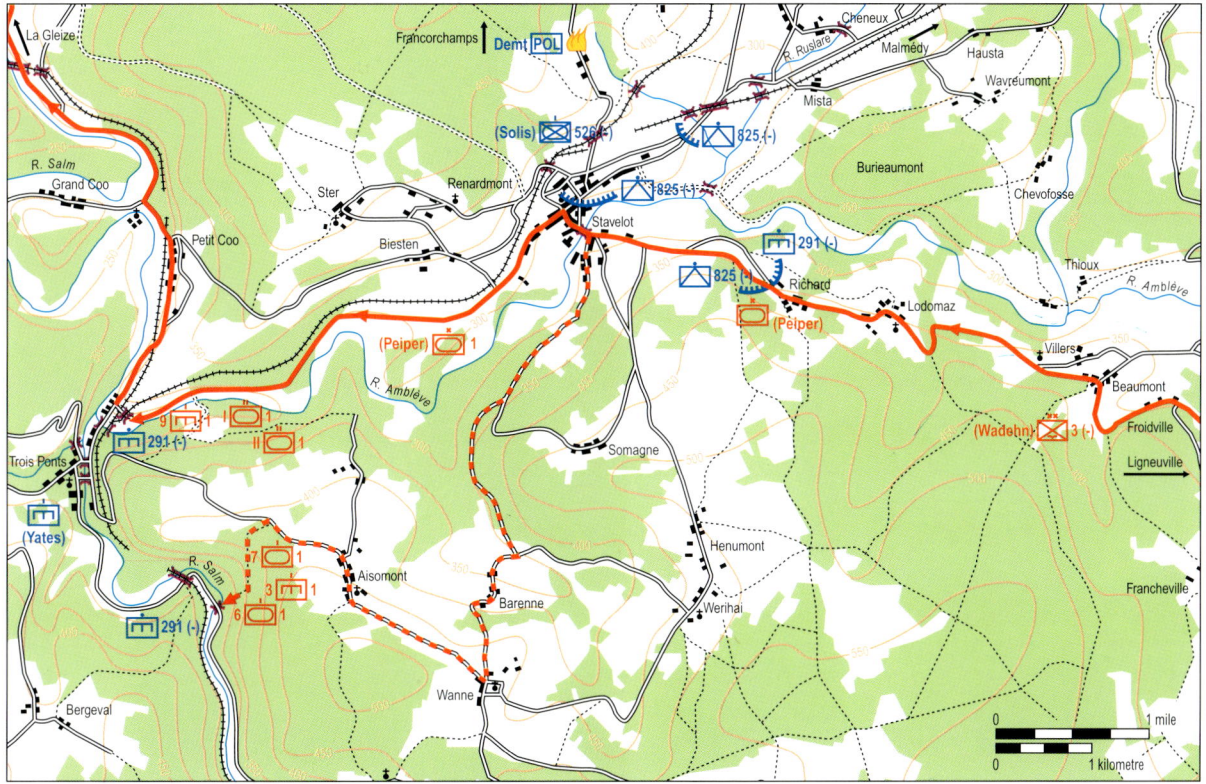

From Stavelot, where he missed the American fuel dump to the north, Peiper tried a two-pronged attack at Trois Ponts which was thwarted by U.S. engineers.

frantically laying mines across the road. German combat engineers charged forward, scattering them, and quickly lifted the mines. Then, as the leading Panther rounded the corner at the far side of the underpass, the American 57mm gun crew opened fire, damaging a track. But there was room for another tank to squeeze past in low gear, and one round of HE demolished the gun and its heroic four-man crew. However, they had bought just enough time for Yates' engineers to finish laying their charges, and the Amblève bridge went up in a cloud of dust, smoke and debris.

Peiper's southern task force was also thwarted as it approached Trois Ponts from the southeast, for the southern bridge over the Salm also blew up in their faces. They would have to travel all the way back to Stavelot to rejoin the main road and the rest of the Kampfgruppe. So Trois Ponts was out as a crossing place and all Peiper could do was reluctantly turn his men away from the inviting Werbomont road on to the

narrow track towards the hilltop village of La Gleize on Rollbahn D. Was there another way round? It seemed so. From here, Peiper's maps showed a minor road stretching southwest, skirting Stoumont to the south, back on to Rollbahn E west of Trois Ponts and only a couple of miles from Werbomont.

The column reached La Gleize without incident by 1300 hrs and scouts reported the first bridge over the Amblève on the new route miraculously intact at Cheneux. Because it was on such a narrow byroad, the 'damned engineers' had missed it. But, hardly had Peiper's leading tanks crossed this about an hour later than his whole column – which did now stretch for 20 miles – came under concerted aerial attack by fighter-bombers from the 365th Fighter Group and two squadrons from other groups. Incredibly, only two Panthers and about a dozen other vehicles were lost, but the advance was delayed until about 1600 hrs when fog descended to hide the Kampfgruppe from the air.

The delay had, however, given Colonel Anderson time to despatch a truck loaded with TNT and a handful of engineers towards what was obviously the next

16/12/1944	18/12	20/12	22/12	24/12	26/12	28/12	30/12	6/1/1945	13/1	20/1	27/1	3/2	7/2
pages 42-49,58-59,70-73,77,87-91				60-61,74-76									

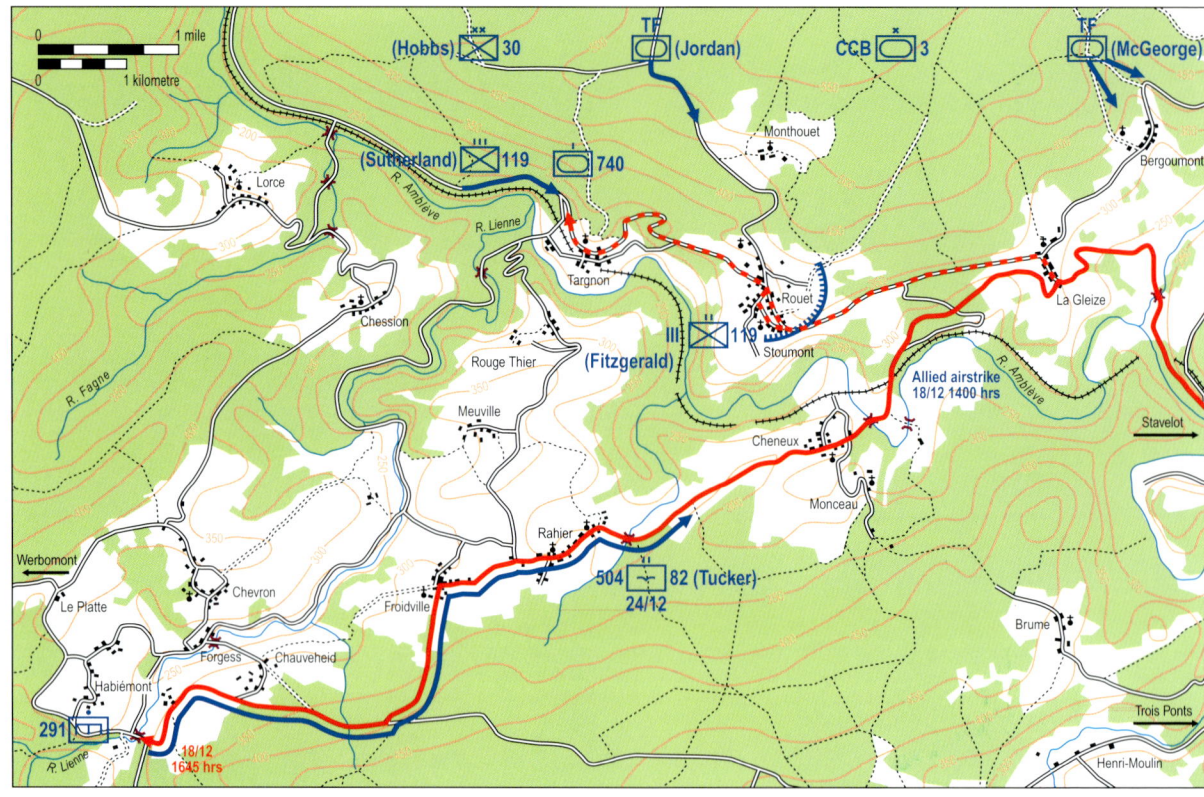

Peiper attempted to circumvent Stoumont through Cheneux but was blocked at Habiémont and failed later to break through from La Gleize to Stoumont.

bridge on Peiper's route, close to the hamlet of Habiémont over the small, but steep-banked, River Lienne. Anderson's men were just in time and blew the bridge at 1645 hrs when the first Panzers appeared out of the gloom.

Kampfgruppe 'Peiper' retreated and hid its tanks back in the woods around La Gleize. Another day wasted. Peiper's mood matched the winter night even though welcome reinforcements had reached him at about midnight in the form of the reinforced reconnaissance battalion under SS-Sturmbannführer Gustav Knittel, together with a small column of fuel tankers. Other news was bad, though, because Knittel reported that he had only just managed to get through Stavelot, which had been recaptured by the Americans. Peiper simply told Knittel to turn the bulk of his Kampfgruppe around first thing in the morning – by now 19 December – and retake the town. In fact, by this time Priess and Mohnke had also realised Peiper's

situation was perilous, and the rest of the Leibstandarte battlegroups were converging to try to extricate him. In the end, though, only SS-Sturmbannführer Herbert Schnelle's II/2 SS-Panzergrenadier Regiment managed to get through at about 1200 hrs on 20 December.

On 19 December Peiper had only one source of inspiration. Werbomont was clearly out but, equally clearly, with Stavelot in enemy hands, no-one else would want Rollbahn D, which debouched on the Meuse north of Huy. He would revert to it: first objective, Stoumont, which he had tried to bypass the day before. By this time, though, Eisenhower's reshuffling of Allied reserves had brought the 30th Infantry Division into play, and the town was defended by Lieutenant-Colonel Roy C. Fitzgerald's III/119th Infantry Regiment plus eight towed anti-tank guns and two 90mm anti-aircraft guns.

Peiper launched his attack at about 0700 hrs, before daybreak, but there was no sign of the sun an hour later because a heavy mist blanketed the landscape. One American 90mm gun knocked out a Tiger, and four other tanks were immobilised by

16/12/1944	18/12	20/12	22/12	24/12	26/12	28/12	30/12	6/1/1945	13/1	20/1	27/1	3/2	7/2
pages 42-49,58-59,70-73,77,87-91				60-61,74-76									

bazookas, but the German infantry prevailed and Stoumont itself was soon theirs. Not for long, though, because the 119th Regiment's commander, Colonel Edward M. Sutherland, had been busy preparing a surprise. From the direction of the railway station 19 Shermans and an M36 of Lieutenant-Colonel George K. Rubel's freshly arrived 740th Tank Battalion loomed out of the mist as dusk began to fall. They were accompanied by Lieutenant-Colonel Robert Herlong's fresh I/119th infantry battalion. Peiper fell back to the eastern edge of the town.

It was the beginning of the end for his Kampfgruppe because next day, 20 December, the powerful two full battalions of the 'heavy' 3rd Armored Division's CCB arrived under Brigadier-General Truman E. Boudinot, temporarily assigned to XVIII (Airborne) Corps whose 504th Parachute Regiment, 82nd Airborne Division, was already to Peiper's south. Boudinot divided his command into three task forces, 'Jordan', 'McGeorge' and 'Lovelady', which attacked along three axes, the latter towards the road between La Gleize and Trois Ponts, cutting off Peiper's logical retreat. With the paratroops of the 504th in Cheneux as well, Kampfgruppe 'Peiper' was surrounded and fell back to the narrow strip of high ground at La Gleize. I and II SS-Panzer Korps were making frantic efforts to save

Peiper's command, with 9 SS-Panzer Division lending its weight to the south of Rollbahn E, but Peiper's pleas on his one remaining functional radio to be allowed to fight his way out cross-country fell on stony ears. The Luftwaffe attempted a supply drop in the evening of 22 December, but the bulk fell into American hands in Stoumont. There was no more petrol or food. Feldwebel Karl Laun from Peiper's attached 84 Flak Abteilung recorded on the 23rd that 'for breakfast we got a double helping of artillery and mortar fire'. That night Peiper told Mohnke on the radio, 'This is the last chance of breaking out'.

Fortunately, there was no snow as Peiper led about a thousand men out of the trap at 0200 hrs on Christmas Eve. He had left behind a small 'forlorn hope' rearguard and a medical officer to look after the wounded. It was a nightmare trek through Wanne and then east for the frozen, starving men, constantly having to hide during the day from American patrols or aircraft, but eventually the survivors did stagger into the arms of Kampfgruppe 'Hansen' on Christmas morning.

Panthers approach Stoumont during Peiper's last attempt to reach the Meuse, which was thwarted by the 740th Tank Battalion. (U.S. Signal Corps)

16/12/1944	18/12	20/12	22/12	24/12	26/12	28/12	30/12	6/1/1945	13/1	20/1	27/1	3/2	7/2
pages 42-49,58-59,70-73,77,87-91				60-61,74-76									

I SS-PANZER KORPS' BATTLES

Kampfgruppe 'Hansen'

Recht-Poteau – December 17-19

Kampfgruppe 'Hansen' reached the little crossroads at Poteau on 18 December hard on the heels of what was left of Colonel Mark Devine's 14th Cavalry Group. The battlegroup commanded by SS-Standartenführer Max Hansen comprised principally the three battalions of his 1 SS-Panzergrenadier Regiment plus 1 SS-Panzerjäger Abteilung and pionier, flak and StuG companies. Hansen had encountered the same problems of congested roads on Rollbahn E that had also delayed Kampfgruppe 'Peiper' on Rollbahn D to his north on 16 December. The paras of 3 Fallschirm Division were pushing on steadily in front of Hansen's battlegroup, but horsedrawn artillery which some optimist had ordered forward to support the anticipated breakthrough now made the road through Hallschlag impassable for his half-tracks. Hansen turned south towards Ormont before heading west again through Kehr and Amblève towards Born, which I/1 SS-Panzergrenadier Regiment reached at about 1030 hrs on 17 December.

Mark Devine's 18th Cavalry Squadron – his 32nd Squadron was back in Vielsalm – had been effectively the only American unit covering the Losheim gap and, attacked by the 12th and 18th Volksgrenadier Divisions on either flank and 3 Fallschirm Division in the centre, had no option but to fall back steadily, initially to Manderfeld. The men of Lieutenant-Colonel William F. Damon's squadron had been spread out in individual platoons through seven widely-separated villages when the attack began, and could not hope to resist. Hansen's Kampfgruppe caught up with them at Born, which Devine had just made his HQ after conferring during the night with the CO of the 106th Infantry Division, Major-General Alan Jones, in St Vith. Outnumbered, and with only Greyhound armoured cars to combat Hansen's Jagdpanzer IV/70s, Devine had to flee again, through Recht and down the Vielsalm road to Poteau, where he again established his headquarters. He now received an order to report to Jones in St Vith, but as the direct route through Vielsalm was blocked by 7th Armored Division tanks moving east, he had to go back along the road he had just vacated. On his return, after dark, he had the misfortune to run into the point of Hansen's Kampfgruppe near the crossroads with the main road from Malmédy to St Vith, and his Jeep ended up in the ditch. Somehow unhurt, Devine and his operations officer made their way on foot back to Poteau but Devine was so unnerved by his experience that he handed over command to Lieutenant-Colonel Augustine Duggan, who had now been reinforced by part of the 32nd Squadron. This was commanded by Major John L. Kracke because its actual CO, Lieutenant-Colonel Paul Ridge, had been infected by the prevailing panic and made an excuse to hurry back to Vielsalm.

A well-known propaganda photo of some of Hansen's grenadiers near Poteau. (U.S. Signal Corps)

16/12/1944	18/12	20/12	22/12	24/12	26/12	28/12	30/12	6/1/1945	13/1	20/1	27/1	3/2	7/2
pages 42-49,50-57,70-73,77,87-91				60-61,74-76									

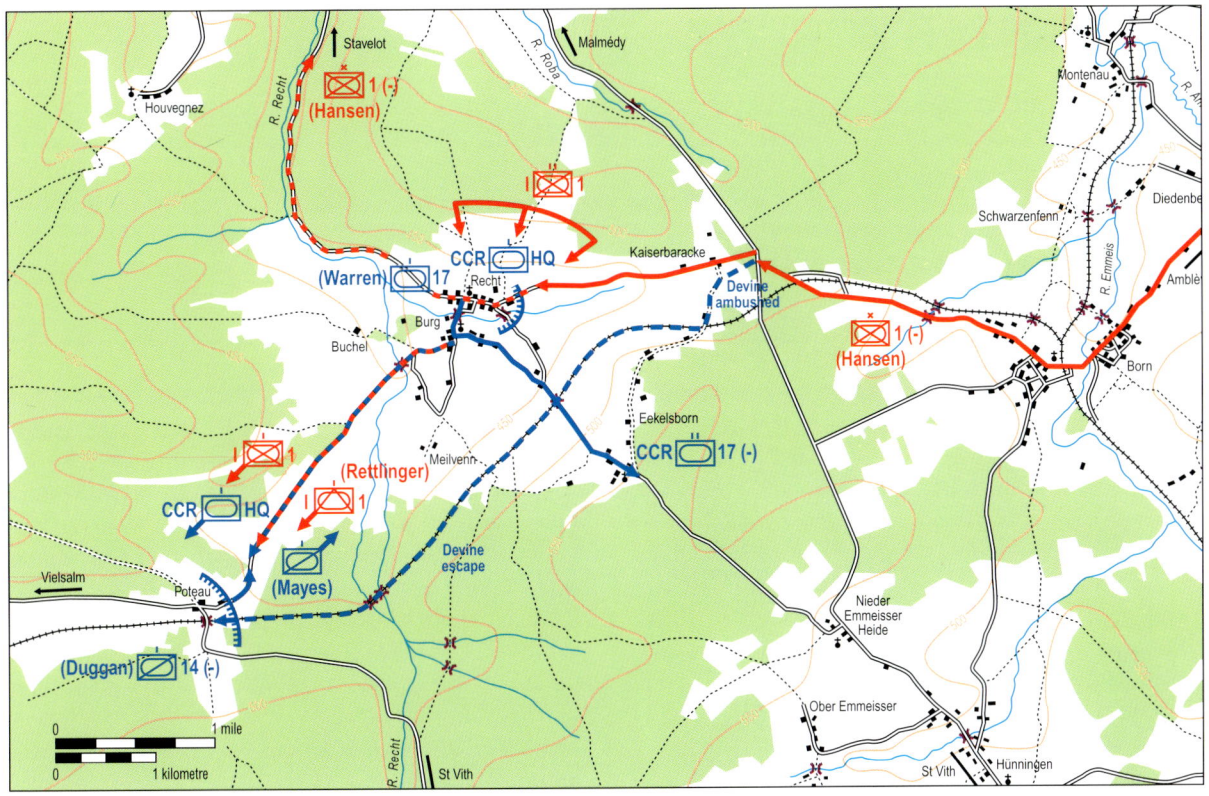

Kampfgruppe 'Hansen's' advance to Recht and Poteau. Colonel Devine was ambushed near Kaiserbaracke. Poteau became of critical importance later during the evacuation of St Vith.

Meanwhile – it was now after midnight – Hansen's vanguard was approaching Recht. This was lightly held by part of of 7th Armored Division's CCR commanded by Lieutenant-Colonel Fred M. Warren, some headquarters troops and a company of 17th Tank Battalion Shermans. Warren had been worried that his tanks had no infantry to defend them from German grenadiers armed with Panzerfausts, and his worst fears were realised when Hansen's I Abteilung burst out of the woods, firing flares to illuminate the tanks. After three-quarters of an hour of confused fighting, Warren ordered his tanks to pull back towards St Vith. He and his headquarters' staff made their way to Poteau where, to his amazement, he found Duggan preparing a counter-attack.

A small task force under Major James L. Mayes, comprising parts of the 18th and 32nd Cavalry Squadrons with six M8 Greyhounds, three M5 Stuart light tanks and three M3 half-tracks, took off up the road towards Recht at 0700 hrs on 18 December. They had barely gone 300 yards when they came under fire from Hansen's grenadiers, supported by Jagdpanzer IV/70s from the Panzerjäger Abteilung. One Greyhound and a Stuart were hit immediately, blocking the advance, and another Greyhound and an M3 seconds later. Deciding that against these odds, discretion was definitely the better part of valour, Mayes hastily withdrew back to Poteau. The uneven fight for the crossroads lasted all morning, for Hansen did not want to leave this threat behind on his flank. When Duggan eventually ordered a withdrawal towards Vielsalm at about midday, Hansen also called off the attack and rolled his column west through Recht on Rollbahn E. Next day he was ordered to swing northwest towards La Gleize, where Kampfgruppe 'Peiper' was in trouble, and cutting cross-country reached Wanne just after the detached task force Peiper had sent to try to get into the southern 'back door' at Trois Ponts had returned disconsolately towards Stavelot. Later, Hansen failed to recapture Stavelot from the Americans.

	16/12/1944	18/12	20/12	22/12	24/12	26/12	28/12	30/12	6/1/1945	13/1	20/1	27/1	3/2	7/2
	pages 42-49,50-57,70-73,77,87-91				60-61,74-76									

I SS-PANZER KORPS' BATTLES

150 Panzer Brigade

Malmédy – December 21-28

As dusk settled over Malmédy on the afternoon of 20 December, the inhabitants of the little town could have been forgiven for thinking the war had passed them by. Apart from some desultory shelling from long-range rail guns, and a heart-stopping period on the 17th when survivors of the massacre at Baugnez were brought in, they had seen nothing of the huge battle raging all around them. Then the Panzers struck out of the fog in the early hours of the morning of the 21st, and by Christmas Allied bombers would have pounded their town to rubble.

Otto Skorzeny's so-called 150 Panzer 'Brigade' was supposed to have infiltrated itself from its starting point at Münstereifel through the Volksgrenadiers clearing the path for I SS-Panzer Korps' Kampfgruppen, and use side roads to close up with the head of the columns. But, plagued by the congested roads which had hindered Hansen and Peiper, two days into the offensive they had hardly moved. Skorzeny therefore suggested that the original plan be scrapped and that his brigade be used as a conventional force to seize Malmédy, which might be needed as an escape route if Peiper ran into serious difficulties, or used as an avenue through which to attack American forces north of the Amblève from the rear. 'Sepp' Dietrich agreed and told Skorzeny to assemble his units between Ligneuville (where Sixth Panzer Armee now had its forward headquarters) and Malmédy.

Oberstleutnant Wolf's Kampfgruppe Z was still too bogged down in traffic to be of immediate use, and had no tanks anyway, so Skorzeny designated it as his reserve and pinned his hopes on Kampfgruppe X (now commanded by SS-Hauptsturmführer Adrian von Foelkersam because Willi Hardieck had been killed by a mine) and Hauptmann Scherff's Kampfgruppe Y. Scherff had five StuGs painted with Allied white stars, and Foelkersam five Panthers disguised, not very successfully, as M10s. Skorzeny also had a handful of M8 Greyhounds and Jeeps, but the rest of his vehicles were German and his men wore a rag-tag mixture of American and Wehrmacht uniforms.

Skorzeny was under the impression that Malmédy was still only occupied by about a company of Colonel David E. Pergrin's 291st Engineer Combat Battalion. However, between 17 and 21 December, the town's defenders had swelled considerably. Disposed in a southeasterly curve, using the railway embankment and the River Warche as natural obstacles, and with minefields guarding the approaches, were, in fact, Pergrin's men, plus I and III/120th Infantry Regiment; 99th Infantry Battalion ('The Norwegians'); 526th Armored Infantry Battalion; a company of the 740th Tank Battalion; and two platoons of the 823rd Tank Destroyer Battalion, all from the 30th Infantry Division which was also blocking Peiper at Stoumont.

Even if Skorzeny had known he was outnumbered, it is difficult to see how he could have planned his attack with any radical differences. He despatched Kampfgruppe Y back up the main road through Baugnez to attack Malmédy from the east and Kampfgruppe X up the winding minor road through Bellevaux-Ligneuvllle and Falize. The attack was scheduled to begin at 0300 hrs on the 21st but a deserter had warned the Americans and Scherff's StuGs and three infantry companies ran into immediate trouble at a roadblock established by the I/120th south of Malmédy, at Géromont. Scherff's leading half-track hit a mine, blocking the road, and American artillery pounded the area using the new proximity fuze. After futilely probing for a weak spot, Scherff abandoned his attack and retired towards Ligneuville at 0500 hrs. Meanwhile, driving north from Falize on the secondary road, Foelkersam split his force at 0430

16/12/1944	18/12	20/12	22/12	24/12	26/12	28/12	30/12	6/1/1945	13/1	20/1	27/1	3/2	7/2
pages 42-49,70-73,77,87-91			74-76										

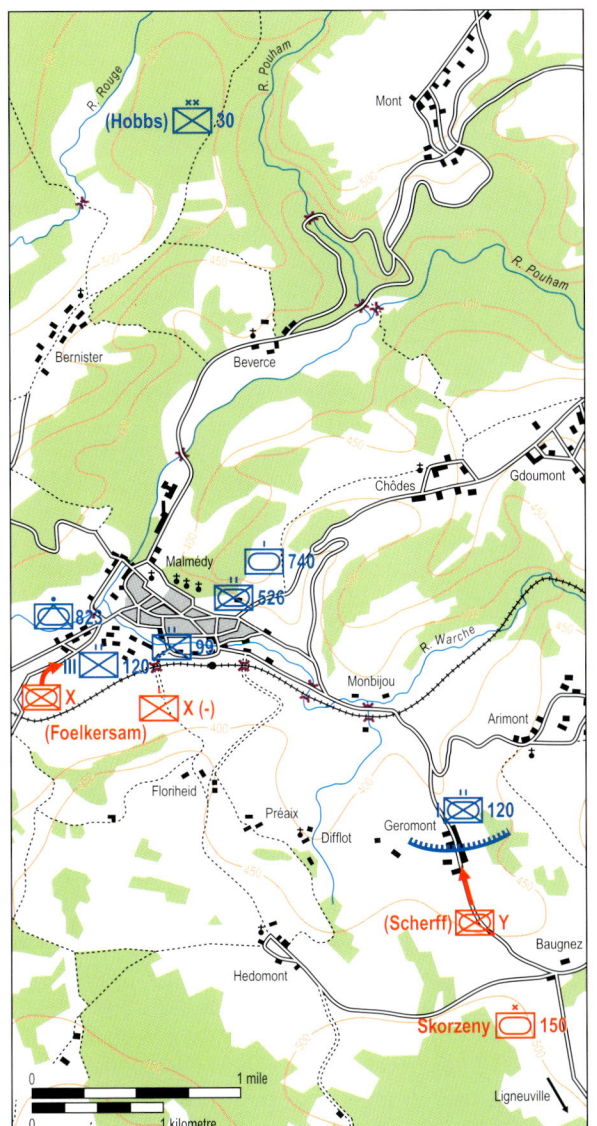

Skorzeny's two Kampfgruppen tried attacking at three points in the Malmédy perimeter but failed to get past the paper mill or railway embankment.

Foelkersam's main force fared little better, because one of his men trod on a trip wire, sending a shower of flares into the night sky. This sector was defended by the III/120th and four M10s from the 823rd whose crews returned the fire of Foelkersam's disguised Panthers. More lightly armoured, and with open-topped turrets, the M10s were quickly despatched and Kampfgruppe X advanced towards a house opposite the paper mill, held by 33 men from Company K under First Lieutenant Kenneth R. Nelson, who decided to fight on despite the fact that a Panther was pumping shells into the building. When Nelson was killed, some of the survivors escaped to join more Company K men in the mill. Private Francis Currey picked up a bazooka and knocked out the Panther, then stalked the others with rifle grenades, for which feat he was awarded the Congressional Medal of Honor.

Heavy artillery fire was now pouring down around the mill, the bridge and the house from further back, because observers on the hill north of Malmédy thought the Germans had captured them. Two men made a dash from the mill along the railway embankment to report the true situation, and the shelling stopped. But, with all his tanks now knocked out, and only a handful of armoured cars left, von Foelkersam, who had himself been wounded, reported to Skorzeny that he could do no more. Kampfgruppe X retired to the hill south of Malmédy in mid-afternoon.

From their vantage point, Skorzeny's men watched helplessly, on the 22nd, as Pergrin's engineers demolished the river bridges and the railway bridge. They also had a ringside seat next day to witness the astonishing sight of wave after wave of American heavy and medium bombers pounding Malmédy because the 117th Infantry Regiment, on the 120th's right flank, had reported the town captured. Amazingly, the mistake was not corrected immediately, and the bombers returned on Christmas Eve and Christmas Day. Over 200 Belgian civilians and at least 300 American soldiers lost their lives in the raids, which General Carl Spaatz of the U.S. Ninth Air Force referred to as 'alleged'.

Skorzeny's 150 Panzer Brigade was finally pulled out of the line on the 28th and its men returned to their parent units.

hrs, detaching one infantry company to continue heading straight up the road while his main body cut across the fields to the west, towards a bridge on the road from Stavelot over the Warche. The detached company ran straight into withering fire from the 'Norwegians' deployed behind the railway embankment and the leading Panther hit a mine, brewing up and blocking the road again. The infantry courageously charged the railway embankment several times, suffering very heavy casualties from machine-gun fire and grenades, but were unable to get over the top and after two hours the survivors fell back.

16/12/1944	18/12	20/12	22/12	24/12	26/12	28/12	30/12	6/1/1945	13/1	20/1	27/1	3/2	7/2
pages 42-59,70-73,77,87-91			74-76										

SIXTH PANZER ARMEE

II SS-PANZER KORPS

SS-Obergruppenführer Wilhelm Bittrich's II SS-Panzer Korps was initially assigned a secondary role in 'Herbstnebel' but, after, the failure of Priess' I SS-Panzer Korps to break through in the north, it was reorganised and re-assigned, 'belatedly', in Heinz Guderian's words, to operate alongside Fifth Panzer Armee either side of the St Vith salient. Yet, in the end, it was 'Das Reich'

SS-Obergruppenführer Wilhelm Bittrich had been a fighter pilot in World War 1 and a stockbroker before rejoining the armed forces after Hitler's rise to power.
(Bundesarchiv, Koblenz)

which made the deepest penetration by an SS forma-tion into American lines. Guderian, back on the east-ern front, was not involved in 'Herbstnebel' and the brief comments on the operation in his widely read memoirs are, in this case, largely misinformed opinion written with the blessing of hindsight.

Like I SS-Panzer Korps, II Korps had been formed in Russia to spearhead the Kharkov and Kursk offen-sives in 1943, and was fighting around Tarnopol when news of the Allied landings in Normandy caused it to be rushed to the west. Both its 9 and 10 SS-Panzer Divisions suffered heavy losses and were withdrawn to Holland to refit outside Arnhem. Here, they were instrumental in defeating the British 1st Airborne Division in September, after which 10 SS-Panzer Division was assigned to Balck's Heeresgruppe G, its

---

II SS-PANZER KORPS
SS-Obergruppenführer Wilhelm Bittrich
Stabschef: *SS-Obersturmbannführer Walter Harzer*

2 SS-Panzer Division 'Das Reich' (Lammerding)
9 SS-Panzer Division 'Hohenstaufen' (Stadler)

---

place being taken by 2 SS-Panzer Division.

Dietrich's orders to Bittrich were much shorter then those to Priess: 'II SS-Panzer Korps will be situated close behind I SS-Panzer Korps in order to follow them immediately. II SS-Panzer Korps has the mission either to co-operate with I SS-Panzer Korps to push towards the Meuse or, immediately after having crossed the Meuse, regardless of their flanks being threatened by the enemy, to push towards Antwerp. Permanent contact with I SS-Panzer Korps has to be maintained.'

Like Priess, 'Willi' Bittrich was accustomed to a challenge and, an ambitious man, resented what he regarded as his Korps' subordinate role in the offensive. He had originally joined the Luftwaffe but transferred to the Waffen-SS in anticipation of more rapid promotion. He got his wish and commanded first 8 SS-Kavallerie Division 1942-43, then 9 SS-Panzer Division in Russia before being given command of II SS-Panzer Korps in June 1944 and the rank of Obergruppenführer in August. However, he did not allow any resentment to interfere with his efficiency and had built his two Panzer divisions up so well that they were actually stronger in tanks and assault guns than those in I SS-Panzer Korps. This was fortunate in the light of what happened.

A very confused situation arose over 19-22 December, much akin to Eisenhower's redeployment of divisions between Corps in the American camp over the same period. II SS-Panzer Korps briefly became responsible for 3 Fallschirm and 3 Panzergrenadier

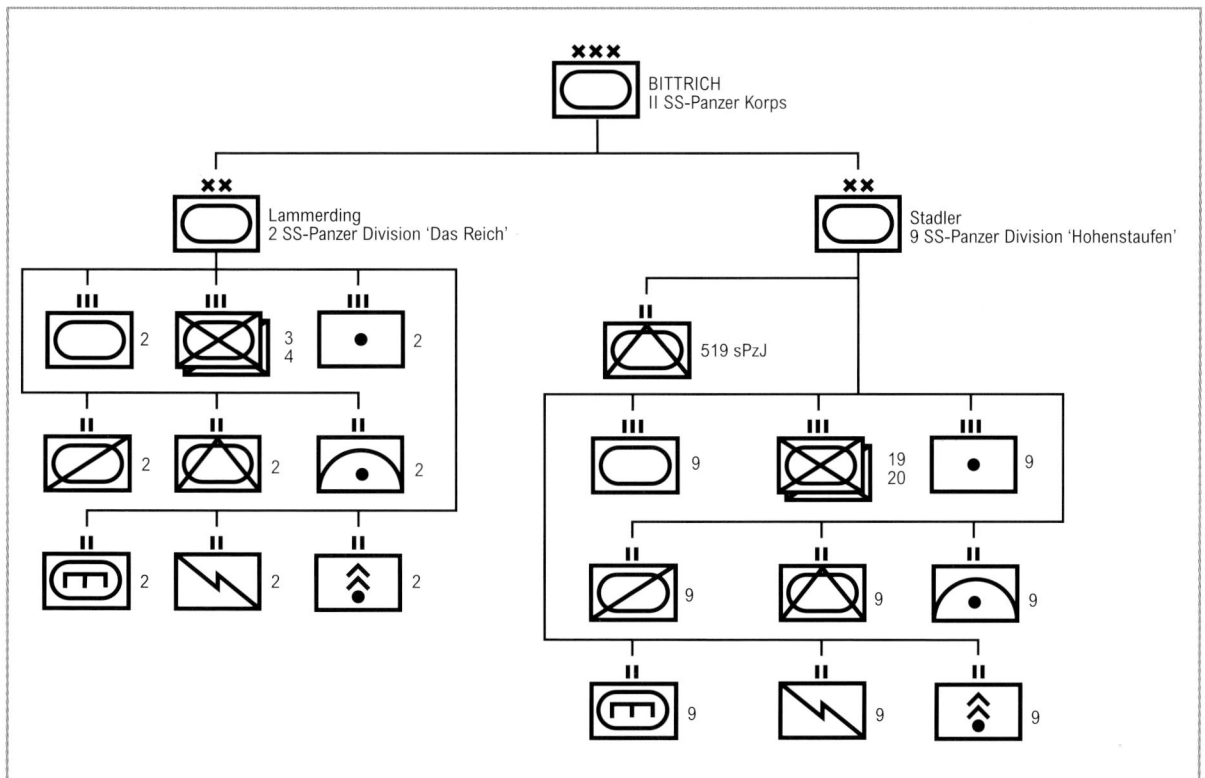

Divisions, and 12 and 277 Volksgrenadier Divisions, 'en route' to LXVII Korps whose commander, Generalleutnant Otto Hitzfeld, had had his headquarters badly bombed, causing considerable disruption. 9 and 12 SS-Panzer Divisions momentarily swapped Korps, while 2 SS-Panzer Division was provisionally taken back into Armee Reserve.

Bittrich's Korps was then assigned the task of clearing the resistance at Dom Bütgenbach and opening up Rollbahn C which Kampfgruppe 'Peiper' had intersected before moving on. But it soon became apparent that the Americans, with more reinforcements arriving hourly, were not going to be dislodged from the northern shoulder, so 12 SS-Panzer Division was pulled back to recuperate from its long ordeal and 2 and 9 SS-Panzer Divisions were reinstated in II SS-Panzer Korps.

This was now given a new mission: to shift its weight south of I SS-Panzer Korps' remaining units, 1 SS-Panzer Division and 150 Panzer Brigade, and join the Fifth Panzer Armee's LXVI Korps assault around St Vith. Once past this stumbling block, the roads to the south gave II SS-Panzer Korps an avenue, albeit a narrow one, to exploit between the rivers Salm in the north and Ourthe in the south, heading straight for the junction of the new U.S. VIII and XVIII (Airborne) Corps boundaries.

Their dividing line bisected the main N15 road from Liège to Bastogne and the Americans had accidentally left two important crossroads virtually undefended, at Manhay just east of Grandmenil and at Baraque Fraiture less than five miles further south. Even though the N15 was not a designated Rollbahn, running north-south rather then east-west, this was an opportunity which Bittrich did his utmost to exploit, and which caused consternation to the Allies.

From here, II SS-Panzer Korps could have headed west towards the Meuse, on the right flank of the Army's 2 Panzer Division (as it was actually ordered to do); south to lend its weight against Bastogne; or north towards Liège, possibly rolling up the flank of the U.S. 82nd Airborne Division. All of Bittrich's men's efforts ultimately failed due to the reasons given earlier, but not through want of trying. What really finished off II SS-Panzer Korps' hopes of continuing the offensive was the clear blue skies on Christmas and Boxing Days, which brought the IX Tactical Air Command P-38 Lightnings out in droves.

II SS-Panzer Korps was still fighting on 15 January 1945 though, covering the withdrawal of Fifth Panzer Armee's 2, 9 and 'Lehr' Panzer Divisions, when it was finally pulled out and sent to Hungary for a new, equally doomed, offensive.

2 SS-Panzer Division 'Das Reich'

SS-Brigadeführer Heinz Lammerding's 2 SS-Panzer Division was one of the strongest German formations at the beginning of the Ardennes offensive when it assembled at Satzvey. In manpower, Sixth Panzer Armee chief of staff Fritz Krämer estimated that it was at 80% of establishment (although this was probably optimistic) and its 2 SS-Panzer Regiment was almost at full strength with 58 PzKpfw V Panthers in I Abteilung, 28 PzKpfw IVs in the first two companies of II Abteilung and 28 StuG III/IVs in the remaining two companies. Additionally, its 2 SS-Panzerjäger Abteilung had 20 Jagdpanzer IV/70s. And, although its initial orders gave it a secondary role in support of 1 SS-Panzer Division, it actually achieved more and three of its ranking officers, Krag, Weidinger and Wisliceny, won the Oakleaves to the Knights Cross as a result.

The 'Das Reich' Division had almost as long a history as the Leibstandarte. Its parent formation was the SS-Verfügungs (or 'special purposes') Division formed in the late 1930s around the 'Deutschland', 'Germania' and the post-Anschluss Austrian 'Der

---

2 SS-Panzer Division 'Das Reich'
SS-Brigadeführer Heinz Lammerding
Stabschef: *SS-Obersturmbannführer Walter Harzer*

---

2 SS-Panzer Regiment
3 SS-Panzergrenadier Regiment 'Deutschland' (Wisllceny)
4 SS-Panzergrenadier Regiment 'Der Führer' (Weidinger)
2 SS-Panzer Artillerie Regiment (Kreutz)
2 SS-Panzer Aufklärungs Abteilung (Krag)
2 SS-Panzerjäger Abteilung
2 SS-Panzer Flak Abteilung
2 SS-Panzer Pionier Abteilung
2 SS-Panzer Nachrichten Abteilung
2 SS-Panzer Nebelwerfer Abteilung
2 SS-Panzer Nachschub Truppe
2 SS-Panzer Werkstatt Truppe
2 SS-Panzer Verwaltungs Truppe
2 SS-Panzer Sanitäts Truppe

SS-Brigadeführer Heinz Lammerding. He was one of the criminals who escaped retribution (unlike Peiper) due to Skorzeny's 'Odessa' organisation. He wears the Demyansk shield on his left arm from his 'Totenkopf' days.
(U.S. Signal Corps)

Führer' Regiments. Commanded by Paul Hausser, the SS-Verfügungs Division took part in the invasion of the west in 1940 but was then disbanded, the 'Germania' Regiment forming the cadre of the new 5 SS-Divislon 'Wiking' while the other two regiments formed the nucleus of 2 SS-Division 'Reich', later renamed 'Das Reich'.

In 1941 the division was prominent in the invasion of Yugoslavia, the then commander of its Aufklärungs Abteilung, Fritz Klingenberg, taking the surrender of Belgrade virtually single-handed. During the invasion of Russia the division fought well through the battles of Smolensk and Kiev before being stopped at the gates of Moscow. 'Das Reich' suffered 60% casualties (10,000 men) in the Soviet winter counter-offensive and was sent to France during 1942 to be rebuilt as a Panzergrenadier division.

Command temporarily passed to Wilhelm Bittrich, then Walter Krüger with Hausser's promotion to CO of the new I SS-Panzer Korps for the spring offensive of 1943 which recaptured Kharkov but set the scene for the disastrous battle of Kursk in the summer. The division suffered further heavy casualties around Kiev later in the year and was moved back to France to refit as a Panzer division. In June 1944, moving up to the Normandy front, members of 'Das Reich' were responsible for one of the worst Waffen-SS atrocities of the war on the western front when over 600 French men, women and children were slaughtered at

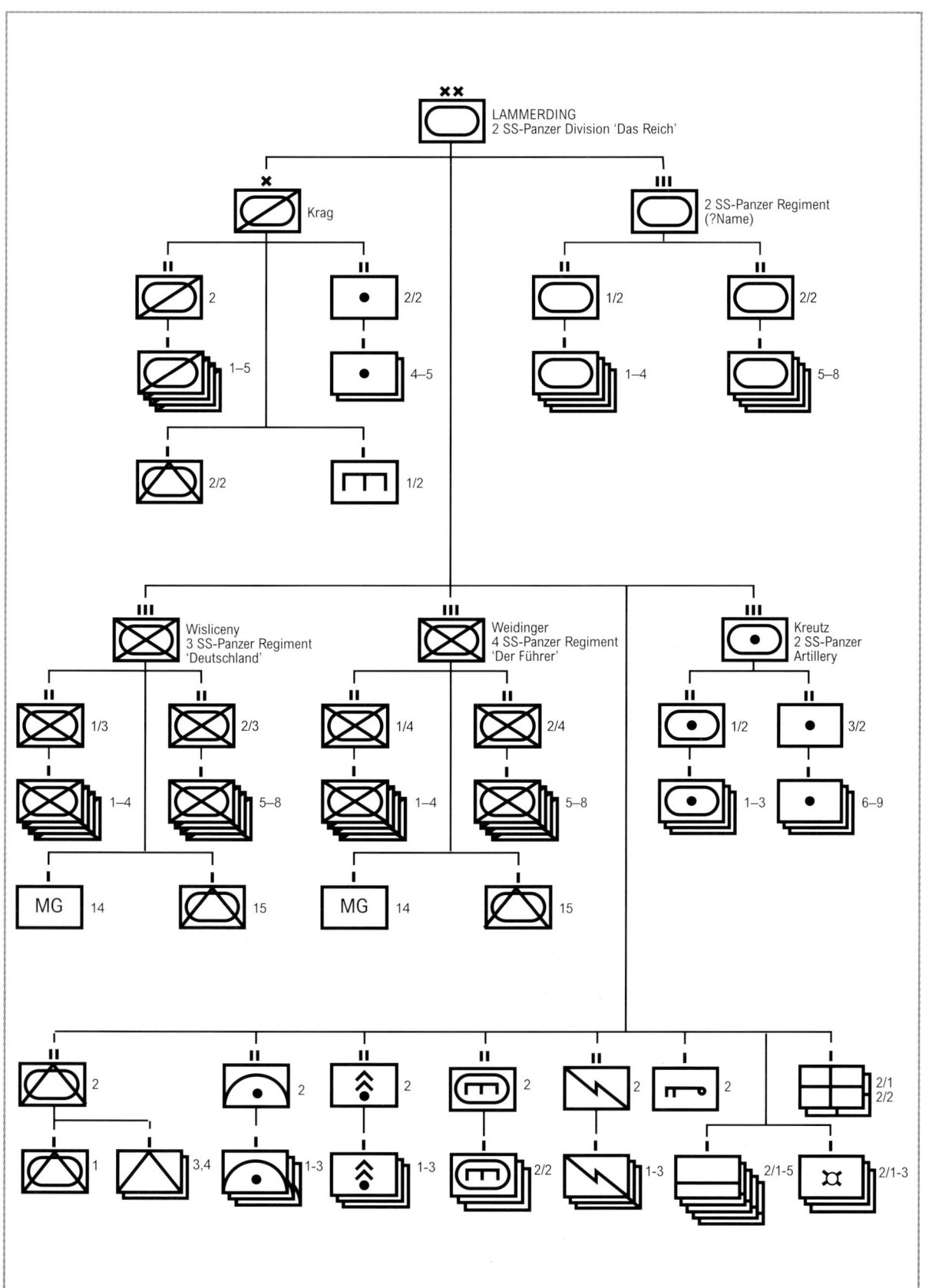

Oradour-sur-Glane in reprisal for the abduction and supposed murder of a single SS officer by the Resistance. (His body was never found.)

The division's commander, 38-year-old Heinz Lammerding, was unmoved by the slaughter and said after the war that he 'approved' because it was 'necessary to provoke terror'. Disliked by almost all of his officers and men, Lammerding was a hardcore Nazi who had been a former operations officer with the

---

Kampfgruppe 'Krag'
SS-Sturmbannführer Ernst-August Krag

---

2 SS-Panzer Aufklärungs Abteilung
II/2 SS-Panzer Artillerie Regiment
2/2 SS-Panzerjäger Abteilung
1/2 SS-Panzer Pionier Abteilung

'Totenkopf' Division in Russia and then with the infamous SS-Brigadeführer Erich von dem Bach-Zelewski's 'anti-partisan' forces, signing hundreds of death warrants for people who had no right of appeal.

Another Himmler in embryo, Lammerding could not have succeeded as a field commander without a dedicated staff and competent regimental C0s who largely made his tactical decisions for him. After the war, he was sentenced to death by a war crimes tribunal but

went into hiding and did not die, unlamented but still a free man, until 1971. Despite Lammerding, one might safely say, 'Das Reich' fought hard in Normandy. Lammerding himself was wounded and his successor, the CO of 2 SS-Panzer Regiment, Fritz Tychensen, was killed, leaving the much more capable and popular artillery commander, SS-Obersturmbannführer Karl Kreutz, in temporary charge. Trapped in the Falaise pocket, 2 SS-Panzer Division fought its way out with its surviving 450 men and 15 tanks.

Withdrawn to Germany, it refitted at Paderborn during October-November. Here, it is, perhaps, worthwhile to sow a seed of doubt about the priority given to the refitting of the SS-Panzer divisions at the expense of army units. It did happen, and I and II SS-Panzer Korps were certainly taken out of the line before any army units allocated to 'Herbstnebel'. But consider: the army itself largely controlled the level of manpower allocated; the Waffen-SS did not have its own Ordnance Office and was dependent on the Wehrmacht in this respect; it did not produce its own equipment (and often had to depend upon army 'cast-offs', even though these sometimes turned out to be superior!); and it did not have a separate system of

Losing its left track to an Allied Sherman or bazooka shot, a forlorn Panther of I/2 SS-Panzer Regiment after the battle at Manhay.
(U.S. Signal Corps)

SS-Sturmbannführer Ernst-August Krag was a highly popular officer and an accomplished pianist.
(U.S. Signal Corps)

SS-Obersturmbannführer Günter Wisliceny had been a coal miner before joining the Waffen-SS.
(U.S. Signal Corps)

acquisition and distribution. All requisitions were forwarded through army channels.

Despite this, 'Das Reich' did manage to get some priority and, commanded by Lammerding again, attacked behind and to the left of I SS-Panzer Korps through to the south of St Vith. This move, beginning on 20 December, led 'Das Reich' into Fifth Panzer Armee's LXVI Korps' area of operations but, instead of 2 (and 9) SS-Panzer Divisions being allocated to Manteuffel, the Korps itself was temporarily transferred to Dietrich's Sixth Panzer Armee instead.

The reinforced reconnaissance battalion under SS-Sturmbannführer Ernst-August Krag, despite a lack of fuel which delayed it for a day, circled round behind the St Vith 'horseshoe', threatening the defenders from their southwest and precipitating their withdrawal, already a foregone conclusion because of the presence of 9 SS-Panzer Division and Kampfgruppe 'Hansen' from the Leibstandarte, plus the newly arrived Führer Begleit Brigade, to their north and east. Krag bottled up a substantial part of the U.S. 112th Regiment, 28th Infantry Division, which had already

SS-Obersturmbannführer Otto Weidinger. After the war he wrote the definitive history of 'Das Reich'.
(U.S. Signal Corps)

narrowly escaped destruction on 'Skyline Drive', and only some 200 men escaped back to 82nd Airborne Division lines.

Meanwhile, the rest of the division had been waiting east of Houffalize for fuel tankers to reach them, but on 22 December a convoy got through and SS-Obersturmbannführer Otto Weidinger's 4 SS-Panzergrenadier Regiment was able to move out. Advancing parallel to Kampfgruppe 'Krag', he defeated a small American task force at the Baraque de Fraiture crossroads on the 23rd but the rest of the division was still waiting for fuel, which finally arrived on Christmas Eve. That evening, SS-Obersturmbannführer Günter Wisliceny's 3 SS-Panzergrenadier Regiment and three companies of Panthers from I/2 SS-Panzer Regiment, headed north to attack the next crossroads at Manhay.

This was defended by the CCA of 7th Armored Division, which had already had one encounter with 9 SS-Panzer Division outside St Vith, and was now starting to pull out as part of a planned northeasterly withdrawal to straighten and shorten the American lines. After a short, very confused fire-fight illuminated solely by flares, Wisliceny's force broke through at Manhay. The road to Grandmenil and Erezée lay open. However, 7th Armored quickly rallied and counter-attacked, supported by fighter-bombers, and Erezée marked the high tide mark of 2 SS-Panzer Division's advance.

Part of the division was later cut off and forced to surrender during Patton's counter-offensive but the remainder was sent to Hungary in January 1945 with Sixth SS-Panzer Army and, resisting stubbornly all the way, retreated into Austria. After a heroic defence outside Vienna, the 'Das Reich' survivors finally surrendered to American troops at the end of April when they heard of Hitler's death.

9 SS-Panzer Division 'Hohenstaufen'

SS-Oberführer Sylvester Stadler's division was reportedly up to about 75% of establishment when it was thrown into the affray north of St Vith. According to the *Gliederung der Heeresgruppe B für den befehlen Angriff,* its I Panzer Abteilung had 35 PzKpfw IVs and its II Abteilung 39 PzKpfw IVs plus 28 StuG III/IVs, while the Panzerjäger Abteilung could field 21 Jagdpanzer IV/70s and 28 StuGs. Best known for the part it played in defeating the British and Polish paras at Arnhem in September 1944, 'Hohenstaufen' was a late war formation raised, unusually for the SS, through conscription. Although Hitler authorised its formation in December 1942, the lack of volunteers forced Hans Jüttner – head of the SS-Führungshauptamt – to draw the necessary manpower through the Reicharbeits-dienst (compulsory labour service).

Despite this, the division's first CO, Willi Bittrich, demanded and got a high level of competence from his troops, who were capably led by a cadre of junior officers and NCOs from the Leibstandarte and 'Das Reich' Divisions. They also benefited from a full year's

---

9 SS-Panzer Division 'Hohenstauffen'

SS-Oberführer Sylvester Stadler

Stabs Kompanie

---

9 SS-Panzer Regiment (Telkamp)
19 SS-Panzergrenadier Regiment
20 SS-Panzergrenadier Regiment
9 SS-Panzer Artillerie Regiment
9 SS-Panzer Aufklärungs Abteilung
9 SS-Panzerjäger Abteilung
9 SS-Panzer Flak Abteilung
9 SS-Panzer Pionier Abteilung
9 SS-Panzer Nachrichten Abteilung
9 SS-Panzer Nebelwerfer Abteilung
9 SS-Panzer Nachschub Truppe
9 SS-Panzer Werkstatt Truppe
9 SS-Panzer Verwaltungs Truppe
9 SS-Panzer Sanitäts Truppe
519 schwere Panzerjäger Abteilung (Heer) (attached)
    (later to 3 Fallschirm Division)

SS-Oberführer Sylvester Stadler was the former regimental commander of 2 SS-Panzer Division and loathed its CO Lammerding.
(U.S. Signal Corps)

training at Amiens before they were despatched to the Eastern Front in March 1944. They saw action for the first time at Tarnopol the next month, when they helped stall the momentum of the Russian advance and rescued the Leibstandarte and other units trapped in the Kamenets-Podolsk pocket. The division was then posted to Poland before being hastily recalled to France in June to help in the battle for Normandy. Like all the Panzer divisions, 9 SS suffered heavily from the

attentions of rocket-firing 'Jabos' outside Caen and Mortain whilst trying to stem the Allied advance. During this period, Bittrich was promoted to Korps commander and his place taken by SS-Standarten-führer Müller until he was killed on 14 July. 'Das Reich' veteran Sylvester Stadler, former CO of 4 SS-Panzergrenadier Regiment, then took over for the remainder of the war.

'Hohenstaufen' emerged from the Falaise pocket with a mere 460 men and fewer than 25 tanks and was withdrawn to the outskirts of Arnhem to rebuild, its ranks being filled by a large number of Volksdeutsch from southern Russia. After the battle of Arnhem, 9 SS-Panzer Division was pulled back to Münstereifel to refit for 'Herbstnebel'.

It assembled near Schönau over 13-14 December with the task of supporting I SS-Panzer Korps. When it became apparent that the northern assault was running into difficulties, 'Hohenstaufen' was moved south and ordered to support Kampfgruppe 'Hansen' by advancing towards it along Rollbahn E. The division reached its new start line near Manderfeld on 18 December, but further progress was slow due to traffic

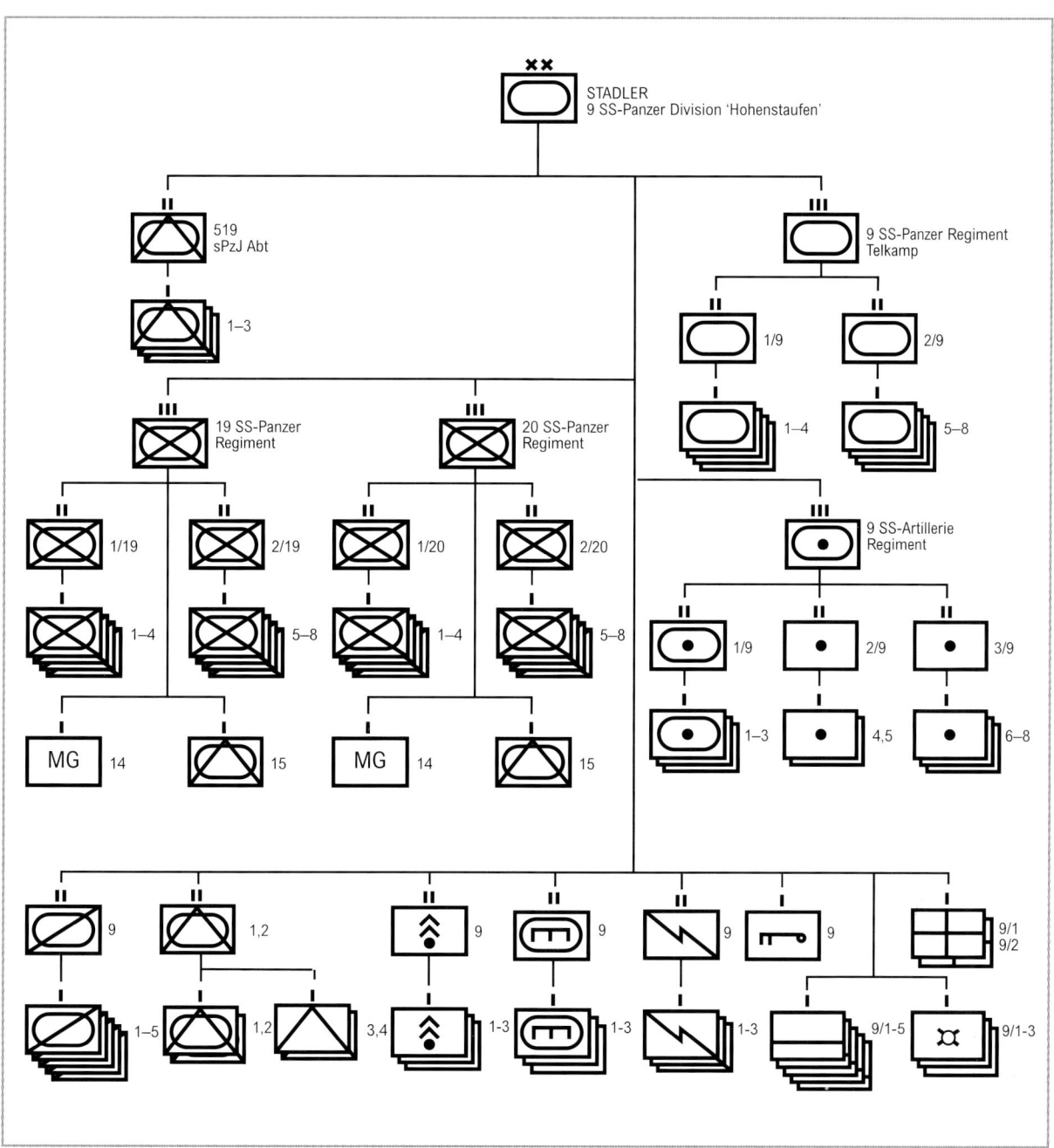

congestion and the acute shortage of fuel. On the 21st the division's vanguard commanded by SS-Sturmbannführer Eberhard Telkamp, CO of 9 SS-Panzer Regiment, attacked from Recht towards Vielsalm, its route being blocked by CCA of 7th Armored Division at Poteau. By this time, though, Montgomery had already agreed to St Vith's evacuation, so Telkamp was denied a victory. Two days later, 19 SS-Panzergrenadier Regiment had reached Grand-Halleux on the River Salm. On the other side it faced the 82nd Airborne, but they were already pulling

back to a new, shorter line Manhay-Trois Ponts. 9 SS-Panzer Division followed closely. By the 29th, however, the Americans had consolidated their new defence line and next day the division was pulled back and replaced by the 12th Volksgrenadiers.

A fortnight afterwards, 'Hohenstaufen' was withdrawn completely to be sent to Hungary as part of Sixth SS-Panzer Armee. Failing to relieve Budapest, it continued to resist stubbornly during the retreat into Austria, and Stadler finally surrendered to American troops near Steyr in April 1945.

II SS-PANZER KORPS' BATTLES

Kampfgruppe 'Krag'

Salmchâteau – December 21-23

With the capture of St Vith by Volksgrenadiers of LXVI Korps on 21 December, the American 'horseshoe' defence line began to collapse like a slowly-deflating balloon with its 'neck' in the narrow funnel between Vielsalm and Salmchâteau. If his divisions had been able to get there faster, 9 SS-Panzer from the north and 2 SS-Panzer from the south, Willi Bittrich's II Korps could have achieved an even more famous victory than that of LXVI Korps in the Schnee Eifel. The whole of 7th Armored Division, CCB of 9th Armored, and the two battered regiments from the 28th and 106th Infantry Divisions (112th and 224th), would all have gone 'in the bag'.

However, Bittrich's divisions were hamstrung from the start, and even though Ernst-August Krag's Kampfgruppe 'raised such havoc' (according to the U.S. Army official history) at the end; and 'Das Reich' got further west than any of Sixth Panzer Armee's other divisions; Bittrich's efforts were ultimately in vain.

With the failure of I SS-Panzer Korps to break through in the north, 2 and 9 SS-Panzer Divisions had moved south to the vicinity of Jünkerath, east of St Vith, by 20 December. On that day, 2 SS-Panzer Division was temporarily passed to Fifth Panzer Armee control and ordered further south, to Dasburg, but was delayed at Asselborn on the 21st for want of fuel. There was only enough for Krag's reinforced Aufklärungs Abteilung, which included a company of Jagdpanzer IV/70s, a battalion of self-propelled artillery and a company of engineers.

Kampfgruppe 'Krag' set off on the 22nd by a circuitous route well to the south of the St Vith perimeter, via Heinerscheid, to approach the choke point of the Americans' southerly escape route at Salmchâteau through Chérain. Here, one of Krag's pioniers was captured by men of an American task force which was in the process of pulling back towards

Krag, then commander of 2 SS-Panzer Division's Panzerjäger Abteilung, received the Knights Cross from Lammerding in October; after Salmchâteau, he was awarded the Oakleaves. (U.S. Department of Defense)

Gouvy. This was the first intimation the Allies had that 2 SS-Panzer Division was anywhere near St Vith, and the news spurred on their evacuation of the salient.

From Chérain, Krag continued along the minor road via Baclan and Langlir to approach Salmchâteau from almost due west on 23 December, reaching the southern edge of the village at dusk. By this time the bulk of the American troops had succeeded in evacuating the salient, most of them along the northerly route through Vielsalm, which was still protected by a covering force from 7th Armored at Poteau.

What was left, straggling along the steep-sided Salm valley north of Bovigny, was Task Force 'Jones', which Krag had bumped into at Chérain. This rearguard formation, commanded by Lieutenant-Colonel Robert B. Jones, CO of the 814th Tank Destroyer Battalion, 7th Armored Division, consisted

16/12/1944	18/12	20/12	22/12	24/12	26/12	28/12	30/12	6/1/1945	13/1	20/1	27/1	3/2	7/2
pages 42-59,72-73,77,87-91				60-61,74-76									

Task Force 'Jones' was straggling up the northern (eastern) bank of the Salm river with Kampfgruppe 'Krag' blocking its path at Salmchâteau and the Führer Begleit Brigade pressing in from the east.

of two companies of his M10s, a company of M5s from the 17th Tank Battalion, the 440th Armored Field Artillery Battalion with 105mm M7s, and a few surviving M8 Greyhounds from the 14th Cavalry Group. Mixed in with these were a number of stragglers, and a rearguard from the 112th Infantry Regiment which had been left at Cierreux. Unknown to them was the fact that Colonel Gustin M. Nelson, CO of the 112th, had evacuated Salmchâteau as soon as Krag's leading vehicles were spotted, believing there were no more American troops still to the east.

Krag's artillery battalion had been bombarding the village for most of the afternoon, and his infantry now probed cautiously forward. Finding Salmchâteau unoccupied, Krag's men quickly seized the bridge over the Salm, and he positioned Jagdpanzers to cover all approach roads. The leading M5 light tanks of Task Force 'Jones', which sprawled for a mile and a half up the road from Bovigny, thus ran smack into Krag's trap. There was no room for Jones to deploy in the steep-sided valley, and half his M10s were at the back of the column anyway, as a rearguard. Then, to complete his discomfiture, leading Panthers of the Führer Begleit Brigade (which had been pulled out of OKW Reserve for the attack on St Vith) appeared to his rear from the direction of Rogery and Cierreux.

Both German forces fired flares to illuminate the battlefield and their high-veloclty 7.5cm guns made mincemeat of Jones' column. The tail-end M10s were cut off, after engineers blew up a culvert under the road, and were annihilated. Although Jones' gun crews fought back, they were outnumbered and outclassed and their destruction was virtually complete when Oberst Otto Remer, CO of the Führer Begleit Brigade, arrived at Krag's headquarters in Salm-château shortly after midnight. It was now Christmas Eve, and the two men celebrated over a bottle of 'liberated' wine.

Total victory, however, eluded them, because some of Jones' men in the centre of the column discovered a narrow track running west. Fording the Salm, they brushed aside a small rearguard Krag had left at Provedroux, and about 200 of them succeeded in reaching the safety of the 508th Parachute Infantry

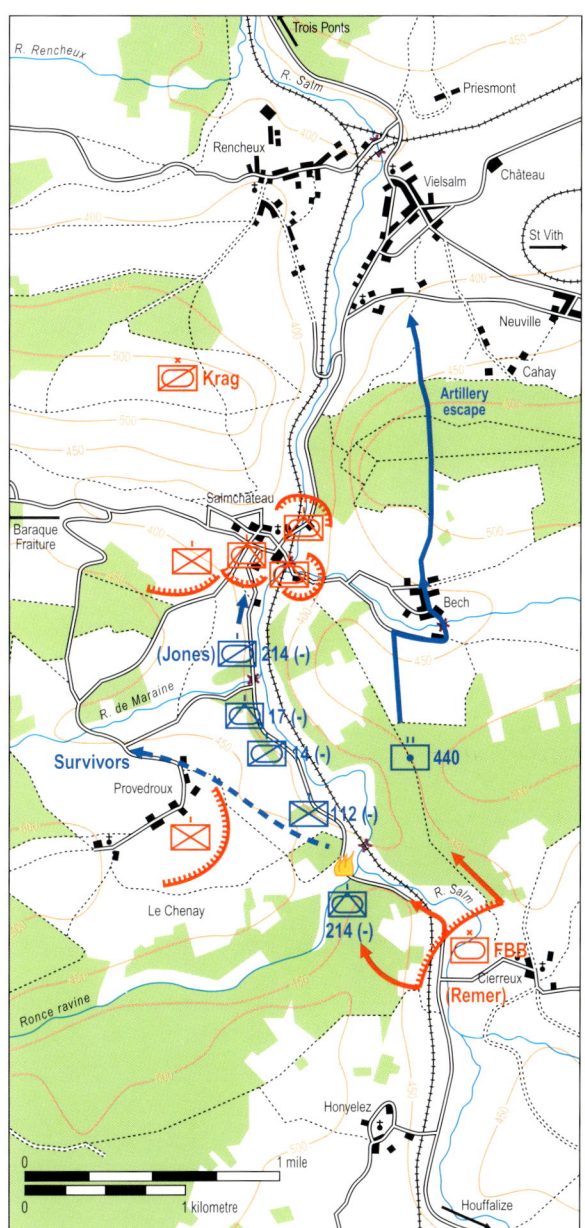

Regiment's lines to the northwest.

Also very lucky to escape Krag's trap was the 440th Armored Field Artillery Battalion, which had been deployed to give Jones' column covering fire if it were needed. Seeing the trap sprung, the M7s formed into a separate column and headed by a narrow track over the hills northwest towards Vielsalm, tearing through the ranks of any of Remer's Führer Begleit Brigade infantry who tried to stop them.

16/12/1944	18/12	20/12	22/12	24/12	26/12	28/12	30/12	6/1/1945	13/1	20/1	27/1	3/2	7/2
pages 42-59,72-73,77,87-91			60-61,74-76										

II SS-PANZER KORPS' BATTLES
4 SS-Panzergrenadier Regiment 'Der Führer'

Baraque Fraiture – December 22-23

The crossroads on the high plateau southwest of the Belgian hamlet of Fraiture seems an unlikely place for a battlefield, but once skirmishers from 560 Volksgrenadier Division (LVIII Korps, Fifth Panzer Armee) discovered on 20 December that they were only lightly held, Lammerding saw an ideal opportunity to exploit the gap at the junction of the 3rd Armored and 82nd Airborne Divisions and drive for the Meuse up the N15 via Manhay and Erezée. To this task he entrusted SS-Obersturmbannführer Otto Weidinger's 'Der Führer' Regiment once a fuel supply column eventually reached it on the 22nd.

Over the preceding two days the original American 'garrison' of three 105mm howitzers from the 589th Field Artillery Battalion, 106th Infantry Division – survivors from the massacre in the Schnee Eifel – had been reinforced by one M15 and three M16s from the 203rd AAA Battalion, and three M5 Stuarts of 'D' Troop, 87th Cavalry Squadron, both from 7th Armored Division; plus the 116 men of 'F' Company, II/325th Glider Infantry Regiment, 82nd Airborne Division. In command of the meagre forces opposing Weidinger was Major Arthur C. Parker III, who deployed his forces in a rough circle around the crossroads.

Weidinger's men quietly took over from the Volksgrenadiers, who had remained to keep an eye on Parker's dispositions, before dawn on 23 December and II Abteilung attempted a surprise assault from the northeast, which was repulsed by the glider infantry under Captain Junior R. Woodruff and the withering firepower from the quad .50 machine-guns on the M16s. Weidinger licked his wounds and reconsidered,

but nearly delayed too long because at about 1300 hrs a platoon of five Shermans from 3rd Armored Division fought their way through his II Abteilung's infantry from the north to bolster the defence.

Weidinger was also bringing up reinforcements: II/2 SS-Panzer Artillerie Regiment with 10.5cm Wespes and 15cm Hummels, SS-Obersturmführer Horst Gresiak's 7/2 SS-Panzer Regiment with PzKpfw IVs, and a company of StuGs. This time Weidinger prepared his attack with more care and began softening up Parker's defences during the afternoon with an artillery and mortar barrage. Again, he had II Abteilung to the northeast, but this time III Abteilung would launch a coordinated assault from the south and west; both Panzergrenadier battalions being preceded by the tanks and assault guns.

Snow had been falling and even in the dusk at 1600 hrs the American tanks, on top of the plateau, were visible to the attackers, while the Germans' own presence was hidden against the backdrop of the surrounding woods. The Shermans had no room to

The crossroads at Baraque Fraiture did not even boast a village, just three farms. The N15 crosses from left to right. II Abteilung attacked from the top left with III Abteilung assaulting from the right. (U.S. Signal Corps)

16/12/1944	18/12	20/12	22/12	24/12	26/12	28/12	30/12	6/1/1945	13/1	20/1	27/1	3/2	7/2
pages 42-59,70-71,77,87-91				60-61,74-76									

The crossroads at Baraque Fraiture with the village of Fraiture itself to the northeast. Vielsalm is off to the right, Manhay to the top left. Parker's three 105mm guns were in the centre of the position, the company of paras in a semi-circle to the north and the AFVs in a rough circle. Weidinger's attack came from three directions, leaving the survivors only one escape route to the northwest.

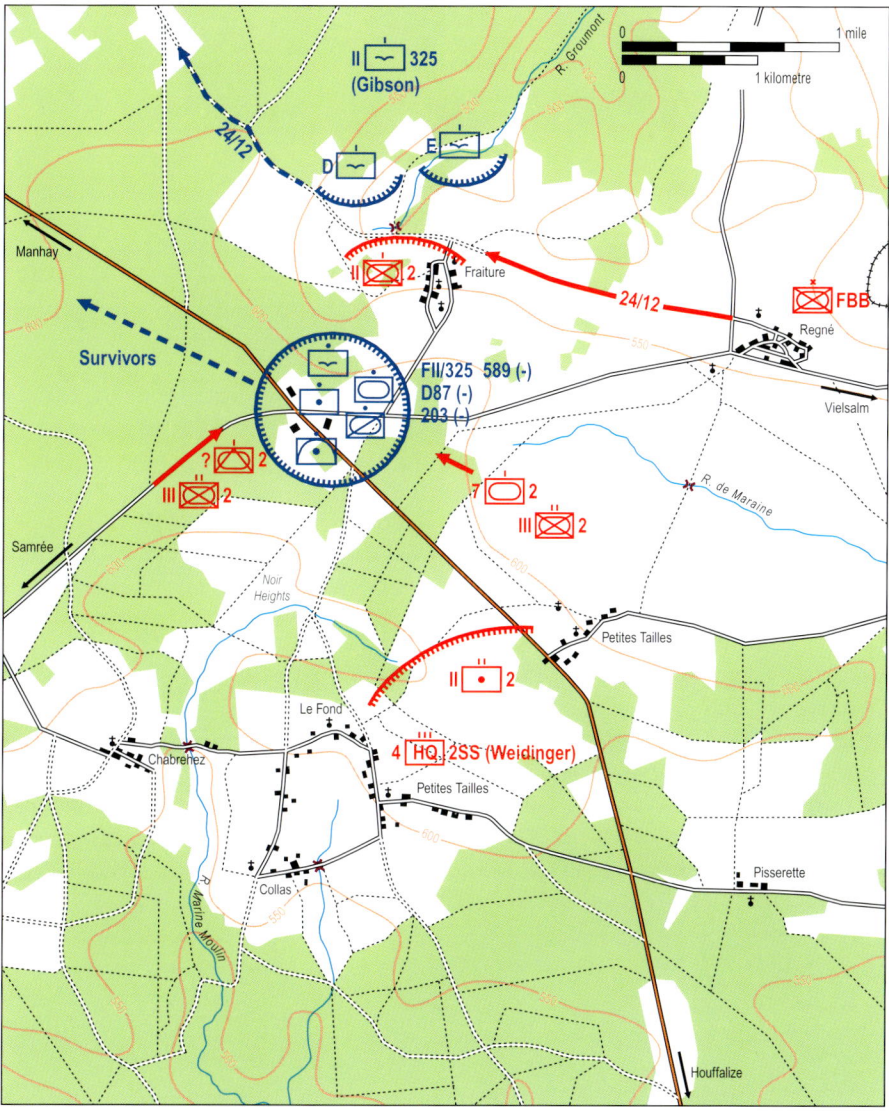

manoeuvre within the perimeter around the crossroads, but to sortie out in a counter-attack would have been suicidal. As it was, the long-barrelled German 7.5cm guns picked them off one by one until eventually only three survived to escape to the north-west. At about 1700 hrs the airborne company commander, Woodruff, radioed for permission to withdraw, but the regimental CO, Colonel Charles E. Billingslea, reiterated Major-General James M. Gavin's orders to all his airborne troops, 'hold at all costs'.

The assorted defenders of 'Parker's Crossroads' did their best but Weidinger's Panzergrenadiers swarmed all over them once the tank menace had evaporated, taking prisoners and destroying 34 half-tracks and Jeeps. A few GIs managed to slip away into the woods rather than surrender, because news of the 'Malmédy massacre' had spread like wildfire; a stampeding herd of cows helped cover the escape of some. Woodruff's men fought on until Billingslea finally allowed them to withdraw at about 1800 hrs; only 44 from the original 116 made it back from Baraque Fraiture. Weidinger was awarded the Oakleaves and Gresiak the Knights Cross for their part in the action. After all their work, though, Lammerding did not use N15 for his attack on Manhay, but minor roads to the east and west.

16/12/1944	18/12	20/12	22/12	24/12	26/12	28/12	30/12	6/1/1945	13/1	20/1	27/1	3/2	7/2
pages 42-59,70-71,77,87-91				60-61,74-76									

II SS-PANZER KORPS' BATTLES

3 SS-Panzergrenadier Regiment 'Deutschland' and

4 Kompanie, 2 SS-Panzer Regiment

Manhay-Grandmenil-Erezée – December 24-27

Kampfgruppe 'Krag' had emptied the first fuel tankers to reach 2 SS-Panzer Division on 21 December, and captured Salmchâteau; the second allocation went to Weidinger's 4 SS-Panzergrenadier Regiment the next day, and he had captured the crossroads at Baraque Fraiture; now, at long last on the 23rd, the rest of the division could begin to move, and Günther Wisliceny was champing at the bit to get his own 3 SS-Panzergrenadier Regiment 'Deutschland' into action.

By Christmas Eve the bulk of the division (excluding Kampfgruppe 'Krag') was assembled in the vicinity of Odeigne and Fraiture, busily rearming and refuelling for the attack on Manhay which would give them access to good lateral roads, through Grandmenil, Erezée and Hotton, towards either Namur or Huy. Lammerding had ruled out a frontal assault straight up the main N15 road because the dense forest on either side would have left his tanks with no room to deploy. In addition, the road itself was blocked at Belle Haie by a task force from 3rd Armored Division commanded by Major Olin F. Brewster. Instead, Lammerding set the 2 SS-Panzer Division's pioniers to widening the secondary roads – actually little more than cart tracks – either side of the N15.

On the right, starting from the hamlet of Fraiture to the northeast of the crossroads, and heading towards Malempré, Lammerding placed Weidinger's 'Der Führer' Regiment; on the left, Wisliceny's 'Deutschland' was to follow up and support 2 SS-Panzer Regiment, itself spearheaded by the Panthers of SS-Hauptsturmführer Pohl's 4 Kompanie.

Quite by chance, Lammerding had probably chosen the weakest spot in the whole American line to attack, because Manhay lay not just at the junction of the 82nd Airborne and 3rd Armored Divisions, but also at the junction of XVIII (Airborne) and the redeployed VII Corps, while many of the troops immediately in front of the SS Panzers had only just escaped from the St Vith salient; these included CCA of 7th Armored Division at Manhay itself. At this precise point in time, with Montgomery just having been given command of all Allied forces 'north' of the 'bulge', there was inordinate confusion in the Allied ranks as to who should take orders from whom. Model, on the German side, obviated such confusion with very clear orders, even while shuffling commands around to suit the very fluid tactical and strategic situation.

To begin with, 'Das Reich's' assault went extraordinarily well, considering the misfortunes which had so far befallen Sixth Panzer Armee. Odeigne fell swiftly – it was only defended by a company of M5s – on 23 December. The main attack began after dark on Christmas Eve – a crisp, clear moonlit night in this sector with the snow hardpacked – and the seven M4s and couple of infantry platoons defending Le Batty (between Odeigne and Manhay) were soon routed by Pohl's tanks and Wisliceny's grenadiers, only one Sherman escaping without damage. About half a mile further north, another ten of 7th Armored's Shermans were quickly despatched. A little later, having reached Malempré on the other side of the N15, 'Der Führer' was also rewarded when Brewster's task force, having been ordered belatedly to abandon its position because German tanks were behind it, ran straight into Weidinger's anti-tank guns. With two Shermans knocked out, Brewster ordered his men to abandon the rest of their vehicles and escape through the woods; he only narrowly escaped a court-martial charge of cowardice.

One of the strangest events in the whole 'battle of the bulge' now occurred. Colonel Dwight A. Rosenbaum's CCA, 7th Armored Division, had received orders to pull back from Manhay to the

16/12/1944	18/12	20/12	22/12	24/12	26/12	28/12	30/12	6/1/1945	13/1	20/1	27/1	3/2	7/2
pages 42-59,70-73,77,87-91				60-61									

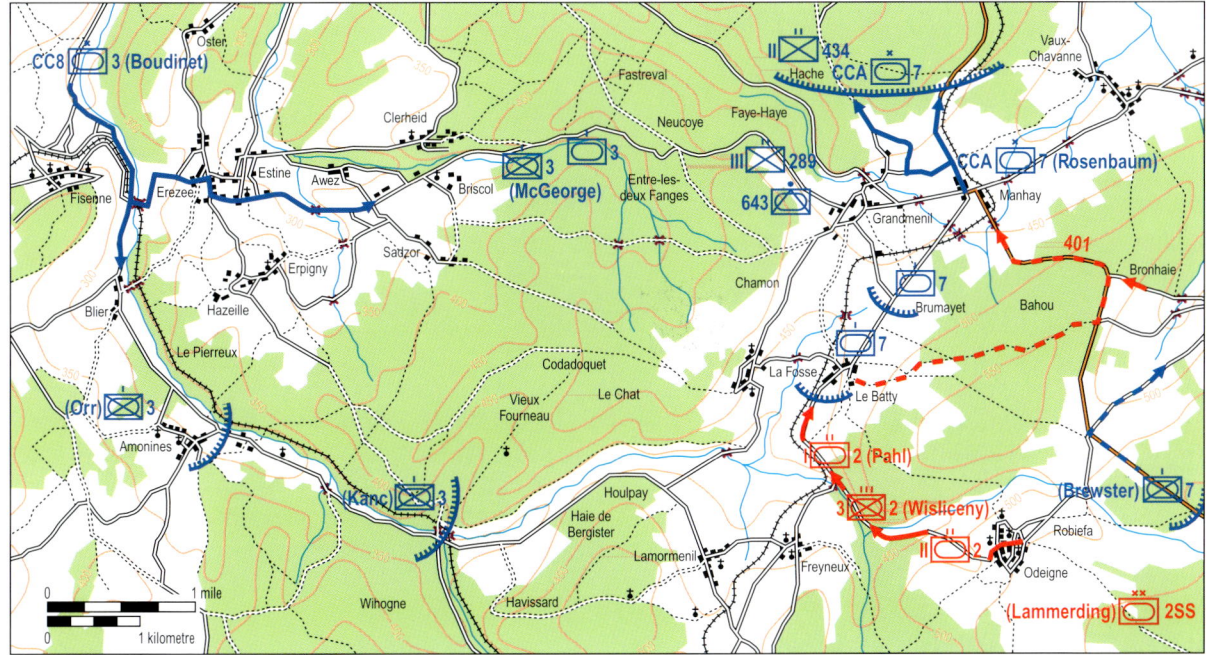

2 SS-Panzer Division's attacks from Odeigne and Fraiture, CCB's withdrawal to the northwest and III/289th's blocking position between Grandmenil and Erezée.

heights behind the crossroads, on the right flank of the 504th Parachute Infantry Regiment. He was in the process of evacuating his command when survivors from the two roadblocks south of the village came running wildly in to report German tanks just behind them. There was total chaos as Rosenbaum's men practically fought each other in their desperation to get out of Manhay. Into this mêlée from up the N15 calmly drove Panther number 401 commanded by SS-Oberschar-führer Ernst Barkmann, who had become separated from Pohl's company in the darkness. In all the confusion, no-one gave his tank a second glance and he headed west towards Grandmenil past a long line of Shermans parked at the side of the road, wondering when on earth someone would cry 'wolf!'. Finally, someone did notice, and the turrets of some of the M4s began swivelling, but they were blocking each other's line of fire. Then a Jeep appeared, heading straight towards the Panther. Realising what was coming towards him, the Jeep driver frantically tried to reverse, but Barkmann's tank hit him. The impact knocked the Panther into the side of a stationary

Sherman and its engine stalled. By this time small-arms fire was rattling against the tank like a hailstorm, but still none of the Shermans had fired. Barkmann's driver got the engine restarted, reversed a couple of feet to get straight, then put his foot down while Barkmann threw smoke grenades out of his cupola. Miraculously, the Panther escaped and turned into the woods to hide the moment it was out of sight of American troops.

Barkmann's solitary 'rite of passage' turned CCA's planned withdrawal into a rout, and when the rest of Pohl's company reached the village, they found only two Shermans protecting the crossroads; these quickly joined the general exodus after a brief exchange of shots. Next stop, Grandmenil, which was only defended by a platoon of three M10s from 3rd Armored Division's 643rd Tank Destroyer Battalion and, behind them, III/289th Battalion of the freshly-arrived and 'green' 75th Infantry Division. Pohl's remaining eight Panthers suffered one more loss but cleared the village. It was now Christmas Day and, although neither side yet knew it, to all intents and purposes it was also the high tide mark of the German offensive.

Lammerding received new orders on 25 December; the Army's 2 Panzer Division was in trouble at Dinant, and 'Das Reich' was needed to take some of the pressure off it. From Erezée, therefore, it was to turn

16/12/1944	18/12	20/12	22/12	24/12	26/12	28/12	30/12	6/1/1945	13/1	20/1	27/1	3/2	7/2
pages 42-59,70-73,77,87-91			60-61										

Just outside Grandmenil, one of Pohl's tanks lies abandoned. It appears undamaged and may simply have run out of fuel. (U.S. Signal Corps)

towards Durbuy and hit the newly-deployed American VII Corps in its flank.

While Lammerdlng was getting organised for the attack, which was to be spearheaded by Wisliceny's 'Deutschland' Regiment, the Americans were also responding to the threat. CCB of 3rd Armored Division, which had been in action against Kampfgruppe 'Peiper' at La Gleize, raced south. First on the scene was a company of M4s and a company of armored infantry commanded by Major Kenneth T. McGeorge which were preparing to attack Grandmenll when they were strafed by P-38s which had mistaken them for Germans. (The Allies painted orange squares on the tops of their tanks for aerial identification, but the Germans had quickly copied this.) Thirty-nine men were killed before McGeorge even launched his attack at 2000 hrs. He got a company of infantry and five tanks into the village but Wisliceny's grenadiers promptly threw them out again.

Brigadier-General Robert W. Hasbrouck's severely depleted 7th Armored Division was now ordered to try to retake the village, but all he could immediately muster out of the confusion was two understrength tank companies and a company of armored infantry from Rosenbaum's CCB, plus II/424th (ex-106th Infantry Division). The tanks could not get past the trees which combat engineers had felled to cover the earlier withdrawal and six were lost to accurate German fire before Hasbrouck pulled them back; the infantry got to within a mile of the village but also suffered heavy casualties and had to give up. On 26 December Lammerding tried to break out of Grandmenil towards the west, but the same felled trees blocked his tanks too, and Wisliceny's infantry were pounded by American artillery – there were now 18 batteries ringing the villages.

Lammerding was forced to evacuate Grandmenil, having to leave some 50 wounded men behind, and McGeorge's little task force recaptured it a second time. 'Das Reich' now faced a new threat from the 325th Glider Infantry Regiment and, with his forces under constant aerial attack, Lammerding was ordered to pull back to Baraque Fraiture. By the end of 27 December, Manhay was also back in American hands. Like Weidinger, though, Wisliceny was also awarded the Oakleaves for this action.

16/12/1944	18/12	20/12	22/12	24/12	26/12	28/12	30/12	6/1/1945	13/1	20/1	27/1	3/2	7/2
pages 42-59,70-73,77,87-91				60-61									

II SS-PANZER KORPS' BATTLES

Kampfgruppe 'Telkamp'

Poteau – December 19-24

The tiny road leading through Poteau, south of Recht, continued to be a battleground after Kampfgruppe 'Hansen' had departed to the northwest to essay a rescue of Peiper's entrapped men. The next unit along the highway was SS-Sturmbannführer Eberhard Telkamp's 9 SS-Panzer Regiment of Sylvester Stadler's 'Hohenstaufen' Division, and Poteau was soon to assume an importance inappropriate to its size, because it guarded the 'back door' to Vielsalm, which the American forces in the St Vith salient would need for their phased withdrawal. At this stage, though, at about midday on 19 December, Stadler just saw a potential menace to his flank and rear if he continued driving west. Over the 19th and 20th December successive waves of infantry from 19 SS-Panzergrenadier Regiment tried and failed to break through. When he received fresh orders to try to rescue Kampfgruppe 'Peiper', Stadler ordered Telkamp to take out the opposition, while the rest of the division headed towards the River Salm west of Grand-Halleux.

After a quick reshuffle of the defences, the force now opposing Telkamp was not just the battalion of 7th Armored Division's CCR and the remnant of the 14th Cavalry Group which had opposed Hansen, but almost the whole of Colonel Dwight A. Rosenbaum's CCA (which would later face 2 SS-Panzer Division at Manhay, west of the Salm). Rosenbaum had about 80 tanks and tank destroyers left after battling the Führer Begleit Brigade, Telkamp a similar number of mostly PzKpfw IVs and StuGs plus the Panthers of his headquarters' company. The trouble is that Poteau is ideally suited for defence, lying at the neck of a steep-sided valley, and Telkamp could not deploy more than half a dozen tanks abreast, either side of the road. CCA, by the same token, could only deploy ten Shermans in the front line, but they were dug in in a semicircle with an excellent field of fire and backed up by M36s of the 814th Tank Destroyer Battalion with hlgh-velocity 90mm guns.

Telkamp himself led the initial assault at about midday on 21 December and ran into a storm of accurate fire, because the defenders had zeroed-in their sights on the spot on the road where Kampfgruppe 'Hansen' had smashed Major Mayes' column from the 14th Cavalry Group. A round from an M36 hit Telkamp's tank almost immediately. His driver was killed and two more of his crew wounded, but their CO was uninjured. Jumping out of his burning Panther, Telkamp tried to rally the attack but as another four of his leading tanks were rapidly disabled, he called the assault off for that day. Over the next two days he continued to keep the defenders pinned down, helped by the arrival of part of the 18th Volksgrenadier Division which had captured St Vith. Realising that the Americans were rapidly withdrawing from the St Vith salient, Telkamp launched another assault at 1035 hrs on Christmas Eve, just as CCA was preparing to evacuate through Vielsalm. This could have been disastrous for Rosenbaum's command, since a withdrawal in the face of an attack is the most difficult military manoeuvre. Fortunately for him, and unluckily for Telkamp's battlegroup, the German armour was caught forming up by a flight of P-38s from the 370th Fighter Group which strafed and bombed the road from Recht.

Telkamp could only watch helplessly as his grenadiers dived for cover and vehicle after vehicle went up in flames. His attack was stillborn and he was unable to interfere as CCA slipped away to the west during the afternoon, discouraging pursuit with accurate artillery fire. In the end it was men of 293 Grenadier Regiment, 18 Volksgrenadier Division, who finally captured Poteau.

16/12/1944	18/12	20/12	22/12	24/12	26/12	28/12	30/12	6/1/1945	13/1	20/1	27/1	3/2	7/2
pages 42-59,70-73,87-91				60-61,74-76									

SIXTH PANZER ARMEE

LXVII KORPS

The weakest of Sixth Panzer Armee's three Korps, Generalleutnant Otto Hitzfeld's LXVII Korps had been formed as a reserve in 1942 and was part of Fifteenth Armee during the defensive operations following the Allied breakout from the Normandy beachhead. It was then transferred to Dietrich's command for 'Herbstnebel' and, to begin

Generalleutnant Otto Hitzfeld was a highly experienced officer well versed in armour and infantry co-operation but, because his Korps was reinforced piecemeal, was unable to achieve his objectives.
(Christopher Ailsby Historical Archives)

The over-optimistic objectives of Hitzfeld's LXVII Korps. They would have been lucky to have reached Eupen, let alone Liège.

LXVII KORPS
Generalleutnant Otto Hitzfeld
Stabs Kompanie
272 Volksgrenadier Division (Kosmalla)
326 Volksgrenadier Division (Kaschner)
3 Panzergrenadier Division (Denkert)
(from 19/12 – 26/12/1944)
246 Volksgrenadier Division (Körte)
(from 28/12/1944)
(Attached from Armee Reserve)
17 Volks-Werfer Brigade (88 and 89 Regimenten)
405 Volks-Artillerie Korps

with, only comprised two understrength Volksgrenadier divisions, 272 and 326. Later, 3 Panzergrenadier Division was attached, but when this was transferred further south after it became apparent that the attack in the northern sector had failed, it was replaced briefly by 246 Volksgrenadier Division until this, too, was ordered south.

Model's intentions for the Korps, given its lack of manpower and the fact that its total armoured element

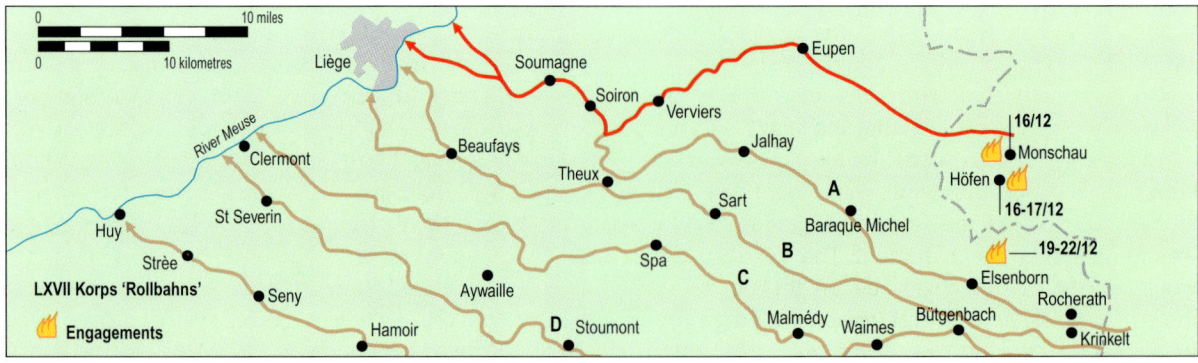

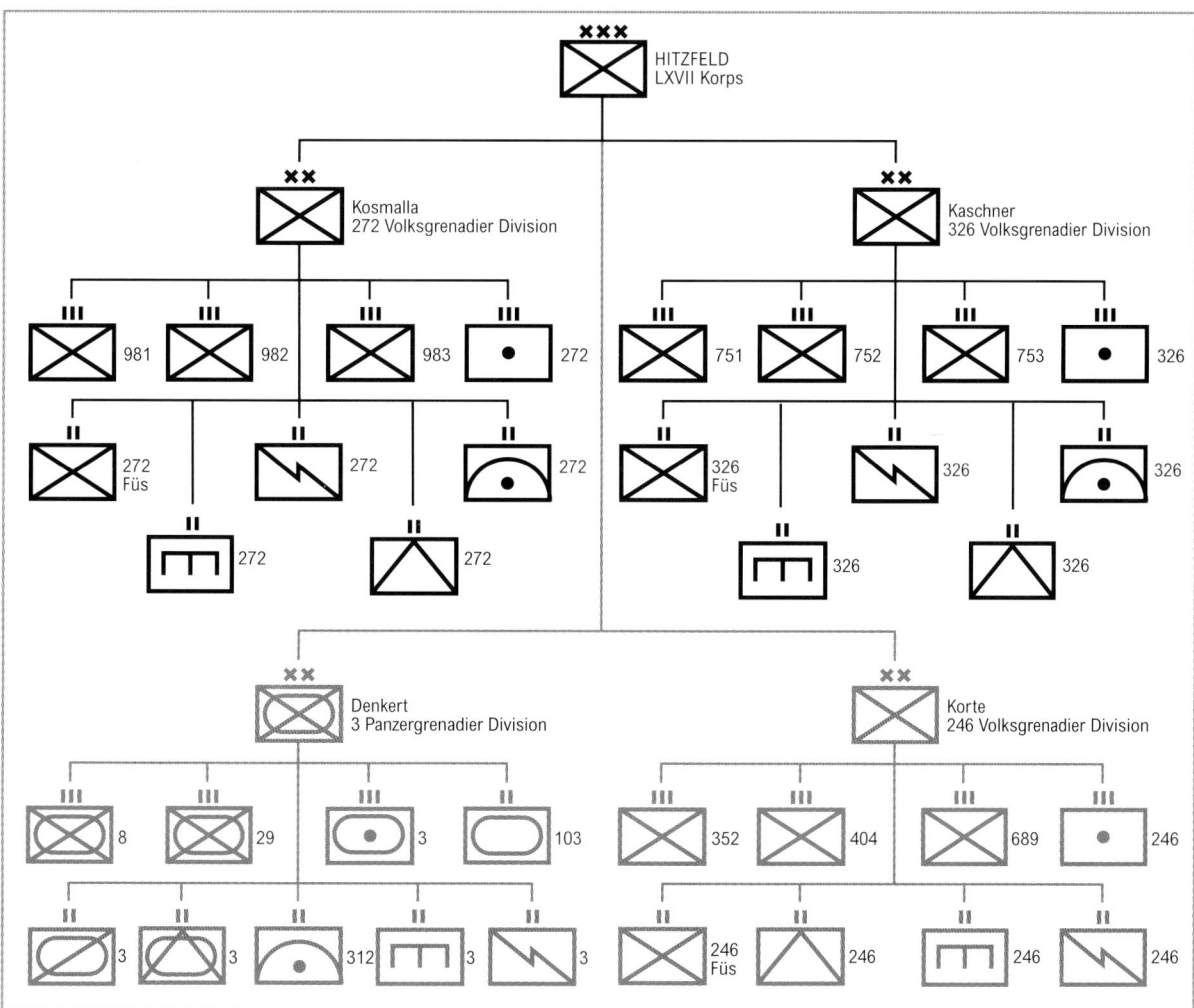

was the ten Jagdpanzer 38(t) Hetzers in 272 Volksgrenadier Division, appeared optimistic to Hitzfeld. A regular Army officer who had earlier commanded 102 Infanterie Division in Russia, and latterly the Infantry Training School at Döberitz, he appreciated the difficulties his men would face breaking the well dug-in American infantry facing them. What he did not realise was the weakness of the opposition immediately opposite him: to the north of Monschau just a single cavalry squadron, and to the south at Höfen a single battalion of the 99th Infantry Division.

On the face of it, Hitzfeld's men should have enjoyed a virtual walkover, but their task was made more difficult because Model had limited their artillery support by ordering that the historic town of Monschau, with its many old timber-framed buildings, was to be spared bombardment. The Volksgrenadiers would, therefore, effectively be on their own – and the Americans had a secret weapon. Model's orders to Hitzfeld instructed the Korps to 'break through

the enemy positions on both sides of Monschau. After having crossed the Mützenich-Elsenborn road (Rollbahn A) and turned northwest, it will then establish a fixed defensive front approximately on the line Simerath-Eupen-Limbourg-Liège.' In practical terms, on foot and with only horsedrawn guns, Hitzfeld's men would have been fortunate to have reached as far west as Eupen, let alone Liège.

It was not to be. 272 Volksgrenadier Division was already heavily engaged at the beginning of the offensive and took no part, leaving just the weak 326th for the attack at Monschau. This was repulsed with heavy losses and even when 3 Panzergrenadier Division's weight was added to that of I SS-Panzer Korps' 277 Volksgrenadier Division, the infantry failed to break through on to Rollbahn A. Thereafter, the 272nd was returned to Fifteenth Armee to await the Allies' suspended offensive over the River Rur north of Monschau once they had eradicated the 'bulge', while the 326th was transferred to Fifth Panzer Armee.

272 Volksgrenadier Division

Although part of LXVII Korps, Oberst Georg Kosmalla's division was placed on Sixth Panzer Armee's extreme right flank and played only a minor role in the offensive. It was supposed to attack north-west through Konzen towards Mariaweiler and Guerzenich but on 16 December it was already heavily engaged against the U.S. 78th Infantry Division at Kesternich. It remained on the defensive and on the 19th December it was transferred to Fifteenth Army.

An original 272 Infanterie Division was raised, like the 277th, from elderly reservists in 1940 but was then promptly disbanded without having seen action. A new 272nd was formed during the winter of 1943/44 under Generalleutnant Friedrich Schack and sent to a training area near Perpignan in southern France. It was seriously understrength in June 1944 but was still

---

272 Volksgrenadier Division

Oberst Georg Kosmalla

Stabs Kompanie

---

981 Volksgrenadier Regiment
982 Volksgrenadier Regiment
983 Volksgrenadier Regiment
272 Volks-Artillerie Regiment
272 Füsilier Bataillon
272 Panzerjäger Abteilung
272 Flak Abteilung
272 Pionier Abteilung
272 Nachrichten Abteilung
272 Nachschub Truppe
272 Werkstatt Truppe
272 Verwaltungs Truppe
272 Sanitäts Truppe

Oberst Georg Kosmalla had commanded both an infantry regiment and another division in Russia prior to Herbstnebel'.
(Christopher Ailsby Historical Archives)

ordered to Normandy where it came to the relief of the badly-mauled 1 and 12 SS-Panzer Divisions in July.

Virtually wiped out at Falaise, the remnants of the division were gathered at Döberitz, just outside Berlin, where their Korps' commander had been Kommandant before his appointment for 'Herbstnebel'. Here, during October/November, they absorbed 575 Volksgrenadier Division which had only been formed a month earlier, as part of Himmler's 'Replacement Army' programme. Schack was promoted to command of LXXXI Korps and replaced by Georg Kosmalla, who had previously commanded 6 Infanterie Regiment and then, briefly earlier in 1944, 32 Infanterie Division in Russia.

In November the division was fighting in the Hürtgen Forest and came under severe pressure from Walter Gerow's V Corps which was heading towards the Rur and Urft dams to prevent the Germans from opening their floodgates. As had already happened outside Antwerp, when the dykes were broached, this would have created a difficult barrier. The American attack was halted to allow reserves to respond to the emergency in the Ardennes but 272 Volksgrenadier Division had to remain in the line, still under heavy pressure. Its precise strength at this time is unknown although one of its anti-tank companies was equipped with ten Jagdpanzer 38(t) Hetzers. (Although there were not many of these left at this stage of the war, this tank destroyer – a diminutive cousin to the Jagdpanther, but based on a Czech light tank chassis – was actually more effective than the bulkier weapons which equipped most of the Panzerjäger battalions.)

After the failure of the Ardennes offensive, during which Kosmalla was seriously wounded, the 272nd, now commanded by Generalmajor Eugen König (ex-12 Volksgrenadier Division), was forced during February 1945 to retreat slowly when the Allies resumed the drive east and ultimately ended back behind the Rhine. Reduced to a mere handful of men, the division was finally surrounded alongside so many others in the Ruhr pocket where it met its end in April.

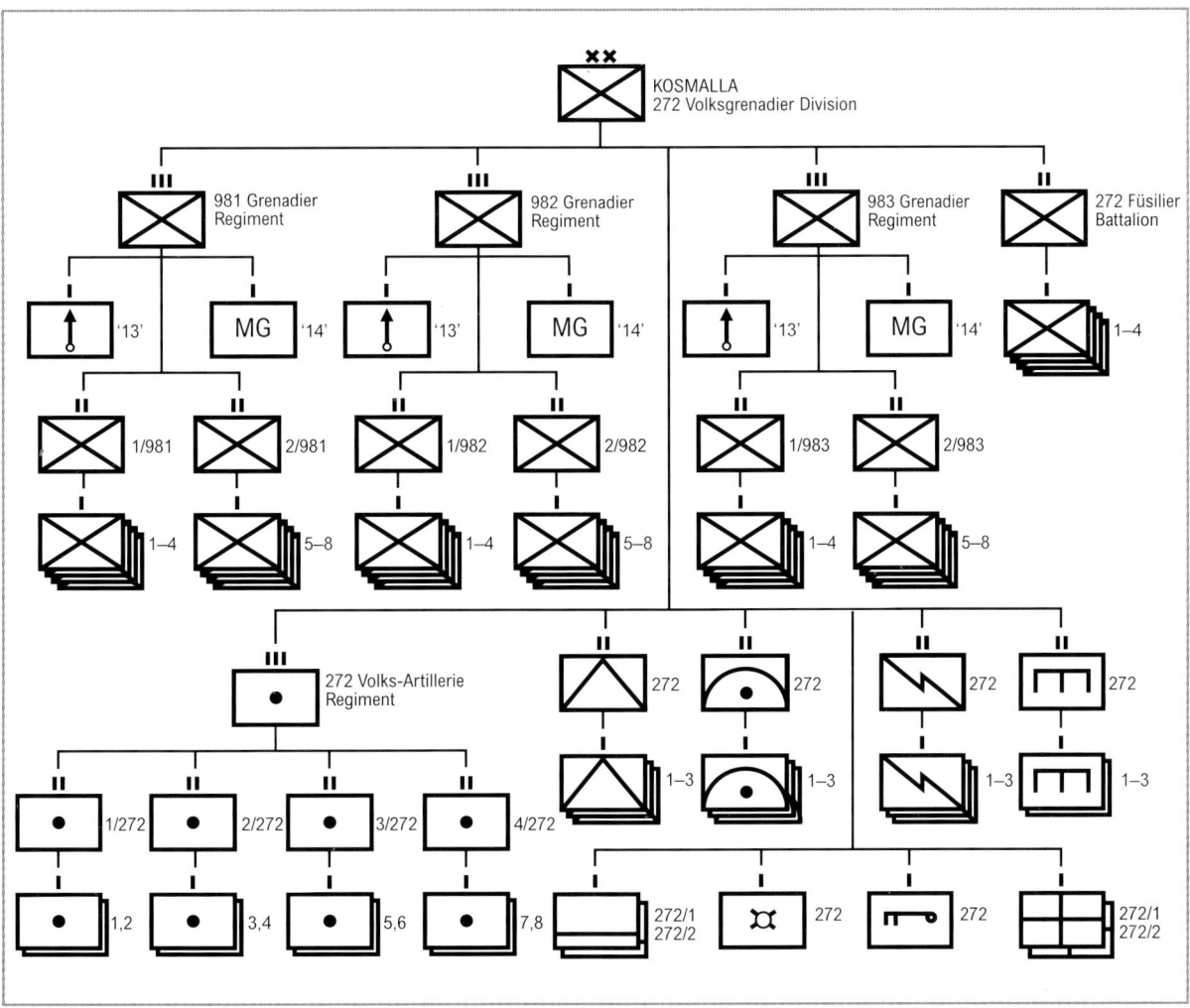

326 Volksgrenadier Division

Generalmajor Dr Erwin Kaschner's division was originally intended to have joined Fifth Panzer Armee for the Ardennes offensive but because it was deficient in transport, lacking enough horses to pull its artillery, it was assigned a more static role in Otto Hitzfeld's LXVII Korps where it was faced south of Monschau merely by the U.S. III/395th Infantry Regiment but, like the flanking 272 Volksgrenadier Division on its right, was unable to make any headway.

The 326th was called into being in 1942 and, although it was only partially trained, it formed part of the occupation force in Vichy after the Anglo-American

'Torch' landings in French North Africa in November. In January 1944 it was moved to northern France to help repel the expected invasion in the Pas de Calais but, when this failed to materialise, the 326th was sent to Normandy where it relieved 2 Panzer Division in the line. Commanded by Generalleutnant Viktor von Drabisch-Wächter, the inexperienced division was overrun at Caumont and only a handful of survivors escaped from the Falaise pocket.

Like the 277th on its left flank, the 326th was rebuilt in Hungary, absorbing the 579th Volksgrenadier Division which was in the process of being formed from Volksdeutsch personnel. It was sent to the Rur

326 Volksgrenadier Division

Generalmajor Dr. Erwin Kaschner

Stabs Kompanie

---

751 Volksgrenadier Regiment
752 Volksgrenadier Regiment
753 Volksgrenadier Regiment
326 Volks-Artillerie Regiment
326 Füsilier Bataillon
326 Panzerjäger Abteilung
326 Flak Abteilung
326 Pionier Abteilung
326 Nachrichten Abteilung
326 Nachschub Truppe
326 Werkstatt Truppe
326 Verwaltungs Truppe
326 Sanitäts Truppe

Infanterie Regiment in Russia. Here, it helped hold the line in the Hürtgen Forest before being reassigned to 'Herbstnebel'.

The division was one battalion short at the beginning of the Ardennes offensive and a second had to be loaned to 272 Volksgrenadier Division because of the pressure from the U.S. 78th Infantry Division around Kesternich. Nor did Kaschner have any assault guns or tank destroyers, his allocation having 'disappeared' to another unit – not uncommon at this time, given the haste with which the forces for 'Herbstnebel' were assembled. (It is possible that these were some of the guns 'acquired' by 3 Panzergrenadier Division.)

The depleted division did, nevertheless, succeed in reaching Höfen before it was repulsed and in January 1945 was south of St Vith. It was badly mauled in February during the retreat through the Schnee Eifel, by now part of LIII Korps of Brandenberger's Seventh Army. The remnants retreated across the Rhine and in April the division was finally destroyed in the Ruhr pocket.

river line in December, now commanded by Dr Kaschner, former commanding officer of the 486th

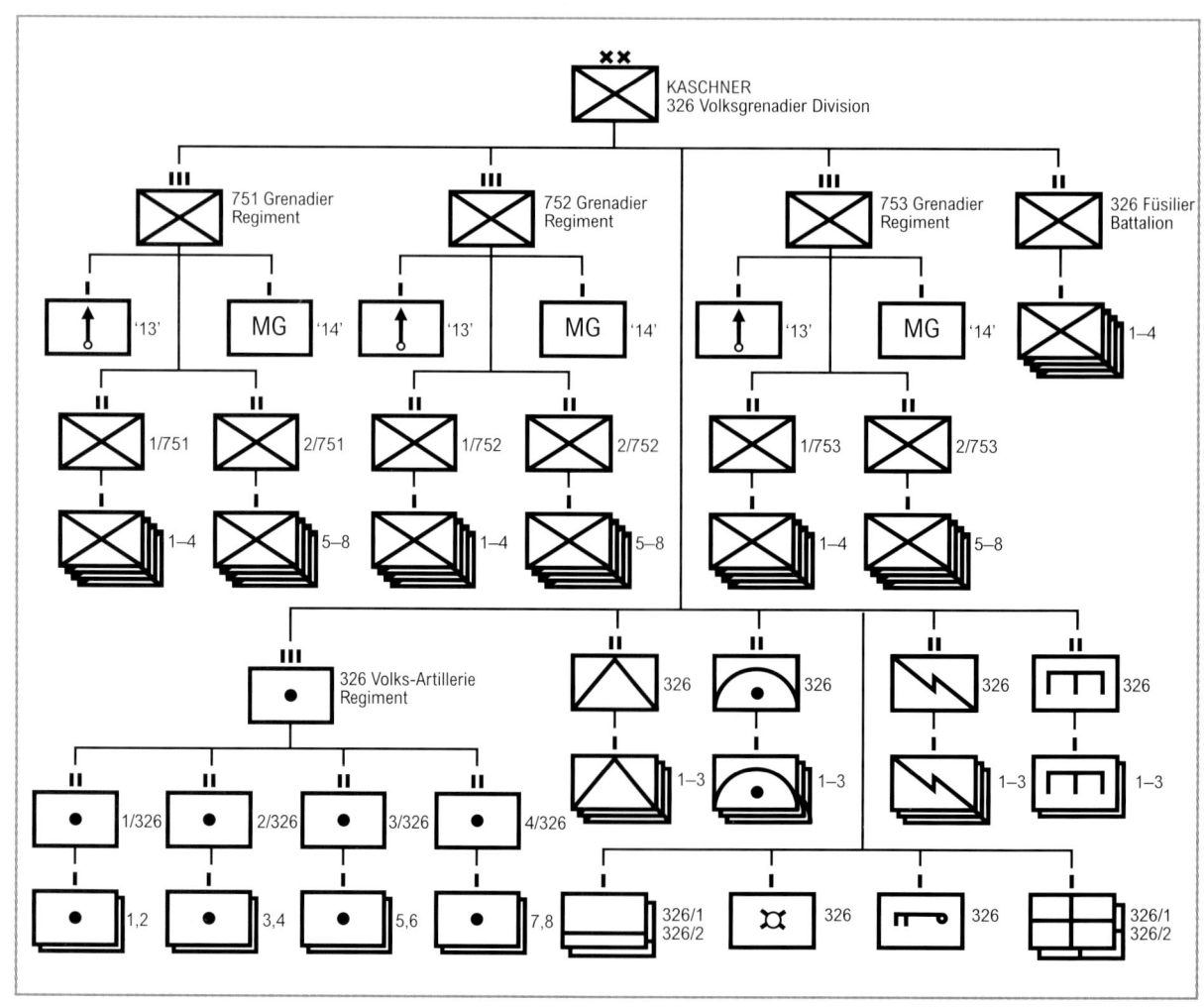

3 Panzergrenadier Division

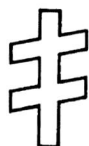

Originally in OKW Reserve, Walter Denkert's 3 Panzergrenadier Division was assigned to Sixth Panzer Armee on 19 December to bolster LXVII Korps during the assault on Elsenborn ridge. Even this additional support was insufficient to achieve a breakthrough, and on 26 December the division was transferred to Fifth Panzer Armee and moved out of the northern sector.

The division's 'family tree' is complicated. It was formed in France in June 1943 around personnel from the former 386 Infanterie Division (mot), which itself had been brought into being in October 1942 under Generalmajor Kurt Jesser, and stationed in southern France; the original 386 Infanterie Division having been formed and disbanded in 1940 without seeing action. But 3 Panzergrenadier Division's traditions and fighting élan stemmed from 3 Infanterie Division, a peacetime formation which had fought well in Poland

---

3 Panzergrenadier Division

Generalmajor Walter Denkert

Stabs Kompanie

---

103 Panzer Abteilung
8 Grenadier Regiment (mot)
29 Grenadier Regiment (mot)
3 Artillerie Regiment (mot)
103 Panzer Aufklärungs Abteilung
3 Panzerjäger Abteilung
312 Flak Abteilung (mot)
3 Pionier Abteilung (mot)
3 Nachrichten Abteilung (mot)
3 Nachschub Truppe (mot)
3 Panzer Werkstatt Truppe
3 Verwaltungs Truppe (mot)
3 Sanitäts Truppe (mot)

Typical of the weather conditions at the start of 'Herbstnebel' which prevented air operations. Grenadiers, with a Panzerfaust team in the foreground, trudge up a ridge in the fog and snow.
(U.S. Signal Corps)

and France in 1939-1940. Re-formed as a motorised division for the invasion of Russia, the 3rd took part in the initial drive on Leningrad, commanded by Generalleutnent Fritz-Hubert Gräser, then was switched south to the belated assault on Moscow and

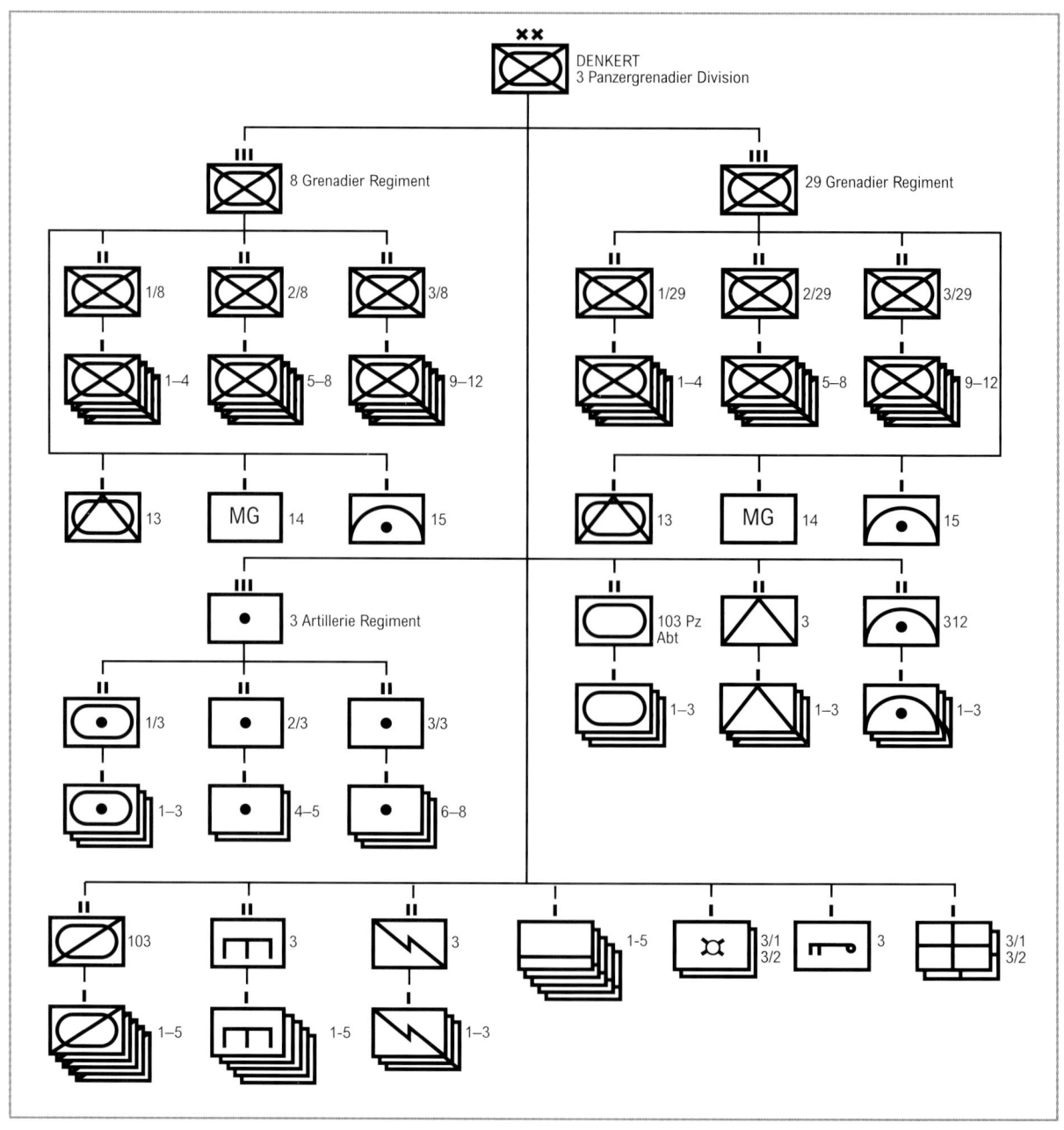

suffered heavily during the Soviet 1941-1942 winter counter-offensive. Transferred to Heeresgruppe Süd, it fought its way across the Don but then became one of the unfortunate divisions entrapped in Stalingrad the following winter, all but a handful of its personnel entering Soviet captivity in February 1943, including its then commander, Generalleutnant Helmuth Schlömer. The survivors formed the cadre of the new 3 Panzergrenadier Division which absorbed the untried personnel of 386 Infanterie Division and trained during the summer in France. The new division was ably led by the man who had command-

ed the 'old' formation in 1941, Generalleutnant Gräser.

Sent to Italy after the fall of Sicily, the division performed well despite the majority of the men's inexperience, opposing the Allied landings during the hard-fought battle of Salerno in September 1943. After retreating to Cassino, they were next thrown in to the beachhead at Anzio. When the Allies finally succeeded in breaking out, the division retreated through Rome to Florence in May-June 1944, then was withdrawn to France in August, temporarily commanded by Generalmajor Kurt Cuno when Gräser was promoted to lead LXVIII Panzer Korps in Russia.

Generalmajor Walter Denkert shared a distinction with Rommel, having previously commanded the Führer Begleit Bataillon.
(Christopher Ailsby Historical Archives)

The division next fought southeast of Aachen in the Hürtgen Forest during November, again suffering heavily but inflicting a price, before being taken into OKW Reserve. At the beginning of the Ardennes offensive 3 Panzergrenadier Division had 12,000 men, but its Panzer Abteilung had only 41 StuG III/IVs (some of them 'stolen' from a Volksgrenadier division) and no tanks. However, its Panzerjäger Abteilung was at almost full strength with 25 Jagdpanzer IV/70s. By the time the division was released from reserve to LXVII Korps and began deploying for its assault south of Monschau on 18-19 December, the Americans had succeeded in pulling back on to Elsenborn ridge itself from where their commanding position gave their artillery a field day.

Denkert's Panzergrenadiers launched a succession of costly and futile assaults before the attack was cancelled and they were re-assigned to Manteuffel's Fifth Panzer Armee. Later, 3 Panzergrenadier Division put up a dogged defence as it retreated slowly through the Schnee Eifel and back across the Rhine where it was finally trapped and encircled near Köln in April 1945.

The division fought a delaying action southeast of Paris before being pulled back to Metz. It suffered heavy casualties during the defence of the fortress and the survivors were withdrawn to the east of Aachen so the division could be rebuilt again during October-November 1944. Its latest CO, Generalmajor Walter Denkert, had formerly been a Guard Commander at the Führerhauptquartier.

246 Volksgrenadier Division

Oberst Peter Körte's division had already had an eventful war when it was first transferred from LXXXI Korps of Fifteenth Armee to LXVII Korps on 28 December 1944, temporarily replacing 3 Panzergrenadier Division. Then it was reallocated to Fifth Panzer Armee in January 1945 to be held as a reserve during the last-ditch attempt to capture Bastogne and, finally, assigned to Seventh Armee. But, after the U.S. Third Army broke through at Pruem, it was forced on to the defensive and by March was in full retreat through the Schnee Eifel, its commander was killed in action, and the survivors surrendered shortly afterwards south of the Mosel. 246 Infanterie Division was formed at Trier in September 1939 and played a successful role in the assault on the Maginot Line the following summer. Its men then enjoyed a year's respite on reserve duties before being flung into the maelstrom of the Russian front in January 1942, commanded by Generalmajor Müller-Bülow. Here, the division fought on the northern flank of Heeresgruppe Mitte, checking the Soviet Twenty-Second Army at Belyy. The battle of Smolensk followed in spring 1943

but, after the disastrous stalemate at Kursk, the Russians counter-attacked in overwhelming force north of the salient and the 246th was forced into retreat from Rzhev. By this time it was down to

---

246 Volksgrenadier Division

Oberst Peter Körte

Stabs Kompanie

---

352 Volksgrenadier Regiment (List)
404 Volksgrenadier Regiment
689 Volksgrenadier Regiment
246 Volks-Artillerie Regiment
246 Füsilier Bataillon
246 Panzerjäger Abteilung
246 Pionier Abteilung
246 Nachrichten Abteilung
246 Nachschub Truppe
246 Werkstatt Truppe
246 Verwaltungs Truppe
246 Sanitäts Truppe

Kampfgruppe size and, after surviving its third Russian winter, was surrounded at Vitebsk in July 1944, most of its men going into captivity.

Those who escaped formed the cadre of the new 246 Volksgrenadier Division, raised in Prague from Bohemian Volksdeutsch personnel and a number of disgruntled Kriegsmarine sailors. They were rapidly whipped into shape by their new commander, Oberst Gerhard Wilck, and entrained to eastern France at the end of September.

At the beginning of October 1944 the 246th was sent to relieve 116 Panzer Division at Aachen. The town was pivotal in the Allied drive to the Rhine and the U.S. XIX Corps, Ninth Army, and VII Corps, First Army, encircled it. The unfortunate 246th was pounded remorselessly by a prolonged air and artillery bombardment followed by a determined assault by the 1st Infantry Division, later supported by 3rd Armored. The struggle, street by street and house by house, lasted from 13-21 October before Wilck surrendered

the city. Amazingly, a large number of men succeeded in escaping to the east and instead of being disbanded, 246 Volksgrenadier Division was promptly rebuilt yet again. It absorbed the remnants of 49 Infanterie Division, which had been even more severely mauled north of Aachen, under its new commander, Peter Körte, and was earmarked for 'Herbstnebel'.

However, by the middle of November the division was so heavily involved in the battle for the Hürtgen Forest that it could not be disengaged. Attrition on both sides was high and by the end of the month the division was down to little more than the size of a battalion. Finally withdrawn at the beginning of December, the battle-weary survivors now found their ranks filled with Luftwaffe personnel with little or no experience of ground combat.

Despite this, when it was later assigned to Seventh Armee, Brandenberger considered it one of his best divisions – a strange reflection on the once mighty Wehrmacht.

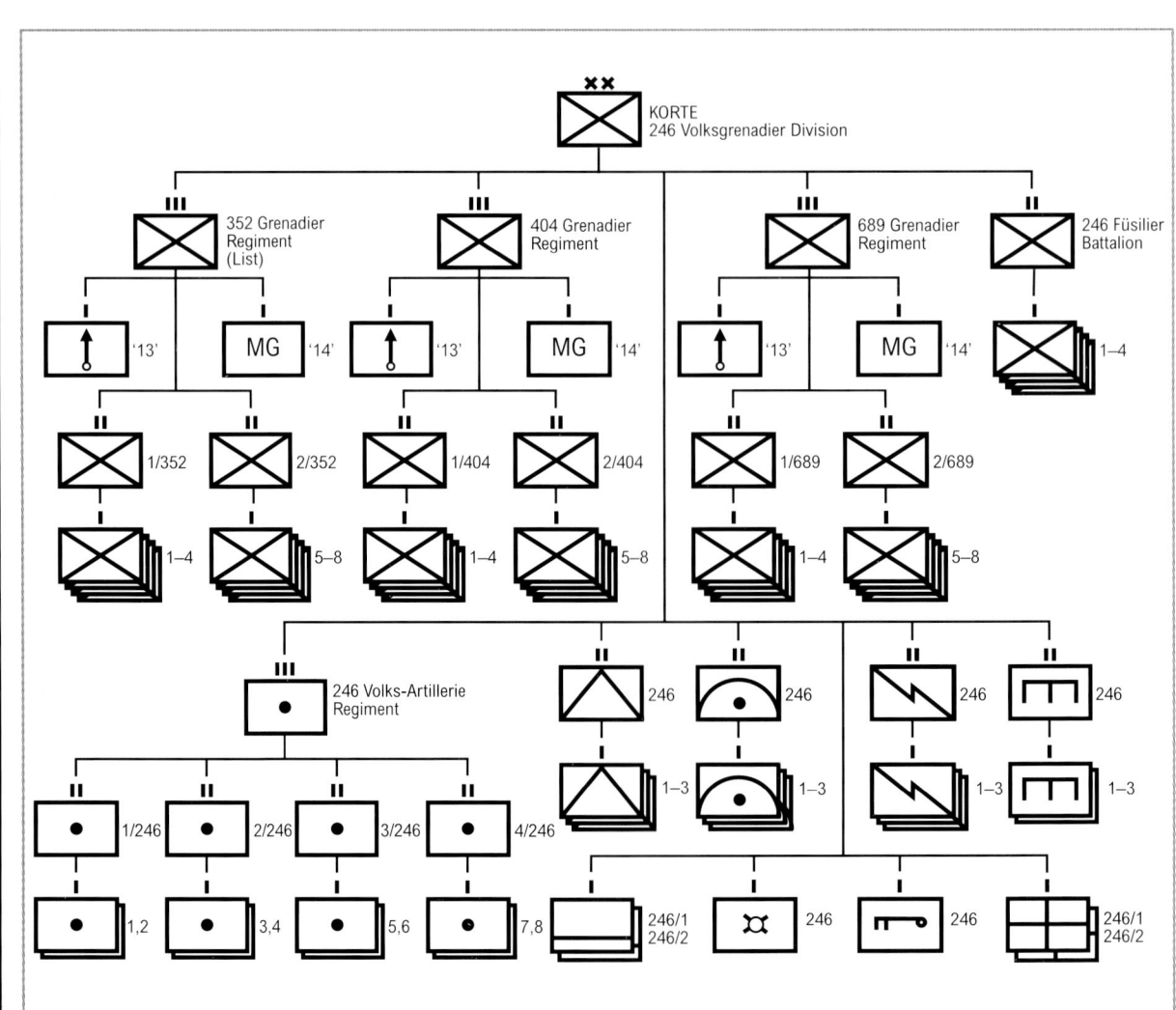

LXVII KORPS' BATTLES

326 Volksgrenadier Division

Höfen-Monschau – December 16-17

To begin with, the attack by 326 Volksgrenadier Division either side of Monschau was interpreted by Allied intelligence as a riposte to 2nd Infantry Division's offensive towards the Rur and Urft dams through Wahlerscheid. However, it was quickly realised that the attack was not a simple spoiling operation, but part of something much bigger. In this sector, however, just as in the Losheim gap, the U.S. Army had very little with which to resist the assault, and Generalmajor Dr Erwin Kaschner's assault should, in theory, have succeeded.

Even though 326 Volksgrenadier Division was understrength, particularly in artillery, Model had recognised this fact and assigned two whole Volks-Artillerie Korps and two Werfer-Brigaden in support. They were specifically ordered not to fire on the historic little German town of Monschau itself, but to direct their fire north and south in a creeping barrage extending west towards Eupen (where, although the Abwehr did not know it, Major-General Leonard Gerow had his V Corps' headquarters). Nor was there any fire directed at Wahlerscheid, for news of the 2nd Infantry Division's attack here earlier in the night had not actually yet filtered upwards. The barrage in the Monschau sector laster only 25 minutes before the grenadiers began advancing at 0600 hrs in the reflected illumination from search-lights aimed at the clouds – a trick invented by Montgomery. Apart from forcing the Americans to dive deeply into their foxholes, and knocking down some telegraph poles, the shellfire inflicted little damage but did fully alert the GIs of Lieutenant-Colonel McLernand Butler's III/395th of the 99th Infantry Division at Höfen, and those of Lieutenant-Colonel Robert O'Brien's 38th Reconnaiss-ance Cavalry Squadron to their north (the lynchpin between V and VII Corps).

A divisional attack against one battalion of infantry and one squadron of cavalry sounds like a walkover, but three factors mitigated against it. In the first place, Kaschner did not have a whole division for the attack, but only three battalions; one of the others was late arriving, one had gone to help 272 Volksgrenadier Division to the north, and one was too far away, having been relieved at Wahlerscheid only hours before the assault. In the second place the Americans, having been there for a month, were well dug-in with overlapping fields of fire. And in the third place, seeing the German attack developing, the CO of the 405th Field Artillery Group, Colonel Oscar Axelson, took the bold step of ordering his 196th Battalion to use the still top-secret POZIT proximity fuze. This made the high explosive shells burst overhead the German infantry, causing a degree of panic as well as horrendous casualties (Kaschner lost 20% of his assault force on the first day).

The attack against Höfen was spearheaded by I/751 and I/753 battalions whose men were simply shot to pieces from close range as they emerged from the mist. Three of them actually fell into American foxholes, and about 30 were captured in the village itself, but the remainder simply fled. To their north, I/752, attempting to break through between Monschau and Höfen, ran into accurate fire from the 37mm cannon of the cavalry squadron's M5s. The division's first attack was over in less than two hours.

Next day, 17 December, Kaschner launched a second attack north of Monschau, across the railway tracks towards the high ground at Mützenich. This went in at 0700 hrs, preceded by another artillery barrage, and broke through the line of Troop B of the 38th Cavalry Squadron, but was repulsed by accurate fire from the 62nd Field Artillery Battalion. Shortly afterwards, the American line was reinforced by the

16/12/1944	18/12	20/12	22/12	24/12	26/12	28/12	30/12	6/1/1945	13/1	20/1	27/1	3/2	7/2
pages 42-59,70-73,89-91				60-61,74-76									

Höfen and Monschau lie in a bend of the River Rur, which produced a salient in the U.S. lines. V Corps' attacks north and south towards the Rur and Urft dams were planned additionally to seal this off, but the German offensive pre-empted this. The two-pronged attacks by 326 Volksgrenadier Division were aimed at Höfen and Mützenich.

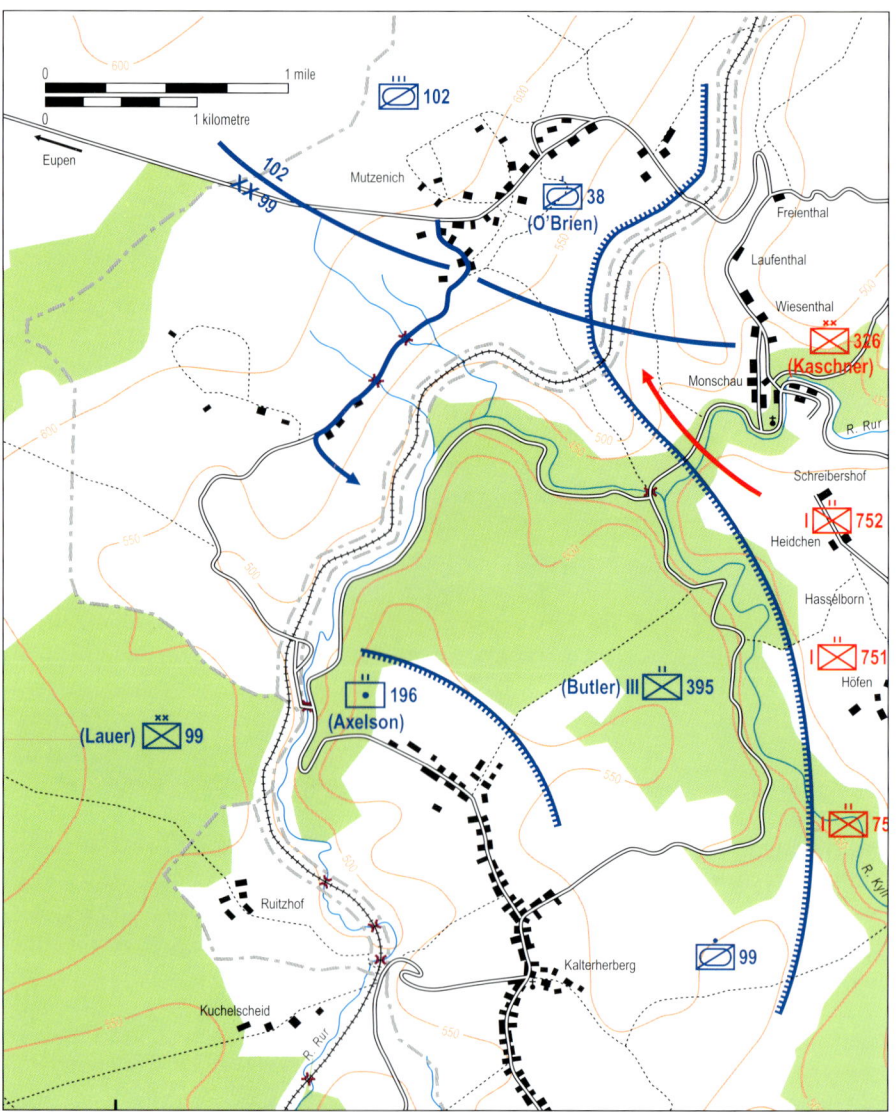

47th Regiment, 9th Infantry Division, which prevented any further attack on this sector.

Nevertheless, LXVII Korps' commander Otto Hitzfeld ordered Kaschner's division to try again on 18 December. By this time their II/753 battalion had rejoined and this was put in the van, reinforced in successive waves by the surviving companies of the other battalions.

Again, Höfen was the objective, and the assault went in three hours before dawn. Again, though, the shellfire from the 196th Field Artillery Battalion was murderous, and although the grenadiers got amongst the first half-dozen houses on the eastern edge of the village, they were thrown back and about 40 were taken prisoner. Daunted though he may have been, Kaschner made one last effort at about 0900 hrs supported, according to the U.S. Official History, by 'ten tanks'. These may actually have been the Jagdpanzer 38(t)s of the Panzerjäger Abteilung, or StuGs borrowed from 272 Volksgrenadier Division. Again, artillery fire won the day for the Americans, even though their forward command post in a three-storey house on the edge of the village was besieged by determined grenadiers. 2nd Lieutenant S.D. Llewellyn called for fire on his own position in three five-minute intervals, which broke up Kaschner's last attack which he called off at 1200 hrs.

16/12/1944	18/12	20/12	22/12	24/12	26/12	28/12	30/12	6/1/1945	13/1	20/1	27/1	3/2	7/2
pages 42-59,70-73,89-91				60-61,74-76									

LXVII KORPS' BATTLES

3 Panzergrenadier Division

Elsenborn Ridge – December 19-22

When Generalmajor Walter Denkert's 3 Panzergrenadier Division was released from OKW Reserve on 18 December to join the battle south of Monschau for Elsenborn ridge, it stepped onto the floorboards of a very confused stage with a constantly shifting spotlight. The leading motorcycles of its Aufklärungs Abteilung reached Hellenthal at about 0415 hrs on 19 December to find themselves temporarily attached to II SS-Panzer Korps instead of the Army's LXVII Korps because of the disruption caused by Allied bombing on Otto Hitzfeld's headquarters. They were not alone, because 12 SS-Panzer Division and 12 and 277 Volksgrenadier Divisions and 3 Fallschirm Division had also been transferred to Bittrich's command from I SS-Panzer Korps, while his own 2 SS-Panzer Division had gone to Fifth Panzer Armee and 9 SS-Panzer to I SS-Panzer Korps. While confusing, this situation merely mirrored a similar situation in the Allied camp but, whereas Eisenhower, Bradley and Montgomery compounded the question marks, Model was quite clear in where he wanted his forces redeployed.

Denkert's task was clearly delineated: his men were to reinforce 277 Volksgrenadier Division and, once and for all, clear the twin villages of Krinkelt and Rocherath. Unfortunately for him, he was too late on two counts.

In the first instance, had his division been released from reserve earlier, it could have exploited the ten-mile gap between the sole III Battalion of the 395th Regiment, 99th Infantry Division, at Höfen, and the remainder of the regiment which was covering 2 Infantry Division's withdrawal from Wahlerscheid. This could – and battles are often composed of 'what ifs' – have rolled up the northern flank of the U.S. V

Sturmgeschütze of an unidentified assault company moving up to the attack. (U.S. Department of Defense)

16/12/1944	18/12	20/12	22/12	24/12	26/12	28/12	30/12	6/1/1945	13/1	20/1	27/1	3/2	7/2
pages 42-59,70-73,87-88			60-61,74-76										

Corps and, if launched in concert with a northward drive from Büllingen by Kampfgruppe 'Peiper' on 17 or 18 December, have resulted in a singular victory.

In the second instance, by the time 3 Panzergrenadier Division was in a position to begin deploying, the American commander on the spot (Major- General Walter Robertson) had already agreed with V Corps' CO Leonard Gerow that the 'twin villages' should be abandoned once all the survivors from the forward battalions of the 99th Infantry Division had safely passed back through his own 2nd Division's lines, and that a new defence should be constructed on Elsenborn ridge itself. Robertson's southern f'lank, meanwhile, was rapidly being secured by the 1st Infantry Division, and his northern by the 9th.

Robertson issued his orders at 1345 hrs on 19 December just before Denkert's leading troops – I/8 Panzergrenadier Regiment and 103 Panzer Abteilung's StuGs (they had no tanks) – relieved Kampfgruppe 'Müller' and entered the affray in 277 Volksgrenadier Division's sector northwest of the twin villages. That day, they encountered little opposition apart from the constant artillery fire, because the American foxholes in the semicircle Rocherath-Krinkelt-Wirtzfeld were being systematically evacuated. Denkert's grenadiers, riding on the backs of the StuGs, took over tanks and SP guns which had been abandoned during the earlier attacks and succeeded in getting some of them back into a semblance of fighting order; even if they could not move, many of their guns could still fire.

Robertson's withdrawal on to Elsenborn ridge was complete by 0200 hrs on 20 December and Denkert launched his first assault which finally captured Krinkelt and Rocherath – both empty of the enemy – just before daylight. His grenadiers were attacking uphill into prepared positions of the 99th Infantry Division which had a commanding field of fire from the ridge, and were checked with considerable losses. New to this battle, though, the grenadiers were game and followed orders to attempt two further attacks the same day but with the same result. The American field artillery was too accurate and, even though they lacked the Panzergrenadiers' automatic firepower, the GIs could pour a withering fire into the German ranks with their M1s and BARs from sheltered positions.

Denkert began reassembling his assault companies before dawn next day, 21 December, but they were spotted forming up and artillery fire broke their ranks before they even began another attack. The following day they were a bit luckier, but it was a tenuous victory. By this time, indeed, Model had virtually decided there was no future in attempting to secure the flank of Sixth Panzer Armee, and on the same day transferred 326 Volksgrenadier Division to LXXIV Korps of Fifteenth Armee.

On the 22nd, Denkert decided to try attacking a little to the north of Krinkelt and Rocherath, bolstering his as-yet uncommitted 29 Panzergrenadier Regiment with a few companies from 277 Volksgrenadier

A grenadier poses alongside an abandoned American 105mm howitzer near Monschau. (U.S. Department of Defense)

16/12/1944	18/12	20/12	22/12	24/12	26/12	28/12	30/12	6/1/1945	13/1	20/1	27/1	3/2	7/2
pages 42-59,70-73,87-88				60-61,74-76									

The area between Monschau and Elsenborn where 3 Panzergrenadier Division launched successive unsuccessful attacks before it was transferred to the southern sector of the front.

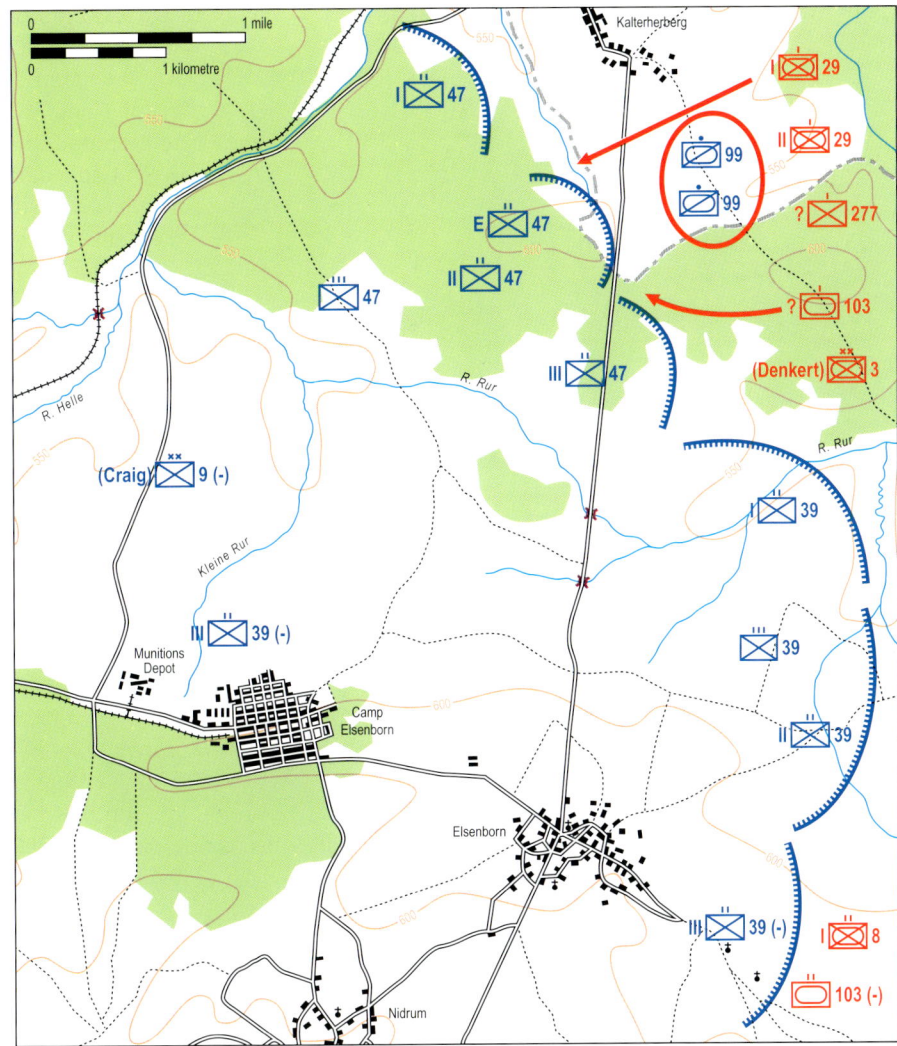

Division. His leading two companies met only initial opposition from two platoons of the 99th Infantry Division's Reconnaissance Troop east of Kalterherberg. Assaulting uphill through a minefield and across a stream, all the while under determined but weak smallarms fire, the grenadiers broke through; for once, the American field artillery was silent. The Germans surrounded the bulk of the two platoons and pushed on about a further thousand yards before they ran into Company E of the 47th Regiment, 9th Infantry Division, which finally checked their advance. The survivors of the two trapped cavalry platoons escaped under cover of darkness.

Denkert had not finished, though, and used his artillery to lay a smokescreen through which subsequent companies could advance to reinforce those already on the ridge. Some of these now ran into elements of the 9th Infantry Division's 39th Regiment on the 47th's flank and, despite supporting artillery fire, were unable to break through. The two regiments of Major-General Louis Craig's division launched a sequence of coordinated counter-attacks on 23 December, well supported themselves now by their own field artillery. This drove Denkert's and Viebig's grenadiers back to their start lines. This finally finished the German assault in the north because that at Dom Bütgenbach by 12 SS-Panzer Division was also terminated at the same time. Thereafter, 3 Panzergrenadier Division was transferred to Manteuffel's command at Bastogne.

16/12/1944	18/12	20/12	22/12	24/12	26/12	28/12	30/12	6/1/1945	13/1	20/1	27/1	3/2	7/2
pages 42-59,70-73,87-88				60-61,74-76									

THE LUFTWAFFE

Just before 1100 hrs on Christmas Eve, 1944, Allied troops in Liège and Namur received an unexpected and unwelcome visit from a Santa Claus in unfamiliar guise. 'Santa' was, in fact, the Arado 234B-2 'Blitz', the world's first operational jet bomber, and the American and British fighters on CAP (Combat Air Patrol) were helpless to intervene, because the invaders were dropping their SC 500 bombs from about 7,000 feet at a speed, in a shallow dive, of some 560 mph. Flak, according to the German pilots' debriefing reports, was 'moderate'; not a single aircraft was hit and the only casualty was one machine which damaged its undercarriage on landing back at Münster-Handorf. Five of the nine bombs dropped on railway marshalling yards were seen to explode.

Later in the afternoon, the remaining eight Arados made a return visit, scythed unscathed through 'strong formations' of Allied fighters, and repeated the operation successfully twice on Christmas Day despite much heavier flak from a forewarned foe. The only mishap was one burst tyre on landing following the second sortie.

It was a technical triumph for the German aircraft industry but almost an historical footnote for Oberstleutnant Robert Kowalewski's fledgling Stabsstaffel of Hauptmann Dieter Luckesch's 9 Staffel, III Gruppe, Kampfgeschwader 76, because the

Generalmajor Dietrich Peltz commanded II Jagdkorps of Luftflotte 3 during 'Herbstnebel'.
(Christopher Ailsby Historical Archives)

bombing attacks had no effect whatsoever on the ground operations in the Ardennes. Indeed, the plaintive cry to be heard from the German troops on the snow-covered, forested hills throughout operation 'Herbstnebel' – particularly when the skies cleared and the Allied 'Jabos' reappeared – was, 'where is the Luftwaffe?'; which was not an idle question.

Following a conference with Hitler in Berlin on 2 December, Fifth Armee commander Hasso von

Arado 234B-2 from KG 76 which was captured by the Allies after it crash-landed in 1945.
(Author's collection)

LUFTWAFFEN-KOMMANDO – WEST
(Generalleutnant Josef Schmidt)
II Jagdkorps, Luftflotte 3
(Generalmajor Dietrich Peltz)

1 JAGDGESCHWADER (Fighter Wing)
(Oberstleutnant Ihlefeld)
 I Gruppe (Group) (c. 25 x FW 190A-8)
 II Gruppe (c.25 x FW 190A-8)
 III Gruppe (c.30 x Me 109G-14)

2 JAGDGESCHWADER
(Oberstleutnant Bühlingen)
 I Gruppe (c 28 x FW 190A-8/A-9)
 II Gruppe (c.13 x Me 1090-14/K-4)
 III Gruppe (c 29 x FW 19OD-9)
 (attached from 4 Schlachtgeschwader
 [Ground Attack Wing]: III Gruppe (c.40 x FW 19OF-8)

3 JAGDGESCHWADER
(Oberstleutnant Bär)
 I Gruppe (c.20 x Me 109G-10/G-14)
 III Gruppe (c.20 x Me 109G-14/K4)
 IV Gruppe (c.25 x FW 19OA-8)

4 JAGDGESCHWADER
(Major Michalski)
 I Gruppe (c.18 x Me 109G-14/K-4)
 II Gruppe (c.10 x FW 190A-8)
 IV Gruppe (c.7 x Me 109G-14/K-4)

6 JAGDGESCHWADER
(Oberstleutnant Kogler)
 I Gruppe (c.20 x FW 190A-8)
 II Gruppe (c.20 x FW 19OA-8)
 III Gruppe (c.25 x Me 109G-10/G-14)

11 JAGDGESCHWADER
(Oberstleutnant Specht)
 I Gruppe (c.20 x FW 19OA-8)
 II Gruppe (c.30 x Me 109G-14/K-4)
 III Gruppe (c.20 x FW 190A-8)

20 NACHTSCHLACHTGRUPPE (Night Ground Attack Group)
(c.21 x FW 19OF-8/G-3) (attached)

26 JAGDGESCHWADER
(Oberstleutnant Priller)
 I Gruppe (c.46 x FW 190D-9)
 II Gruppe (c.48 x FW 190D-9)
 III Gruppe (c.36 x Me 109G-14/K-4)
 (attached from 54 Jagdgeschwader):
 III Gruppe (c.31 x FW 19OD-9)
 (attached from Luftflotte Reich):
 Einsatzstaffel (Special Duties Squadron) 104 (4 x FW 190D-9)

27 JAGDGESCHWADER
(Major Franzisket)
 I Gruppe (c.20 x Me 1O9G-14/K-4)
 II Gruppe (c.18 x Me 109G-14)
 III Gruppe (c.16 x Me 109K-4)
 IV Gruppe (c.12 x Me,109G-10)
 (attached from 54 Jagdgeschwader):
 IV Gruppe (c.20 x FW 190A-8/A-9)

51 KAMPFGESCHWADER (JAGD)
(Fighter-Bomber Wing, attached)
 I Gruppe (c.37 x Me 262)

53 JAGDGESCHWADER
(Oberstleutnant Bennemann)
 II Gruppe (c.19 x Me 109G-14)
 III Gruppe (c.15 x Me 109G-14)
 IV Gruppe (c.14 x Me 109G-14)

77 JAGDGESCHWADER
(Oberstleutnant Neie)
 I Gruppe (c.43 x Me 109G-14)
 II Gruppe (c.32 x Me 109K-4)
 III Gruppe (c.10 x Me 109K-4)

(Attached from Luftflotte Reich):
1 Nachtjagdgeschwader (Night Fighter Wing)
Gruppe (c.14 x Bf 110)
3 Nachtjagdgeswader
Gruppe (c.20 x Bf 110)
101 Nachtjagdgeschwader
Gruppe (c.30 x Bf 110 & Ju 88)

Note: numbers of aircraft listed are approximate because they changed from day to day depending upon serviceability.

Manteuffel asked Walter Model what he should tell his troops about air support for the coming offensive because, he said, 'in our sector of the front we never see or hear a German aeroplane these days'.

Model replied: 'The Luftwaffe is being deliberately held back. Göring has reported that he has three thousand fighters available for the operation. You know Göring's reports. Discount one thousand, and that still leaves a thousand to work with you and a thousand for Sepp Dietrich.'

So where were they when both Panzer Armees so desperately needed them? Part of the answer lies in the earlier quotation from Generalleutnant Siegfried Westphal, and the Arado 234 is one of his culprits. For the most part, though, the German fighter-bombers were, as Model had said, being held back quite deliberately for a special operation. Even then, his estimate of the number of aircraft which could be made available to support 'Herbstnebel' fell far short of the truth, as the accompanying table for II Jagdkorps clearly shows.

In addition to those Geschwader listed, a small number of other Luftwaffe units was assigned to support 'Herbstnebel': KG 76 with its Arado 234s and KG 66 with Ju 88s; SG 4, a dedicated ground attack wing, with more FW 190s; NJG 2 with Ju 88 night fighters; and NSG 1 and 2 with obsolescent Ju 87 Stukas.

This assembly of power was itself only created by virtually denuding Germany of aerial defence against Allied bombing during the second half of December

(I/KG 66) in the Mediterranean in 1942, he later took over Fliegerkorps IX which did its best to disrupt the D-Day landings despite the overwhelming Allied aerial superiority.

This superiority was just one of Peltz's dilemmas in December 1944. In addition, not only was fuel for his aircraft as short as it was for the vehicles in the land offensive, but he faced the same consideration as the Allied air forces' commanders – the weather. His pilots could not support the Panzer divisions in virtually zero visibility, with the cloud base down to the hilltops and snow falling. And when the skies did clear briefly, they brought out swarms of American and British fighters. II Jagdkorps could have scrambled to give battle – but its pilots would have been watching their fuel gauges all the time, and their endurance would have been strictly limited. On top of this, any Allied aircraft losses, no matter how heavy, could be replaced in a week or two, whereas the Luftwaffe was virtually bankrupt.

Reichsmarschall Hermann Göring was also aware of this unpalatable truth, and the reason he deliberately held back his squadrons – just as Model told Manteuffel – was for an operation as audacious, but ill-fated, as 'Herbstnebel' itself. This was operation 'Bodenplatte', which loosely translated means 'Groundstrike'. If, Göring reasoned quite correctly the Luftwaffe could not keep the Allied fighters away from the Wehrmacht's tanks by indulging in air-to-air combat, they could achieve the same effect by destroying them on the ground. But this, too, depended on favourable weather conditions, so the operation was delayed time after time. The result, when it finally took place on New Year's Day 1945, was a case of 'too little, too late' for Sixth Panzer Armee and Heeresgruppe B as a whole. If the operation had gone ahead earlier, on Boxing or Christmas Day, for example, in conjunction with the Arado 234 attacks on Liège and Namur – well, anything might have happened. As it was, the 'Hangover Raid', as it was dubbed in RAF and USAAF circles, was still a partial success but with a high price. It was planned in as much secrecy as 'Herbstnebel' had been and achieved complete surprise even though an 'Ultra' intercept on 16 December had alerted British Intelligence to II Jagdkorps' headquarters move from Holland. Some 900 aircraft took part, and 18 Allied airfields in Holland, Belgium and France were attacked. The most successful results were achieved by JG 3 against Eindhoven where two waves of fight-

1944, apart from two Jagdgeschwader. The II Jagdkorps Gruppen brought together on eleven airfields to support 'Herbstnebel' comprised principally Messerschmitt 109s, which by this stage of the war were really showing the limitations of their design, and Focke-Wulf 190s. The latter were certainly the equal of most Allied fighters, but the Luftwaffe had already lost so many of its most skilled pilots in five years of war that the calibre of the 'new boys' was as much a problem here as it was on the ground, in the individual tank crews and Volksgrenadier platoons.

These problems were assuredly recognised by Generalmajor Dietrich Peltz, commander of II Jagdkorps, which had been entrusted with the task of supporting 'Herbstnebel'. Too young to have seen service in the First World War, Peltz had joined the fledgling Luftwaffe in 1935 and flew Ju 87 Stukas in Poland and France before converting to the twin-engined Ju 88, Germany's most versatile combat aircraft of the war. Rising rapidly to command of his own Gruppe

Focke-Wulf FW 190F-8 as used by III/JG 2 was the Luftwaffe's most potent ground-attack aircraft and could carry rockets and bombs. (Author's collection)

ers, attacking from different directions, caught two squadrons of Royal Canadian Air Force machines taxiing out prior to take-off. JG 1 also achieved success at St Dennis and Maldegen; as did JG 26 at Bruxelles-Evère and Bruxelles-Grimbergen, and JG 27 at Bruxelles-Melsbroek (where one casualty was Field Marshal Montgomery's personal C-47).

Attacks by JG 2 and JG 4 against St Trond were a partial success, as were those by JG 11 against Asch (although the geschwader commander was killed) and by JG 53 in the most southerly raid of all on Metz-Frascaty. JG 6 inflicted only minor damage at Volkel (where its own commander's FW 190 was shot down and he was taken prisoner after baling out); and it was a similar story for JG 77 at Deurne and JG 4 at Le Culot. Aircraft of JG 3 and JG 27 also attacked targets of opportunity at Gilze Rijen without noticeable effect, and Ophoven, Heesch and Woensdrecht were awarded similar by-blows.

The result of the operation was 156 Allied aircraft written off and a similar number damaged, mostly on the ground. A few were already in the air, and there were some dogfights, but others were shot down as they attempted to scramble, as at Eindhoven. The official Royal Air Force history states that, 'had the execution of the operation been equal to its conception, very severe damage could have been achieved. In the event there were too few good leaders and too many young pilots who lacked not courage but experience.'

For the Luftwaffe, however, 'Bodenplatte' was a real disaster. Nearly 300 fighters were lost along with 214 virtually irreplaceable pilots, 151 killed or reported missing in action. The USAAF history records that, 'it was one of the worst single days for human and aircraft losses the Luftwaffe ever experienced and the military effect on the Allies, save for some embarrassment, was truly negligible'. Ironically, about a third of the Luftwaffe's losses, some 85 aircraft, were the victims of 'friendly' flak. An entire corps of anti-aircraft guns, Generalleutnant Wolfgang Pickert's III Flakkorps, was assigned to 'Herbstnebel'. In the northern sector its 2 Flak Division, with 21 heavy (8.8cm) and 23 light/medium (20/37mm) batteries, was brought up to support Sixth Panzer Armee. In addition, Model had ordered that all army and SS flak abteilungen were to come under air force control so that their efforts could be coordinated by Luftwaffen-Kommando-West. His orders for the flak units specified that their main task was 'to protect the attacking spearheads and units on the march, especially at narrow points, bridges, over terrain offering no cover, etc'. III Flakkorps was to 'accompany the movements of the Heeresgruppe and will, depending on the air situation, add its fire to the artillery preparation barrages'. However, 'flak will be used against ground targets only in cases of crisis or for rapid elimination of obstacles to troop movements'.

To safeguard the strike aircraft for operation 'Bodenplatte', Luftwaffe liaison officers with the ground forces were instructed to fire golden signal rockets as soon as they received the codeword 'Goldenregen'. This was to alert the flak gunners to the fact that friendly aircraft could be expected approaching from their rear. Nothing, unfortunately, was said about those aircraft returning from their sorties, and this was where most of the casualties were incurred. C'est la guerre.

WARGAMING THE ARDENNES – AXIS NORTHERN SECTOR

The successful wargamer depends on the same factors that influence real battlefield victories, and the 'big battalions' are rarely a decisive factor. Surprise and determined speed of execution are the key factors. OK, what's new?

The Axis player representing 'Sepp' Dietrich in any game, whether on computer, a game board or a conventional table with model tanks and figures, automatically has the advantage of surprise, and must use this to the maximum advantage. If the game demands that you deploy your forces as Dietrich did, you have one hand tied behind your back, but you can cut it free by immediately halting your infantry – leaving them for 'mopping up' – and unleashing your Panzer kampfgruppen to take the initiative on day one. The right turn at Büllingen for Peiper referred to earlier could change the whole course of events. Elsenborn ridge will be yours, the U.S. 99th Infantry Division decimated, and a second fuel depot at Stavelot in your hands a day later. Take it from there...

If the game allows flexible choice in the initial set-up, spread your Panzers and Jagdpanzers more evenly along the five Rollbahns. I know as well as you do that splitting your forces is not usually advisable, but take the narrow roads and the weather into account, the lack of air support, and in this instance the exception proves the rule. A totally unconventional, almost sacrilegious, suggestion is to pack your leading columns with Panzergrenadiers and bridging units to make sure the Panzers can 'roll'.

The 'Battle of the Bulge' also provides numerous opportunities for 'skirmish' type games on a company or even squad level, with one or two tanks or tank destroyers on each side and a handful of infantry. Given the nature of the terrain and the fact that you are the attacker, you must maximise the firepower advantage of a higher proportion of automatic weapons to counteract your opponent's ability to use selective firepower from concealed and sometimes dug-in positions.

And always remember, hesitation is your worst enemy!

SELECT BIBLIOGRAPHY

Cole, Hugh M. *The Ardennes: Battle of the Bulge.* United States Army in World War II, Office of the Chief of Military History, Washington D.C., 1965.

Crookenden, Lieutenant General Sir Napier, *Battle of the Bulge 1944.* Ian Allan, Shepperton, 1980.

Davies, W. J. K. *German Army Handbook.* Arco Publishing, New York, 1984.

Downing, David. *The Devil's Virtuosos.* New English Library, London, 1977.

Ellis, Chris. *The German Army 1933-1945.* Ian Allan, Shepperton, 1993.

Elstob, Peter, *Hitler's Last Offensive.* Secker & Warburg, London, 1971.

Kessler, Leo. *SS Peiper.* Leo Cooper, London, 1986.

MacDonald, Charles B. *The Battle of the Bulge.* George Weidenfeld & Nicolson, London, 1984.

Mitcham, Samuel W. *Hitler's Legions.* Leo Cooper, London, 1985.

Pallud, Jean Paul. *Battle of the Bulge Then and Now.* Battle of Britain Prints International, London, 1984.

Pimlott, John. *Battle of the Bulge.* Bison Books, London, 1990.

Price, Dr Alfred. *The Luftwaffe Data Book.* Greenhill Books, Lionel Leventhal Ltd, London, 1997.

Quarrie, Bruce. *Encyclopaedia of the German Army in the 20th Century.* Patrick Stephens, Wellingborough, 1989.

Richardson, William, and Seymour Freidin. *The Fatal Decisions.* Consul, London, 1965.

Strawson, John, *The Battle for the Ardennes.* B.T. Batsford, London, 1972.

United States Military Intelligence Service. *Order of Battle of the German Army, 1944.* U. S. War Department, Washington D.C., 1944.

---- *Order of Battle of the German Army, 1945.* U. S. War Department, Washington D.C., 1945.

COMPANION SERIES FROM OSPREY

ELITE
Detailed information on the uniforms and insignia of the world's most famous military forces. Each 64-page book contains some 50 photographs and diagrams, and 12 pages of full-colour artwork.

NEW VANGUARD
Comprehensive histories of the design, development and operational use of the world's armoured vehicles and artillery. Each 48-page book contains eight pages of full-colour artwork including a detailed cutaway.

WARRIOR
Definitive analysis of the armour, weapons, tactics and motivation of the fighting men of history. Each 64-page book contains cutaways and exploded artwork of the warrior's weapons and armour.

CAMPAIGN
Concise, authoritative accounts of history's decisive military encounters. Each 96-page book contains over 90 illustrations including maps, orders of battle, colour plates, and three-dimensional battle maps.

MEN-AT-ARMS
An unrivalled source of information on the organisation, uniforms and equipment of the world's fighting men, past and present. The series covers hundreds of subjects spanning 5,000 years of history. Each 48-page book includes concise texts packed with specific information, some 40 photos, maps and diagrams, and eight colour plates of uniformed figures.

AIRCRAFT OF THE ACES
Focuses exclusively on the elite pilots of major air campaigns, and includes unique interviews with surviving aces sourced specifically for each volume. Each 96-page volume contains up to 40 specially commissioned artworks, unit listings, new scale plans and the best archival photography available.

COMBAT AIRCRAFT
Technical information from the world's leading aviation writers on the aircraft types flown. Each 96-page volume contains up to 40 specially commissioned artworks, unit listings, new scale plans and the best archival photography available.